Essence of a Manager

Krishna Pillai

Essence of a Manager

Springer

Dr. Krishna Pillai
Frejs Väg 4
61234 Finspång
Sweden
krishna.pillai@kkpms.com

ISBN 978-3-642-17580-0   e-ISBN 978-3-642-17581-7
DOI 10.1007/978-3-642-17581-7
Springer Heidelberg Dordrecht London New York

Library of Congress Control Number: 2011921515

© Springer-Verlag Berlin Heidelberg 2011
This work is subject to copyright. All rights are reserved, whether the whole or part of the material is concerned, specifically the rights of translation, reprinting, reuse of illustrations, recitation, broadcasting, reproduction on microfilm or in any other way, and storage in data banks. Duplication of this publication or parts thereof is permitted only under the provisions of the German Copyright Law of September 9, 1965, in its current version, and permission for use must always be obtained from Springer. Violations are liable to prosecution under the German Copyright Law.
The use of general descriptive names, registered names, trademarks, etc. in this publication does not imply, even in the absence of a specific statement, that such names are exempt from the relevant protective laws and regulations and therefore free for general use.

Cover design: WMX Design GmbH, Heidelberg, Germany

Printed on acid-free paper

Springer is part of Springer Science+Business Media (www.springer.com)

Forewords

Krishna Pillai is probably the most internationally experienced manager I have ever met. While he was born and brought up in India, to me as an Englishman, he always appeared to be culturally quite British – we certainly share the same sense of humour. This doubtless comes from the time he spent early in his career working as a research engineer in the UK. Yet he is a Swedish National and when I first met him in the late 1990s he was running ABB's operations in Japan. We met with  the formation of the ABB Alstom Power JV, itself a very large international organization where we created a new global HQ in Brussels bringing together senior managers from 17 countries under one roof. Subsequently Alstom bought out ABB's interests and we all relocated to Paris. At my request Krishna took over as Alstom's Country President in India.

We have stayed in touch since I left Alstom 6 years ago and I was delighted when he asked me to write a foreword to his book. Krishna has a wealth of hands on managerial experience in multiple cultures and cross cultural organizations. He has brought this experience to bear in writing this book which, reflecting Krishna's own style is thoughtful, practical and pragmatic.

Studying this book should help the aspiring manager avoid many of the pitfalls of working in cross-cultural environments and accelerate their overall development as an international manager themselves.

London
25 August 2010

Nick Salmon
Chief Executive
Cookson Group plc.

This is a book by a manager about managers but it is not just for managers. It is for anyone who is interested in the way people behave and function around the world. It is not a management manual and yet it is a map for navigation and a guide for behaviour which can be valuable for practising managers at all levels. It is not a handbook of cultural differences across different countries but it deals with the fundamental drivers which lie deeper than language or culture and which control human behaviour.

I first met Krishna Pillai when I was the Country Manager for ABB in Japan. Krishna and his sales team from Sweden – after having successfully penetrated the Japanese power market by selling one power plant to the Electric Power Development Corporation in competition against Hitachi and another to Kyushu Electric Power Company against the formidable opposition of Mitsubishi – were attempting to penetrate the even more parochial and insular mesh of politics and business that exists on the island of Okinawa. In the event they did not succeed but they gave Marubeni a run for their money. Soon afterwards Krishna moved to Japan to head ABB's joint ventures with Kawasaki Heavy Industries; one for industrial steam turbines and one for large gas turbines. He closed the one and grew the other. Closing any enterprise – let alone a joint venture – in Japan poses its own challenges and he was no doubt especially motivated by all those who advised that it could not be done. Even though the market in Japan was developing very slowly for large gas turbines he operated "outside the box" and utilised opportunities in Korea and China to ensure survival. Later he capitalised on the boom in the US to grow the joint venture's gas turbine business. In time they succeeded in the Japanese market as well with power plants at Mizushima and Chiba Mill for Kawasaki Steel. After Japan we went our separate ways when I moved to France and he went on to head the Indian operations of Alstom when ABB divested its power generation activities to Alstom.

Born in India and educated in England, Krishna has lived and worked in England, Sweden, Japan, India and Germany. No doubt this varied background has contributed to his understanding of behaviour across cultures and across boundaries of nationality and language. He crosses effortlessly from Europe to Asia to the Middle East to the Americas. He has been able to deal successfully with a diversity of people ranging from workers on the shop floor and trade union leaders through academics, scientists and politicians to Government Ministers and CEOs of large multi-national companies. He has exhibited a love of learning which, as he mentions himself, he hopes will never stop which leads naturally to his ability to teach.

In this book he weaves together his central thesis about the qualities of a good manager which he illustrates by anecdotes and his own experiences. He uses quotations liberally to illustrate his points and these have been selected with great care and are remarkably apposite. He uses a dry humour with metaphors and analogies from science and engineering and history and the financial world. He treats and clarifies diffuse matters such as the use of power and judgement and communication and motivation in a rigorous and precise yet easily comprehensible way.

This book is not just for managers. But it should be required reading for every young manager or student on an MBA course. It would benefit all managers who must deal internationally. It could be useful in team-building and change management situations for executives and in management teams. And, for any reader who is interested in such things, this book is a fascinating story of real human behaviour around the world.

Horn, 14 September 2010

Bo Dankis
Chairman
Gadelius Holding KK, Tokyo
Swedish Trade Council, Stockholm

Preface

Wittgenstein asserted that we cannot step out of our language by means of language. He got this wrong. When misunderstandings arise, some find refuge in blaming differences of culture and language as barriers to communication. I find this a feeble excuse. I get intensely irritated when I hear a statement such as "You can take a Japanese out of Japan but you cannot take Japan out of a Japanese", not just because it is puerile and offensive but because it exhibits a resignation of attitude and a laziness of mind. It denies the sapience in *Homo sapiens*.

Culture and language are the means to communication; they are not barriers. No doubt they are intertwined and culture can only be properly represented as values which in turn can only be articulated and described by language. But culture is a consequence of sapience, and language is merely a tool. They are not the drivers of human behaviour. It is not necessary to be a linguist or a cultural specialist to communicate across languages and cultures. But it does require an awareness of where differences lie. Whether using Japanese or Mandarin or Spanish or Tamil or any of the various forms of English found around the world, it is being aware of the differences in language and culture which allow them to be used as the tools that they are. And being aware of the differences in these tools enables the penetration of the "packaging" to reach the underlying and common drivers of human behaviour.

Since receiving my first wage packet as an engineering apprentice in England in 1964, fresh from completing school in India, I have had the good fortune to be active in academia, industry and the corporate world over the subsequent 45 years. I have been stationed in England, in Sweden, in Japan, in India, in Germany and then in Sweden again. During this time I have reported directly to at least 200 different individuals of some 18 nationalities who were either my direct managers or their superiors (not including reporting to company Boards of Directors and many thousands of shareholders at Annual General Meetings). I have visited some 40 countries and have managed operations in over 50. Over the years, in excess of 800 individuals of over 25 nationalities have reported to me directly as their manager or as their superior's superior and for whose performance I have had some responsibility. I have probably interviewed around 1,000 individuals to appoint some 200 of them as managers. I estimate that I must have had meaningful interactions with between 6,000 and 10,000 individuals in managerial positions. They have been colleagues, customers, suppliers, competitors, partners, consultants, academics, politicians or civil servants in government. They have been men and women of all ages and have come from across all continents.

I have found managers worthy of respect and admiration across all the countries I have worked in, and among all the nationalities I have worked with. I have also found incompetence and stupidity and cowardice and lack of integrity and questionable ethics in all countries and with all nationalities. I have found skilled professionals and rank amateurs everywhere. There have been examples of clumsy beginners and lords of the dance. But underneath the veneer of culture and language, the primal driving forces for managerial behaviour have been much the same all over the world.

But differences do exist. They exist just above the level of the primal drivers. I have found that these show up first as differences of attitude and subsequently in behaviour. Fundamental values are not so very different between peoples around the world but the variations on these basic values are endless. Culture and language and religion are inextricably linked with differences of nuance in values and value systems. The values of an individual and his surrounding environment in turn strongly influence the attitudes and behaviours he exhibits. The "Essence of a Manager" lies here, in getting under the surface of the outer veneer and addressing the fundamental drivers of human behaviour.

It has been a fascinating and an educational journey which still continues. There has been and still is something new to learn every day; about technology, about science, about commerce, about governing and governance, about ethics and integrity, about bribery and corruption, about human relationships, about human behaviour, about cultural differences, and, above all, about the common drivers of human behaviour which lie beneath the outer packaging of culture and language and religion. I have been lucky with, and am profoundly grateful to, all my immediate superiors who have – without exception – given me the room to learn and to grow. I cannot think of any one of my colleagues and subordinates who did not have something to teach me. Even those people who I have not had much respect for or just did not get on with, have provided opportunities to learn – even if only as behaviour to be avoided.

From my personal reservoir of experiences I find I have developed very decided opinions about many areas of management and people and relationships and behaviour. These have hardened over the years and appear – at least to me – to be insights which may have some value for others. This work is not intended to be a scientific treatise with a hypothesis followed by the collection of evidence leading to an analysis and a synthesis of data to formulate a new scientific law or a better hypothesis. I hope that I have by now outgrown the stereotyped attitudes of the right or the left and no longer have any particular political agenda. In any case, I have never had much time or respect for political correctness. I am hopeful therefore that the opinions I put down – and which I hold at times very strongly – are as objective as they reasonably can be but which are no doubt coloured by faulty and inaccurate memory.

I count myself fortunate to have had a great deal of satisfaction and a fair share of fun in all my assignments. I hope I have demonstrated over the years that you don't have to be sad to be serious. But, it is all just opinion – my op-ed column rather than "hard news". However, not everything Wittgenstein had to say was wrong. The world is indeed a totality of facts and not just an accumulation of things. And what I do not know and cannot speak about, I must pass over in silence.

Finspång, Sweden   Krishna Pillai

Contents

1 The "Manager" as a Species 1
   Homo sapiens sapiens manageralis 1
   Species Definition 3
   Habitat and Behavioural Traits 4
   What Makes for a "Good" Manager? 14
   Profile of a "Good" Manager 17
   Visualising the Profile 20

2 Have the Power, Do the Thing 23
   The Ability to Mobilise Actions 23
   Power 26
   From Having "Power" to the "Exercise of Power" 30
   Assessment by the Use of Hypothetical Scenarios 33
   The Proper Exercise of Power 34

3 "A Daniel Come to Judgment" 39
   Infamous Judgments 39
   The Nature of Judgments 40
   Judgment in Managers 44
   Willingness to Make Judgments 46
   Soundness of Judgments 49
   What Makes for "Bad" Judgments 51
   Recognising the Ability 54

4 Communication: Hearing What Isn't Said 57
   The Elements of Communication 57
   Communication for the Manager 60
   From Meaning to Message to Communiqué and Back Again 65
   Cross-Cultural Communications 66
   The Feedback Loop 69

	Conversations for Communication	70
	Identifying a Good Communicator	72
5	**Inescapable Networks and Relationships of Mutuality**	**75**
	Networks for a Manager	75
	The Nature of Networks	75
	Human Networks and Personal Networks	78
	Relationships	82
	Escalation of Engagement	86
	Relationships Across Cultures	89
6	**The Strength of Ten**	**93**
	The Materials Analogy	93
	Character Traits	96
	Strength of Character	97
	Stress and Strength	100
	Developing Strength of Character	105
7	**The Red Badge of Courage**	**109**
	Of Bravery and Courage	109
	Courage Across Cultures	114
	Courage in the Work Place	116
	Creating a Culture of Courage	119
	Courage with Peers and Superiors	122
8	**"Praise Loudly, Blame Softly": The Art of Motivation**	**125**
	Of Carrots and Sticks	125
	Of Psychology and Theories of Motivation	128
	From Theory to Practice	131
	The Size of the Stick	133
	The Sweetness of the Carrots	135
	When Carrots Rot	142
9	**No Confidence Without Integrity**	**145**
	My Integrity or Yours	145
	Values, Morals, Law and Ethics	148
	Business Ethics on the Grand Scale	151
	Ethics in the Workplace	158
	Managing with Integrity	162
10	**A Touch of Class**	**165**
	"A Man for All Seasons"	165
	Classy Is as Classy Does	167
Index		**171**

Chapter 1
The "Manager" as a Species

Managers are born locally but their habitat is global. Culture and language are the wrapping around the fundamental drivers of human behaviour and this behaviour is universal. It is this universality of the drivers of human behaviour which allows "managers" to be considered as a species. In any enterprise appointing the right people to the right positions is critical to its success. But success can only be judged after the event and choosing mangers is concerned with the likelihood of success. "Goodness" in a manager is similar to an asset in a balance sheet. It is different to "success" or "failure" which can be likened to a profit and loss account. A manager improves by strengthening his balance sheet and finding the right manager is an assessment of his balance sheet. There are nine fundamental attributes to look for in a "good" manager and these are both necessary and sufficient. It is the "goodness" of the manager which increases the probability of success.

Homo sapiens sapiens manageralis

All organisations would like to have successful managers. How should we find managers who will be successful? Should we confine ourselves to those who have been successful or should we appoint managers who are inherently "good"? Is the "goodness" of a manager then of any predictive value and discernible? What then makes a "good" manager?

The category of people I have most experience of is managers.

Frederick W. Smith
A manager is not a person who can do the work better than his men; he is a person who can get his men to do the work better than he can.

In the simple version, biologists might consider species to be "*populations of organisms that have a high level of genetic similarity*". Building on Darwin's description of the name of a species as "*one arbitrarily given for the sake of convenience to a set of individuals closely resembling each other*", we can modify the biologists' formulation slightly to consider using the term species for "*populations of individuals that have a high level of behavioural similarity*". For the sake of convenience, and for the purpose of describing and analysing managerial behaviour, I consider the "manager" to be such a species.

> manager *n.*
> 1. One who handles, controls, or directs, especially:
>   a. One who directs a business or other enterprise.
>   b. One who controls resources and expenditures, as of a household.
> 2. One who is in charge of the business affairs of an entertainer.
> 3. *Sports*
>   a. One who is in charge of the training and performance of an athlete or a team.
>   b. A student who is in charge of the equipment and records of a school or college team.
>
> *The American Heritage® Dictionary of the English Language, Fourth Edition copyright ©2000 by Houghton Mifflin Company. Updated in 2009.*

While the verb "to manage" still retains its meanings of "to cope with" or "to take care of", it has evolved to encompass meanings such as "to take charge of", or "to direct" or "to control" or "to lead" or "to supervise" or "to achieve a purpose". The derived noun of "manager" has become a catch-all title. The use of the word "manager" has become ubiquitous. It has come to be used to describe a variety of jobs or functions but also serves as a rank or a title in many organisations.

Everybody today is a manager in some respect. Most people are managers of at least their own finances or their leisure time. A student at school is a manager of his own schedule, his homework or his extra-curricular activities. A good housewife combines a variety of functions with aplomb and is a General Manager *par excellence*. Individuals manage – as general managers – a range of different activities for and during their annual vacations. A workman manages his tools and his work schedule. A flight attendant manages her passengers. A priest manages his flock.

There are more people occupied today as "managers" than there have ever been! But managers come in all shapes and sizes and forms.

Functional descriptions abound and are the most common: Sales managers, Communications managers, IT managers, Purchasing managers, Supply Chain managers, Administration managers, Project managers, Bank managers, Personnel managers, HR managers, Account managers, Team managers, R & D managers, Technology managers, Fund managers, Department manager, Engineering managers, Shop managers, Logistics managers, Production managers, Training managers, Factory managers and Manufacturing managers.

A location rather than a function may be the focus: Office manager, Site manager, Region manager, Country manager, Lobby manager, Laboratory manager, Floor manager, and District manager.

"Manager" may be appended to a process or to abstract concepts: Complaints manager, Business manager, Commercial manager, Quality manager, Relationship manager, Change manager, Innovation manager, Welfare manager, Health & Safety manager, Risk manager and Compliance manager.

The word "manager" probably occurs more often than any other on business cards and in job descriptions today. This applies not only in the business and corporate worlds but even in the areas of sports, entertainment and culture. It is wide-spread in virtually every field and even in governmental and non-governmental organisations. Tournament managers, School managers, Promotions managers, Programme managers, Wedding managers, Hospital managers, Event managers, Funeral managers, Funding managers, Festival managers, Cultural managers, Operations managers, Facility managers, Garage managers, Games managers and Traffic managers.

A designation as a "manager" may represent a rank or a hierarchic level within an organisation: General Manager, Executive Manager, Corporate Manager, Senior Manager, Junior Manager, Deputy Manager, Assistant Manager, Trainee Manager and even Deputy General Manager. An entire class may be referred to as top managers or middle managers or line-managers.

Species Definition

For the purposes of this work let us therefore take a member of the species "manager" to be someone:

1. Appointed to his position
2. Vested with some specific authority
3. Given access to and control over defined resources
4. Charged with the realisation of goals or targets (explicit or implicit)
5. Answerable to his appointees (or their designate) for the means and methods used towards the realisation of his targets
6. With the promise of a pre-defined reward which may be fixed or variable or both

A "manager" is born the first time he is appointed to be responsible for at least one other person's performance and has the authority to dispose of the other's time and efforts. He remains a manager usually for the rest of his working career even if he is elevated to positions where the label of "manager" is superseded by more fashionable titles of Director or Chief Executive Officer or the like. A manager today may have (and – within an organisation – usually does have), a number of subordinates subject to the authority vested in him. These subordinates are then – within the scope and constraints of their own contractual employments with the same employer – at his disposal in the realisation of his goals. Subordinates in turn may well be managers in their own right. A rule of thumb is that a manager should not have more than about six or seven direct subordinates, though in practice this is sometimes up to twenty direct subordinates. However, having subordinates is not a necessary requirement to be a manager as defined above. A Project manager or a Purchasing manager – for example – might have no direct subordinates but they can be vested with the authority to co-opt people and other resources from within an organisation to achieve their objectives. Managerial rewards may be fixed or be a variable, performance-based compensation or be a combination of the two.

Rewards are usually monetary but may also be in kind (for example as various perquisites or as shares or as stock options).

I focus here on people appointed to be managers.

The selection and appointment of managers in the business world is perhaps the single most important internal exercise in determining an organisation's future. The success of any organisation depends primarily on having the right people in the right place at the right time. It is now well recognised that manager selection and development is critical and crucial. A great deal of effort is therefore put into assessing individuals and their capabilities and in their training and development. It is also well recognised that appointing a manager is relatively easy to do but that rectifying a poor selection is difficult and disruptive and time-consuming. Appointing the "wrong" people as managers probably has the most far-reaching and negative consequences of any for an organisation.

Habitat and Behavioural Traits

In my experience, the entire range of attitudes and behavioural patterns exhibited by managers are present everywhere in the world. It would be quite wrong to assume that certain managerial traits are unique or exclusive to any particular region or country or that absolute distinction can be made about managerial behaviour in different countries. No doubt some specific behavioural patterns predominate in certain areas of the world or with certain types of organisations. Therefore, it is possible and very instructive, to make some generalisations which can be linked – for the most part – to types of organisations or to countries or to regions of the world.

Enterprises and their managers in the Asian countries share common features of how they interact commercially with each other, socially or with government. The same can be said for those in, say, South America or Europe or Scandinavia. Bureaucrats, the world over, share similar pressures from their politicians. Japanese and Korean and Chinese managers share many social attitudes. Managers in large companies anywhere are subject to the same shareholder demands and are judged to the same performance standards.

But focusing on some of the differences can be very instructive. Managerial behaviour within large organisations in the US is in most respects, very similar to but can often be distinguished from European or Asian behaviour with regard to "hiring and firing". Small workshops in India or China can be differentiated from those in Japan or Sweden on grounds of technology used or the education levels of employees, but they all face the same competitive pressures and constraints. US, Indian and Chinese entrepreneurs have comparable goals and strategies and have much in common though they may not like to admit it. Family-run enterprises everywhere exhibit the same paternalistic – almost feudal – behaviour. South American managers inevitably exhibit a blend of European and US management behaviour but with an overlay of uniquely "country-specific" behaviour which varies from Brazil to Argentina to Chile and to Columbia. There is a strange commonality of the differences between stereotypes of West Coast and East Coast behaviour, whether in the US or in Australia. San Francisco vs. New York can be mapped to Perth vs. Sydney. Similar behavioural differences can be observed in India but here the east –west pattern is reversed between Bombay and Calcutta (and I choose not to use the names Mumbai and Kolkata). The hustle and bustle of Bombay or of Milan can be mapped to New York, as the slowing down of time in Calcutta or in Calabria can be likened to the laid-back attitudes in Perth.

Some caution should be exercised with these generalisations. These are but my perceptions and should be treated as such. I use examples and analogies. But examples are only illustrations of an opinion and do not in themselves constitute evidence. Similarly, my use of analogies is for illustration and clarification. Analogies cannot be exact or comprehensive and no analogy should be extrapolated too far.

I find for example, that there are distinct behavioural patterns in respect of trust. European managers tend to assume that they themselves are inherently worthy of trust. They are prone to start with the assumption that they are fully trusted, even in a brand new relationship. The level to which they trust others however, can be coloured by perceived nationality traits. Only reluctantly do they modify their assessment as the expected relationships do not materialise. On the other hand, Asian managers can appear to be superficially polite but non-committal and aloof to begin with. They know they start from zero and that they and their counterparts will have to earn and build up the trust in any new relationship before any meaningful interaction can occur. The imbalance of trust can be acute in the case of an Asian manager dealing for the first time with a European manager. Each may have a view of the other which is based on country stereotypes. However, in such instances, European managers generally take more risk. This exposure to personal rebuffs however, can pay dividends in terms of the speed with which a relationship can develop. Asian managers generally start much more tentatively with a distinctly lower presumption of trustworthiness. This slows down the building of a relationship, but reduces the risk of a rebuff and a subsequent loss of face. It is a different behaviour, but perfectly understandable considering the higher measure of risk perceived with being rebuffed.

Often European and American managers tend to view a relationship, for example with a customer, as a somewhat abstract matter which can be kept separate or adjacent to the business to be done. They expect that the relationship will develop automatically as a consequence of establishing business. The relationship is often seen as being parallel to business. Most Asian managers tend to place a relationship with a customer at the centre of their interaction. Subsequent business then is developed as an integral component of developing the relationship. To them, the business is contained within the relationship. In Japan or India a Key Account manager reports first on the quality of his relationships within the customer organisation, and only then on the business volume with that customer. A US or European Account manager usually starts with the volume. Needless to say they are both correct – one has hold of the chicken and the other holds the egg. But matters get complicated and messy when someone tries to break the chicken to make an omelette! But what is worse is when a manager is surprised at the mess when that happens.

A Sales manager from Europe or the US feels his job is done when the contract is signed and he can either deliver a product directly to a customer, or transfer the contract internally to a Project manager or a Product manager for implementation of the contract. His performance and his bonus can then be measured by means of the estimated, "as-sold" profit margin in the contract. But a Japanese or Korean Sales manager sees the completed contract only as the end of one phase of negotiations which merely creates the framework for the next phase of negotiation. In the power generation equipment business where it may take over 12 months to make a sale and where the equipment may be delivered and commissioned a further 18 months or more later, there is ample scope for negotiation after the contract is signed.

My friend, Uchida-san who eventually became Vice President of International Sales at Kawasaki Heavy Industries once taught me that "the Sales manager completes his sale of the first turbine only when he sells the second to the same customer"!

Attitudes to taxes around the world can sometimes be both instructive and amusing. Tax and the paying of tax is a subject that always generates animated, and sometimes very heated, responses which are very similar all around the world. Wherever I have worked I have found that tax evasion is admitted to as being illegal – though sometimes very grudgingly. But few anywhere – and especially in Asia – will take the uncompromising position that it is unethical or immoral. Tax avoidance – as opposed to tax evasion – is of course perfectly legal and has become a major sport in all countries. It has been raised to an art form in many places. It has even become the primary performance target for some Financial and Accounting managers. At the corporate level, finding all the loopholes in legislation to enable tax avoidance (or to transform a case of potential tax evasion into one of tax avoidance) may even provide a decisive competitive edge. In India (and no doubt also in many other places) it is a game to be played by even the most junior of managers. To have escaped paying a tax, and without legal repercussion, is usually a matter for congratulation and celebration! Creativity in matters of tax avoidance can be well rewarded. I found it was not uncommon for Indian managers to have after-tax results (even if the tax was notional) as Key Performance Indicators – something quite unusual in large European organisations where matters relating to tax are usually considered corporate matters and a shielded compartment reserved for the tax avoidance specialists.

In the infrastructure and construction fields, implementation times for a project can run into many years. The management of claims between the contractors and the customer and with tax departments can be a major contributor to the financial success or failure of a project. Perhaps it was their creative attitude, or perhaps just their natural argumentativeness which explains the great success we had with Indian Claims managers operating in South America or Europe or the Middle East.

Corporate rules and regulations are treated very differently in different countries. In Russia they may be ignored with impunity. In India they may be treated merely as proposals which are – sometimes – worthy of consideration. In France or Italy or

Spain, they are seen merely as guidelines which may always be dispensed with, provided – in the sole opinion of the individual – there is sufficient justification to do so. In Germany and also in the UK, there is a much greater respect for the view of the authorities. Here, any pronouncement from Head Office – even if completely trivial or utterly ludicrous – is generally considered to be written in stone and inviolable. The manager in the UK may well point out the failings of such regulations but will follow them anyway but his German counterpart will not even question them. But I hasten to observe that the production of trivial or ludicrous regulations happens everywhere and is not the exclusive preserve of any one country.

Dilbert transcends geography and is hilarious everywhere!

In Japan, corporate rules tend to be overly concise and always written in very general terms. But this allows for many interpretations and can provide much flexibility. It would be considered unethical and is therefore very rare for an individual to have – or admit to – values or a value system deviating from that of the group. However, the flexibility and ambiguity intentionally made available enables most individual variations to be encompassed within the group value system. Here face-saving and protecting the integrity of relationships – both internal and external – will always take priority in the interpretation of corporate rules. A non-compliance with some rigid corporate rule will not generally be permitted to allow the ostracism of an employee. In Germany, in contrast, corporate rules are comprehensive and incredibly detailed, allowing of no ambiguity and little leeway. They always trump an individual's values but it is quite acceptable socially, for an individual to hold different – but subjugated – values (even if the resulting concept of a Corporate Value system applying to individuals who do not all share the same values becomes a paradox). Large European companies love to create PowerPoint slides extolling "Our Values" – usually created by a consultant or a Public Relations or a Communications manager and usually approved by a very select few – perhaps only the CEO. But with very few exceptions, no more time is spent on promoting or propagating these values than the minimum necessary for creating and distributing the slides! In my experience such Corporate Values presentations are more often meant for creating the right image with investors and media rather than actually for governing any behaviour.

In India and Japan and Korea and China, appearance and "form" can seem to be of more importance than "substance". Provided that things appear to be correct – then they must be correct! How one says something can be much more important than what one says. Lack of the proper form may completely disqualify, negate or nullify substance. Results may appear to be sacrificed for the sake of form. Not losing face for example in Japan or not violating perceptions of honour and prestige – *izzat* – in India are perfectly valid and sufficient explanations when some action or behaviour is questioned. In India for example, a pronouncement that "It is a matter of honour – *Izzat ki baat hai*" draws a line in the sand and allows of no further discussion. But this behaviour becomes perfectly rational when one realises that complying with form (maintaining face or maintaining honour) is in fact an integral if unspoken part of the managerial targets to be achieved. In reality, form becomes a part of the required substance. In Germany, on the other hand, substance is crucial but format, rather than form, is also very important. Following the correct protocol and reporting in the correct format is very necessary. Memoranda, reports, meeting agendas or presentations in a non-standard format can cause discomfort and even be considered somewhat anti-social. At the other extreme, in Sweden or Finland, form or format and questions of prestige or ego may be given little value. Substance becomes everything. In fact, relying too much on protocol and tradition and format can be treated with suspicion – as an indicator of a lack of substance.

A Japanese manager's traditional difficulty to say "No" (Never a "No" but always a "*Hai, tadashi...*" – "Yes, but...." or a "We will do our best") may be taken as vacillation by his European counterparts. An Indian manager's bland politeness may be taken as procrastination. And to observe a Japanese manager in India, competing fiercely with his Indian counterpart to avoid any commitments while at the same time, prolonging the conversation, can be surreal. But this is because both recognise that the conversation itself is a vital step in building or maintaining a relationship. Neither is willing to end the conversation and be seen as the one threatening the potential relationship. A Swedish manager's own perception of his straightforwardness and pragmatism can be taken to be blunt and rude behaviour by his Korean counterpart. The caricature of a brash and insensitive American abroad casts a long shadow over US managers wherever they find themselves. While a Korean manager may still be in the early stages of exploring the very possibility of a relationship, his US partner may be already frustrated at not closing the deal.

In Finland, I learned the hard way that if we had not been invited to the sauna then we had not got the order.

While a French or an Italian manager operating in Asia, may very quickly (and usually too quickly) come to the perception that he is being invited to resort to undue influence, the Indonesian counterpart could merely be trying to determine to which restaurant or night-club it is his duty to take his guest to.

When operating in South America my Scandinavian colleague was convinced that an invitation from a senior bureaucrat to "walk in the park" was totally innocent and merely signified a nature-loving host. But it soon became apparent that self-enrichment and not communing with nature was his objective.

An American manager in India thought that his relationship with a vendor was building well when he received and accepted a gift of dried fruits and nuts at Diwali. But he had missed noticing that the bowl carrying the gift was made of sterling silver and his acceptance of the gift had put an obligation upon him.

In all countries and especially in large organisations, some managers – and even some very senior managers – are required only to be "keepers of a process". Maintaining the integrity of the process and avoiding any deviations then become the only objectives required of these managers. The maintenance of processes and the continuity and reproducibility this offers is, of course, bureaucratic but it provides the fundamental benefits that all bureaucracies do – the benefits of resilience and continuity in large organisations. Here avoidance of blame inevitably takes precedence over any result which may be achieved by the process which is being maintained. To be able to deal with bureaucrats in India it is necessary to understand that it is the potential for blame which has to be minimised while the potential for personal gain has to be maximised. In such situations, changing or improving a process is not for the process-keeper but becomes both the challenge and the task for other managers. In large European organisations, I have seen deep schisms develop between the process keepers (generally managers in support services or centralised services such as HR, IT or legal), and the operational managers. The operational, business-oriented entrepreneurs consider the others disparagingly to be the bureaucrats, while they themselves are perceived as being free-wheeling, shooting from the hip "cowboys". It represents the perennial battle in large organisations between those "who are overheads" and those who "do the business". In most private organisations it would be unusual for the CEO to have originated from a support function. It is not surprising that it is only in State-owned organisations, where the bureaucratic tradition is strong, that I have observed that the career path to the Managing Director can be via the Personnel Department.

While US managers would ignore, and European managers would generally fear to tread into, the personal life of their subordinates, a Korean manager would be failing in his duty of maintaining harmony (*inwha*) if he did not. While managers in Europe do spend time in soliciting the views of their subordinates they spend much less time than a Japanese manager does in creating the group consensus (*nemawashi*). This is where the concept of establishing consensus itself varies. In most Asian countries a consensus is something to be created while elsewhere it is often something to be found. In Japan and Korea and China the skilful manager has perfected the art of keeping options open until he can get others to agree with and buy in to the decision he intends to take. He moulds and creates the consensus prior to announcing any decision. This process, known in Japan as *nemawashi*, has agricultural and bonsai origins and means "binding the roots". It is not surprising that dissension after creating the consensus becomes rare. Creating such a consensus requires patience and can be time consuming but subsequent actions can be extremely rapid. In Europe however, a consensus is assumed to exist and something to be found rather than created. This is done fairly quickly by averaging different opinions or by finding that opinion or direction which will likely have the least dissent. But the dissenting opinions are not addressed or taken care of and are consequently repressed but remain preserved to surface later. A few managers still mistakenly believe, especially in Europe, that overruling and suppressing all dissension from among their subordinates is commendable and a proof of their strength. Dissension after finding such a consensus is not uncommon. The advantage here is that finding the consensus may happen relatively quickly but the subsequent course of actions can occasionally get bogged down in petty dissent. Both systems can function well in themselves and I do not presume to judge the one better than the other. But what I have observed is that misunderstandings and conflicts inevitably appear when one system meets the other, and especially if the people involved lack the insight to see the cause of the conflict.

I have found Western (European or US) managers more likely to compartmentalise acts of bribery and corruption as a necessary – if forbidden – tool of business.

As if the hiding of such a compartment makes it go away or cease to exist. Stopping bribery and corruption then requires finding that compartment and eliminating it, but it does not ensure that a new compartment will not spring into existence somewhere else since the underlying ethics involved are rarely addressed. Asian managers are equally prone to these same acts but consider them to be intertwined with particular relationships and not something which can be treated separately from the relationship. Here the avoidance of bribery and corruption requires the breaking of particular relationships and not just by a unilateral change of one's own actions. To break a relationship needs the avoidance of all interactions with certain parties. It carries with it implicitly all the heartbreak and loss of face or the loss of honour that breaking or avoiding a personal relationship entails. But, whether in Asia or in Europe or in the Americas the concept of integrity has – unfortunately in my view – come to mean no more than the demonstration of compliance with laws and regulations. The battle against corruption is not really considered to be a moral or ethical imperative. The discussion, if at all there is a discussion, often ends with a "If we don't do it the competitor will", or "When in Rome do as the Romans do". Compliance has become divorced from integrity and ethics. Sadly the focus is on showing that compliant processes exist and on not being found out. Whether exerting undue influence is right or wrong or whether it is ethical or unethical is not usually a subject of interest. "Compliance managers" have become common – primarily as part of the process of demonstrating compliance – but I have come across only one person carrying the title of "Ethics manager". But even in this case, his task was not concerned with ethics at all, and was focused solely on the paperwork to show compliance.

The "BCA or Business Consultancy Agreement" has been the most common mechanism used by large European and US companies, whether operating in their home countries or abroad, to contract with various Consultants and Lobbyists (middle-men with sticky fingers), to effect payments for "services rendered".

I once was naïve enough to suggest that we would be better served by the transparency that would follow if we were, at least internally, to call these BCA's what they actually were – "Bribery & Corruption Agreements". I still recall the general horror and lack of amusement that this generated with my superiors – but I was much younger then!

But I would also observe that wherever in the world I have operated, the instigation of the bribery and corruption has come mainly from politicians and bureaucrats. Whether in Europe or in Asia, an unexpected procedural delay in the permitting of a large project has nearly always meant that somebody, somewhere, was waiting to be unduly influenced. But, wherever a competitive advantage has been perceived, corporations have been willing and enthusiastic participants, even if only rarely the instigators.

US managers are expected to be and are often involved in firing subordinates or at least in initiating the firing process. Being fired does not carry the same stigma in the US that it might in Europe and definitely does in Asia. European managers are far less involved with dismissals and relocation of the offender within the organisation is usually sought as the preferred solution. Managers tend to pass on the task of removing – or relocating – unwanted subordinates to a Personnel or a HR manager. He in turn is the keeper of the relocation or dismissal process and merely, and dispassionately, initiates the process. This can become a form of systemic cowardice so as to avoid unpleasantness. For both the manager and the HR specialist the objective becomes to minimise the emotional involvement in the dismissal. A Korean or Japanese manager would be considered an abject failure if he could not establish and maintain harmony within his group and eliminate the need to ever consider the dismissal of a subordinate. In the extreme case, where a separation becomes unavoidable, he would still avoid a formal dismissal and instead arrange for and manage a resignation. (And how these "voluntary" resignations are engineered and managed is a story in itself.) But even this would lead to a considerable loss of face for the manager since a resignation is clearly a major and visible disruption of the harmony in the group.

In the 1980s, a Japanese manager I was slightly acquainted with took the extreme step and committed suicide when he was to be dismissed from the Japanese subsidiary of a US company. This was to have been a dismissal and not a case of redundancy. A terrible personal and a family tragedy and I have great difficulty in comprehending the stigma that he perceived that pushed him over the edge. It came as a revelation though, when I realised that among my own Japanese colleagues this was seen as a tragedy no doubt, but a heroic one where – by his honourable action – he had bypassed the stigma accompanying a dismissal and had actually "protected" the social standing of his family.

While conducting a major downsizing at our Kobe operations during the 1990s, our initial attempts at Voluntary Separation Programmes had poor results, even though the separation packages were constantly improved. But we exceeded our wildest expectations when we finally and properly addressed the real fears of the employees. The fear of how to go about finding another job and the perceived family stigma were the dominant barriers. We were then able to find a variety of ways by which the employees' honour and his family's status could be protected. Once we fully realised the employees' fear of the unknown process of finding another job we made this the central part of the exercise. In the event, we helped over 80% of those to be separated to find a new position within 6 months of the decision to implement a separation (but made sure that their date of termination was the last working day prior to their starting their new employment). All except three individuals (out of over 300) found, or were found, new employment within 12 months.

A few years later, I found this approach, of focusing on the employees' fears of stigma and family status, worked very effectively also in India where we carried out major downsizing at four different factory locations. Two of the factories were located in large cities (Calcutta and Madras) and two were in fairly remote locations. It was only with the support of the unions that we managed to properly identify the different fears of the employees. In addition to assistance in finding new jobs, we provided some with assistance in maintaining their family homes as part of their termination packages. This was particularly effective at factory locations which were rather remote. Remarkably, it was also at these locations where the cost of providing such assistance was relatively low. An additional factor that worked very well at the urban locations was to address the aspirations of some of the factory workers where we had identified them to be entrepreneurs at heart. By including some old machine tools in some of the packages, some foundry patterns for others and some old computer servers for a few, we were able to assist them to start-up small businesses of their own. This was effective even at the remote locations, but here we needed to commit to some volume for their new businesses, but this was not necessary at the urban locations. We not only exceeded our downsizing targets but also created a new resource pool – but the latter was more by accident rather than by design. Virtually overnight we found we had created a new pool of vendors who were very familiar with our products and our IT infrastructure and to whom we could then out-source work. Two years later when we started expanding again, this pool of competent and qualified sub-suppliers was invaluable.

Many organisations have developed elaborate structures of formal managerial grades which specify limits of authority and regulate promotions and remuneration. The managerial grade structures in large organisations can be as rigid and as uncompromising as in military organisations. With all grades and sub-grades, a large organisation may often have 12 and sometimes as many as 16 distinct managerial levels from the Managing Director or CEO down to the Trainee manager. The title of "manager" can even require incumbents to don de facto uniforms (with unofficial but strict dress codes requiring for example the wearing of dark suits or sober ties or no tie at all or no sports blazers or only white shirts or no jeans or no ladies slacks and so on). The dress code may differ from one rank in the organisation to another. Many companies have explicitly rejected dress codes – ostensibly to encourage a spirit of creativity – and sometimes have only succeeded in creating new dress codes! I have found it amusing when organisations have introduced so called Casual Fridays – and I have introduced these myself – to escape the unofficial dress codes (to demonstrate or to encourage a creative working environment) only to find that yet another dress code has evolved applying to the Fridays! Some Japanese and Korean companies insist – especially at factory locations – that all employees wear the same uniform to demonstrate solidarity and the equal value of all individuals. But as happens with the army in China, the managerial or hierarchical grade structure is unaffected by the superficial uniformity of dress, and remains absolutely intact. Very often, perquisites are related to the "rank" one holds within an organisation. Visible perks can become very important. Whether the rank carries with it a car and which type of car; whether a chauffeur is included and whether he has a uniform; whether housing is provided and does it have a garden or servants attached; whether children's school costs or health care or invitations to social functions are included can all have a profound social impact on neighbours and relatives and can clearly modify the behaviour of those involved.

The social impact cannot be neglected. When I was heading the Alstom Group in India, I replaced a rigid, 1970s style, managerial grade system (which had time-based promotions of grade unrelated to the content of the job), with a job and performance evaluation system. Initially there was much resistance. My Engineering manager responsible for some 200 engineers was a key supporter of the change.

At the salary review immediately following this change, I was greatly taken aback when he requested me privately to ensure that the expected progression of his visible perks in the old grade system – in this case a shift to a bigger company car with a chauffeur– be maintained at all costs. He was even willing to accept a salary reduction in return! It took me a little while and it was only after visiting him socially at his home that I came to fully comprehend the enormous pressures on him which resulted from what was visible to his family, his neighbours and his friends. In this particular case, he was planning and expecting to fulfil his obligations to get his daughter "married off". He and his family were intensively seeking the "right" bridegroom and were themselves subject to due diligence checks being carried out by the families of prospective grooms. The visible accoutrements of his managerial position were not at all irrelevant or unimportant in this process!

For the young today, a "manager" may be merely a "suit" and can be a term of disparagement. The title and trappings can subsume a person's identity. At one time the term "General Manager" described the highest level of manager in an enterprise and who was responsible only to the owners. He was an over-manager and was necessarily responsible for and supervised all the other subordinate function-specific managers. Usage today more often signifies a hierarchical position or rank rather than describing the multiplicity of functions being supervised. It is not uncommon in these days – and especially in Asia – to hear someone define himself as being "a General Manager – a GM" or as "a DGM (Deputy General Manager)". In India, for example, a "GM" commands a higher dowry than a "DGM" in the marriage stakes. But it is only in one Indian state-owned enterprise that I have found a "JADGM – a Junior Assistant Deputy General Manager" representing a coveted status. Some parents aspire for their children just to be "managers". If you come across a Mr. Manager Singh in Delhi it is because his parents had clear aspirations for his career! In Japan to be appointed a *"Bucho"* (General Manager) – irrespective of in which organisation – gives a high status and is an integral part of one's identity. It is sufficient for a person to be introduced socially as a *"Bucho"*. No further detail is necessary for a first introduction. A *Bucho* in a customer organisation may decline to meet, at the work-place or socially, with a lowly *Kacho* from a supplier. That could be an inappropriate loss of face and an unacceptable breach of protocol. It could however be perfectly permissible for a supplier *Bucho* to call on a customer *Kacho* or to invite him to a round of golf! Socially, a *Bucho* is of sufficiently high status that he can be addressed as *Bucho-san* rather than by his name. To be elevated to be a *Jicho* (Department manager) from a *Kacho* (Group Manager) gives you a larger desk and a larger entertainment allowance and is known to do so!

A Manager is assumed to be a part of The Management (as opposed to Labour). He is expected to identify with the owners of and to represent the larger enterprise he may be a small part of. The difference in work-place compensation levels between labour and management is greatest in the developing countries and the relative status in society mirrors this. In social interactions it becomes a class divider. A manager in India or Malaysia just does not mingle socially with "workers". It would be rare but could happen from time to time in Japan or the UK but would not be at all uncommon in Scandinavia. Social status is important not just for the individual concerned but also for those around the individual.

A few weeks after taking up my appointment as a Managing Director in Delhi, I borrowed a rather old and dilapidated car from the car pool – an Ambassador – to attend a meeting with a customer at a rather posh hotel. This was noticed and the next day I was roundly told off by my secretary for "damaging the company reputation" and "not showing a proper respect for my seat"! Of course what I had damaged was the status he enjoyed.

But in spite of all these differences of managerial behaviour, which are very real and which cannot be glossed over, the primal drivers remain the same. The fears all over the world are also much the same even if they do differ in nuance. But it is the manager's individual attributes rather than national characteristics which are important. I have seen Indian managers succeed in European or US environments and vice versa. Japanese managers have done wonderfully well in South America, It was with great trepidation we once appointed a Polish manager in Germany but our fears were entirely misplaced. I have seen Czech and Brazilian managers also operate fluently in Germany. Eastern European managers have adapted very quickly to manage and manage very well in Indonesia and Malaysia and Australia. There have been plenty of failures of course. Many managers have been quite unable to cope with new environments and new responsibilities and new countries. But nationality or country of origin has no veto on a managers potential to operate – and operate well – in any region of the world.

The origin of a manager is perforce local but his viable habitat is global.

What Makes for a "Good" Manager?

I think it is necessary first to distinguish between what is inherent in an individual as a manager and what he may achieve. Success or failure is a judgment made only after the event – when a manager meets or fails to meet or betters his specified goals or targets. But a manager's performance or his achievement of such targets may be – to a large extent – a consequence of external circumstances and forces entirely outside his control rather than necessarily or exclusively due to his efforts alone. For example, changing fashions, or changing market conditions or the vagaries of weather or Acts of Governments or breakthroughs in technology or Acts of God, usually fall outside the scope of a manager's influence but may have a profound effect on a manager's results. Thus, a "bad" manager may be quite successful – in spite of himself – in good times. A "bad" manager may be "lucky", where I take "luck" to be the beneficial combination of surrounding circumstances which are outside ones control. Equally, in bad times even a "good" manager may not reach his targets and therefore may not be deemed to be successful, but he will usually get the better results. The "good" manager will better anticipate the onset of negative factors outside his control and be better able to mitigate the effects of adverse circumstances. Equally he will be better prepared for the occurrence of beneficial circumstances and be able to maximise the advantages that could be available. To that extent, he "makes" his own luck. I have heard it claimed that managers can be classified as being defensive or reactive types on the one hand (who are effective during a recession for example), or aggressive or predictive types on the other. But these are descriptions of behaviour and not inherent traits. All managers need to be defensive and reactive at times and to be aggressive at others. The "good" manager knows when to be what.

We need to also make a distinction here between "the best possible result" and "the best result possible". The first represents the playing field of possible results and boundaries are set only by where the impossible begins. The second describes the best possible result attainable in the prevailing circumstances on that particular playing field. Managerial targets are usually – if set correctly – within the bounds set by the best possible result. (Targets can be – and sometimes are – set outside the bounds of possible results. Except in very rare cases, such targets become untenable and self-defeating once they are discovered to be outside the range of what is possible.) The "goodness" of a manager however, is concerned with getting the best result possible in the prevailing circumstances, whatever the prevailing circumstances. The rare occurrence of a "good" manager, operating during good times and who is "lucky", is that particularly potent combination which can come close to achieving the managerial Holy Grail – the best possible result. "Goodness" is an inherent attribute of a manager whereas "success" is a value-judgment of what has been achieved – but only and always in retrospect. "Successful" cannot and should not therefore be equated with or substituted for "good".

Success is transient. Just like profit or cash-flow – it is over once it has been recognised. The success counter is set to zero once the success is "booked". Goodness lasts longer – it is like a balance sheet item. This financial analogy is sound. A success once booked – like profit or cash – gets transferred to the goodness in the balance sheet. It is available as a balance sheet item for future results but does not – in itself – ensure such future results. Past successes like previous profits provide a track record and an indication of things to come but do not, in themselves, ensure future success or profit. And just as a lack of profit or a shortage of cash can impair a balance sheet, a lack of success can impair a manager's goodness. Success and goodness are different.

A consistent track record – in any field – is a very powerful indicator. It brings to mind Newton's First Law of Motion, which states that a body continues in its state of rest or motion in a straight line unless acted upon by an external force. The inertia in organisations and other complex systems of human behaviour weighs heavily in favour of things continuing in their present state. For example, weather systems are enormously complex and forecasting weather uses the most sophisticated and complex mathematical models running on the world's most powerful super-computers. But, I believe it still holds good that, statistically, the most accurate weather forecast (or that which is least prone to error) is the simple statement "that the weather tomorrow will be the same as today". Drastically wrong sometimes but more often right than wrong and statistically the most accurate nevertheless. When appointing a manager therefore a track record of previous success is a valuable indicator of things to come. And equally, an indifferent or a poor track record can also indicate what is not likely to come. Inertia cannot be denied and must be given its due.

> Omar Khayyam
> When I want to understand what is happening today or try to decide what will happen tomorrow, I look back.

Of course, a track record in the wrong field may be irrelevant or of limited value and can be highly misleading. It has become a clichéd statement, but it is a true statement nevertheless, that "elevating the most proficient engineer to become the Engineering Manager will surely result in the loss of an engineer and may result in the gain of a bad manager". It is not at all uncommon, and especially in large organisations, that fairly proficient managers in one field get promoted into areas of responsibilities for which they are totally unsuited.

A manager with a history of success in a particular field is not necessarily a good manager in a different area of responsibility. The Peter Principle comes to mind which states that "in any hierarchical organisation employees rise till they reach their level of incompetence". There are dangers and limitations to relying on a track record alone. There is, I think, no doubt that the likelihood of a manager with a proven track record of success being a "good" manager is high. There is also no doubt that the probability of a "good" manager achieving the best result possible is high. From this it follows that the chance of achieving success is enhanced with a "good" manager. Success though does not just require goodness. And goodness does not ensure success. But goodness does predicate achieving the best result possible. In other words, if the goodness is inherent then the track record may follow. To continue with the financial analogy, if the balance sheet is sound then the probability that profits and cash may follow is enhanced.

Therefore it is a much more grounded approach to focus on the goodness of a prospective manager rather than on just his track record of past successes or on trying to make a forecast of his future success. I believe it is possible to assess what makes a person likely to be a good manager. The analogy from the financial world still applies. Selecting a manager is like doing a due diligence on the financial status of a company being considered for acquisition. Looking at the prospective manager's track record is not dissimilar to studying profit and loss statements. Assessing his goodness as a manager is then very much like penetrating and understanding the balance sheet.

Of course, "good" is a subjective term and it is relative and it is in the eye of the appointer. Finding ways of discerning the qualities that are likely to make a person a "good" manager has generated an industry of its own. This quest has spawned a jungle of folk-lore, check lists, interview techniques, intelligence tests, behavioural tests, immensely complicated and – supposedly – sophisticated aptitude tests and assessment techniques. Sometimes I feel it smacks of witchcraft – but that is not to say that the witches' potions may not be effective! They are applied by armies of Human Relations managers, flocks of psychologists and hordes of consultants. It is easy to be seduced by the jargon and the apparent sophistication of the assessment process. It needs to be borne in mind that the qualities to be discerned within each individual represent an enormously complex balance of attributes. It needs to be always remembered that a good score in a test may well reveal someone who is good at taking the test but very little else. It should not be overlooked that having a complicated processes of assessment is no guarantee for being able to penetrate the complexity that makes up an individual. Such complicated methods of assessment – in my experience – can be a very useful complement in a recruitment process but can be misleading and counter-productive and quite dangerous when used alone. Ultimately the qualities to be assessed in the prospective manager represent the value-judgments of the appointer. The assessments – which are all forecasts of future behaviour – are no doubt extremely difficult to make but the basic attributes to look for and the fundamental value-judgments to be made are actually quite simple.

Complexity – I would contend – is best penetrated by simplicity and best deciphered by applying simple principles – consistently. I have generally found that the most penetrating assessment of balance sheets is achieved by sticking to the basics and using relatively simple – but very sharp – analytic tools. This applies also to assessing individuals and their potential to be good managers.

There are a plethora of qualities – sometimes quite contradictory – proposed as being essential to a "good" manager. Leadership and entrepreneurial acumen; vision and strategic thinking; decision making or consensus building; creativity or a structured approach; an extrovert character or an introvert nature; an eye for detail or an eye for the big picture; passion or detachment; intuition or rational thought; involvement or objectivity; intelligence and knowledge; integrity and courage, pragmatism or idealism, to name but a few.

But I would suggest that when trying to recognise the potential that can make a "good" manager it is necessary to revert to fundamentals, to keep things simple. The assessor's own values and value system provide the reference points that are needed. This in turn, of course, requires that the assessor (or the appointer) has a clear and explicit view as to what these values are. I have come to the conclusion that a "good" manager will necessarily – and sufficiently – have certain characteristics or building-blocks of attributes.

> John D Rockefeller
> Good management consists in showing average people how to do the work of superior people.

Profile of a "Good" Manager

To create a complete and consistent "picture" of what to look for in a good manager, I start with the core requirement of a Manager; which is to mobilise the actions necessary to achieve a particular objective. I break this central requirement down into three component parts; firstly the power to mobilise actions, secondly the ability to exercise this power and leading, thirdly, to the ***proper exercise of power***.

Most of the actions to be mobilised will generally be carried out by others. Some of the actors to be mobilised will be the manager's subordinates and some will be his peers and even occasionally his superiors. Others will be members either of his personal networks or of the connected chain of intersecting networks, and some will be total strangers.

Judging when and how and to what purpose power is to be exercised is indispensible to being a good manager. This relies on the manager being prepared and willing to make judgments and on the quality of his *judgment*. I take judgment to be the exercise of mind resulting in an actionable conclusion. This is integral to his choices and decision making. Whether for choosing broad strategies, or for choosing the correct short-term objectives and sub-objectives, or for selecting the right people, or for selecting the actions to be mobilised, or for choosing the right avenues for such action or anticipating other people's reactions or behaviour, the manager's readiness to make judgments and the soundness of such judgments will determine the actions that can be, and need to be, mobilised. The soundness of the judgments will determine the risks involved and the overall level of exposure to risk. It is his judgment which enables his exercise of power and the mobilisation of actions.

But his judgments must be made manifest in many people. The art of **communication**, such that what is perceived by the subject is what was intended by the communicator is what makes desired actions possible. Communication here is not just his meaning, his message and his subsequent "broadcast" but includes also it's "reception" and conversion to meaning in the mind of the recipient. The broadcast itself may be written or visual or verbal or non-verbal or any combination of these. An absence of an expected broadcast may itself be a broadcast. It may be explicit or implied or direct or indirect. The good manager knows how to listen and is aware of what has been heard and comprehended by those he directs his communications to and how actions he desires are consequently generated.

A significant factor in mobilising actions is the activation of one's own networks. Many members of intersecting and connected networks may also need to be energised. For the manager it becomes important not just to have a wide network of his own with meaningful relationships but also in having an understanding of how **networks and relationships** function in general. Many of the actors he needs to mobilise will be members of other networks than his own. Not only must the manager understand how chains of actions will unfold through the various networks, but he must also be able to judge if and when and how he must empower others to perform the actions he needs performed. They may well be part of multiple networks and subject to multiple and conflicting calls to action.

The manager will be subjected to many stresses; from actions not going as planned or because the actors are not performing as they should or because superiors are demanding results or because deadlines are approaching. Making choices and judgments and following through on the basis of these judgments in an atmosphere of stress demands a fundamental and inherent **strength of character**. Every judgment will also be accompanied by a probability of risk. Sometimes the risks will materialise. The exposure to the risk itself, the toughness to accept setbacks and reverses, to avoid despair and resignation, to maintain equilibrium and direction of purpose and the resilience to move on are all contained within his strength of character.

To have a belief in one's own judgments, to be aware of and expose oneself to the risks inherent in the actions pursuant to the judgments made and to hold to the course of action decided in spite of setbacks or opposing views or peer pressure calls for a full measure of *courage*. I take courage and bravery to be almost synonymous but distinguish between the two by taking courage to be the capacity for a regular stream of brave actions. It is courage which keeps the manager forever subordinating his fears, expanding his envelope of available actions and constantly breaking new ground. It is his courage that can help to create a culture of courage in his immediate surroundings and even permeate through the entire organisation.

Most of the actions that have to be mobilised will be carried out by others. In many cases the actions required will be as a chain of actions, reactions and counter actions, where many of the actors will be mobilised only indirectly. The *ability to motivate* people must be applied not just to oneself – but to the entire orchestra of players who must act. Motivation will be needed not only for subordinates but for all the actors who may be required in his chosen chain of actions. This includes superiors, third parties, total strangers and sometimes even competitors and antagonists. Leadership capabilities are closely tied to the ability to motivate others in a particular direction or to a particular goal. A good leader may not necessarily be a good manager but a good manager will always have some leadership capabilities. The good manager must not only choose the players in his orchestra but he must also write the music, orchestrate it and conduct the entire orchestra.

It is axiomatic for me that without *integrity* every other attribute is suspect and rendered worthless. Without a palpable integrity, a manager's judgment becomes suspect, his earning of trust is jeopardised and his motives become questionable. By integrity, I mean here a consistency of behaviour with an underlying set of values. Integrity of purpose, of judgment, of communication, of actions and of relationships must all be present. Without integrity a manager can command no trust, no confidence, and no respect and will lose the power to mobilise any actions.

Finally, the wrapping around all these attributes, the packaging around the individual which completes the picture and makes it a whole is what I choose to call *class*. For each of the first eight attributes there is a threshold level – on the necessarily arbitrary and subjective scale the assessor determines – which needs to be exceeded. It is not necessary that all attributes are present at a very high level, but it is important that they be inter-connected and in balance. A well-rounded individual will be one who exhibits uniformity in the strength of all the other attributes. Class is not his appearance or his clothes or cultural sophistication. Class is style and much more than style; it is integrity and courage and strength and all the other attributes allied to an uncompromising professionalism. I believe that if an individual has one or more of these attributes being dominant or is lacking an attribute, it leads to sharp and ragged edges in a manager's profile and shows up as a lack of class. In this respect class is a holistic picture of the individual describing the shape or a profile of all the other attributes.

These then are the nine key characteristics which together as a package indicate the potential "goodness" of a prospective manager:

1. The ability to properly exercise power
2. Judgment
3. The ability to communicate
4. An understanding of networks and relationships
5. Strength of character
6. Courage
7. The ability to motivate
8. Integrity
9. Class

These nine fundamental attributes are both necessary and sufficient to complete a full profile. I would be reluctant to classify any person as having the potential to be a good manager if any of the above were totally missing from his armoury. It is not necessary to include in this list such attributes as intelligence and knowledge and creativity which are present in all individuals to varying degrees and which are implicit in all of the above. It is not necessary either to include leadership, decision making and vision and strategic thinking in this list. They are all of great importance but they are also all present as consequences or as derivatives of the nine fundamental building blocks. It should be noted that the fundamental characteristics are not separable and do not exist independent of each other. The complete package is what is needed and what should be assessed. These are therefore the areas I would investigate when assessing a prospective manager and I would look to track record and any results from aptitude tests and the like as a complement to, and primarily to illuminate the assessment of, these characteristics.

Visualising the Profile

One way of visualising this profile is to try and quantify each of the first eight attributes (for example as successive vertical bars on a bar chart or on eight radii of a circle) and to consider the ninth – the "class" of the individual – as the shape given by the profile of the other eight. A well rounded shape on a circular chart or a uniform surface on the bar chart would indicate the more rounded personality of a well-balanced individual and is a good indicator of class. One advantage I have found with this technique of visualisation is that it forces the "quantification" of these soft attributes and even if it does not remove any subjectivity in the assessment it enables the assessment to be made visible and communicated to others.

However, the labels I have used above for the fundamental building blocks can give rise to various interpretations and misinterpretations. Each of these needs elaboration to ensure clarity.

In the rest of this work I expand on and develop what I see as the substance of these fundamental nine characteristics. These inherent characteristics can help to find the managers who are "good" or can become "good". The prevailing circumstances will determine success but the good manager will always be able to manage in whatever circumstances that might apply.

Chapter 2
Have the Power, Do the Thing

A manager's task is to elicit the necessary and sufficient actions from all those required to achieve a specific purpose. It is his **social power** *which is a measure of his ability and capacity to mobilise actions from others. But it is his* **exercise of power** *which actually elicits actions. The* **exercise of power** *requires both direction and magnitude. Just the exercise of power and the generation of actions may not achieve his purpose. The actions could be misjudged or incorrect. The wrong actors may have been chosen. They may be incompetent or incapable. The actions may be unnecessary. Power can be dissipated if wrongly exercised. It is by the* **proper exercise of power** *that he can ensure that only those actions that are necessary are taken and that the actions taken are sufficient.*

The Ability to Mobilise Actions

One hears many glib slogans describing what power is:

"Information is Power"
"Knowledge is Power"
"Intelligence is Power"
"Money is Power"
"Rank is Power"

But it would be just as easy to add that none of these – information or intelligence or knowledge or money or rank – would alone constitute power. And it would also be true to observe that all of these together do not necessarily represent or define power. Something else is needed for that.

In physics, energy is the capacity for doing work and power is the rate at which energy is expended in doing work, and work in turn can be expressed as a motive force exerted over a spatial distance. Social power as used in regard to human relations has some distinct similarities. The exercise of social power can be seen as the application of a motive force of social relationship, exerted between humans for the purpose of eliciting certain behaviours or actions. The human actions or behaviours that are summoned can be mapped to "work" in physics. In this analogy the "exercise of power" between humans then becomes similar to "power" in physics. Social power in human relations then maps to "energy" in physics.

Some philosophers take human power to include not only control over others but also the individual's influence over the surrounding environment. I restrict myself to considering the social power between people. This is sometimes categorised as being applied in only one of two ways; either through the use of physical force or through the force of persuasion. However a definition of power between people is elusive. What power is, and what the exercise of power is, has always been a fertile subject for philosophers ranging from Aristotle in ancient times through Thomas Hobbes and Friedrich Nietzsche to Michel Foucault and Steven Luke and Alvin Toffler in more modern times. There is still much debate which now extends to theories of "people power", or for the "power plays" in ice hockey and in Games Theory and the interactions between nations.

In trying to take a practical view of complex philosophical and sociological concepts and apply them to the work-place, I find the approach of Michel Foucault, building on Niccolò Machiavelli, quite useful. They saw social power as being the strategic status of a person within a particular social situation which enabled him to influence and control and dominate others. I find that this is not so unlike my analogy from physics; where I take social power to be the state of an individual which can be applied to enable the mobilisation of actions. It can be taken to be similar to the state of energy of a material which enables, by its release, the doing of work.

Energy exists in materials in a variety of forms; it may be as potential energy or as kinetic energy or as thermal energy or as chemical energy or as nuclear energy. The form of energy is not unlike the different states of human condition that can exist such as respect or wealth or intelligence.

The most basic requirement of a manager – to be a manager – is that, as Edmund Burke put it, he "do the thing", that he mobilise all the actions that are necessary and only those that are sufficient for the achievement of the objectives that he himself defines.

Edmund Burke
> Do the thing and you will have the power. But they that do not the thing – had not the power.

I apply "necessary and sufficient" to actions in the sense of mathematics or logic. The actions then are those which are individually or jointly necessary and which are jointly sufficient. I include within the set of "actions", all primary actions (directly or indirectly mobilised) together with all consequent reactions and any counter-actions.

In the particular context of managerial behaviour, I prefer a more precise and functional formulation:

- Social **power** *is the ability to mobilise actions.*
- The **exercise of power** *is the mobilisation of actions.*
- The **proper exercise of power** *is the mobilisation of the necessary and sufficient actions for a particular purpose.*

The principal states of human conditions which can lead to a force of social relationship and which in turn can mobilise actions include, but are not limited to, the following:

1. Knowledge or skill or expertise
2. Authority earned by skill or knowledge or expertise
3. Force of personality or charisma
4. Physical superiority (or inferiority)
5. Physical force
6. Intelligence
7. Intellectual superiority (or inferiority)
8. Force of argument
9. Authority vested by an acknowledged superior authority
10. Fame and honours bestowed
11. Moral status
12. Age and its corresponding physical states (helplessness or strength or weakness)
13. Wisdom
14. Relationship
15. Social status
16. Wealth

Every individual has these states of human condition to some extent. If the states between two people are different then it is this difference which creates the potential difference of social power. A rich idiot may be powerless with an impoverished intellectual. A helpless infant may have incredibly potent power over an autocratic tycoon. Just as chemical energy or kinetic energy must be harnessed to do work, social power must also be harnessed to be able to mobilise actions. The social power of an individual to mobilise actions then consists of two parts. First, the difference of social power applicable is given by the result of all the appropriate and relevant states of human conditions that he can bring to bear in any particular interaction. Second, his inherent virtues of strength and courage and judgment and communication and integrity, must come into play so that the potential – the difference in states of human condition – is transformed into a motive force. In a manager or a prospective manager therefore, each of the three constituent parts which can lead to the "proper exercise of power" need to be considered separately:

1. Does he have or can he develop social power as the ability to mobilise actions?
2. Can he exercise or learn to exercise this power by which it is translated into actions?
3. Can he exercise the power properly by bringing about all those actions which are necessary but none beyond those which are sufficient for the achievement of his objectives?

Power

Let us take these three parts of our definition in turn.

Power ≫ Exercise of Power ≫ Proper Exercise of Power

First, consider the ability to mobilise actions.

With this particular formulation, "social power" is then a just a description of the potential or the capacity to mobilise actions. As such power is then merely a magnitude, a measure. In the language of physics or mathematics it is a Scalar quantity, though sometimes very difficult to quantify. It is useful here to refer again to analogies from the physical world. Managerial power is analogous to a high voltage potential or to a high water level or a high temperature level, which describe respectively the potentials for the flow of an electric current or the flow of water or the flow of heat. The existence of the potential is necessary but not sufficient to guarantee that a flow will occur. Something else is needed for that. Similarly the ability to mobilise action is not the action itself. Having power does not automatically result in actions. Something else is needed for that. But without the potential existing no flow can occur, and without power no actions can possibly be mobilised. Can this ability itself be described or measured? To address this we need to first look at human actions and the triggers which mobilise such actions.

I take it as an axiom that every voluntary human action is carried out only in response to a request.

The request can be self-generated for one's own actions or it can come from others. Sometimes the request is implied rather than being expressed explicitly. The request can be in any form that can be sensed or detected by the subject. It may be visual, or aural or verbal or written or even unspoken and unexpressed. A smell of burning from the oven can trigger action from the chef; but even though the request to save the meal is not articulated, it is present, self-generated in the chef's subconscious mind. A sound or a picture can trigger actions. A wave of the policeman's hand is a visual cue which can trigger the subject's movement in response to the policeman's request. The request may be disguised. My observation about somebody else's very neat appearance may be a disguised request to my son to get his hair cut. It may be a direct request or indirect. It may be a command or it may be a plea. It may be accompanied by threats of sanctions or the promise of inducements. It may contain the menaces of penalties or the offers of reward. It may call on the fulfilment of obligations or the repayment of debt. It may take the form of a duty demanded or a favour solicited. It may appear to be non-existent but is often present as an anticipated or a perceived request. But, the perception of the request lies only within the perception of the receiver. If the request is not perceived there is no request. Even where no explicit request is made the perception of a request within the receiver is sufficient for the request to exist.

The perceived request is a necessary condition for any voluntary human action. Wherever there is a voluntary action there is always a perceived request – always. But note that a request made is no guarantee of a request perceived. Furthermore, the request perceived by a receiver – if perceived – may not be exactly as the maker of the request intended. Requests may even be perceived where no request is made or intended. (As Henry II probably claimed after his cry of "Will no one rid me of this turbulent priest?" led to his knights perceiving a Royal request for the assassination of Thomas à Becket.)

It does not follow that a request – if and when perceived – will always lead to action. Without sufficient driving force backing up a request (power as we define it here), there will be no discernible action. The desire or motivation of the subject to respond to the perceived request, will determine the effectiveness with which the request is complied with or if it is complied with at all.

We can pursue our analogy from physics a little further. If the voltage or temperature difference is not high enough to overcome the internal resistance of an electric or thermal conductor no discernible current or heat will flow. A "weak" teacher will be ignored when demanding silence in class. Weak in this context could mean lacking sufficient difference in the relative states of the human condition to evoke a response. Weak may also mean a deficiency in an inherent virtue such as courage or strength or communication which can convert the difference of state into a motive force. A politician may not be able to fulfil his election promises even if he fully intended to. Paraphrasing Edmund Burke, "He does not the thing – for he had not the power". To place an individual into the position of a manager where he may be vested with authority but where he has not the power, renders him ineffective and does a disservice to all.

Moreover, even if a request is perceived correctly, and is backed up with sufficient power, the action requested must be within the capabilities and the competence of the receiver. Else the action mobilised – even if performed with great enthusiasm – will not be the desired action. This probably explains why my wife's commands to fix the washing machine are perfectly well understood and can generate frenetic activity on my part, but usually does not succeed in fixing anything!

If a chain of actions is what is needed and the primary subject is required to trigger further actions by others, then the subject's own power to mobilise these further actions comes into play. This is the point where empowerment comes in. Empowerment is not merely the delegating of authority; it is increasing the ability of the receiver to mobilise actions and may include some delegation of authority. The manager can take suitable actions to increase one or other of the states of human condition which confer power on his subject (knowledge, skill, social status, wealth or authority for example), so as to enhance the subject's capability for mobilising actions. But the manager needs to have the insight and judgment as to when empowerment of others is needed or beneficial to achieving his own objectives. Needless to say, he needs also the ability to be able to change one or more of the states of human condition in his subjects so as to empower them.

But the corollary for the good manager is that he does not empower others merely for the sake of empowerment. He does it for the sake of the actions he wishes to mobilise. Empowerment carries risk. Empowering the incompetent is a cardinal sin for any manager! It is putting a loaded gun in the hands of a chimpanzee.

Requests received from others can take many forms:

1. As an "order" from a person of higher rank within the same organisation (Major to Captain, Senior manager to Junior manager, Pope to Cardinal) and bear in mind that such an "order" or "instruction" is not merely a request with an implied sanction, but may also be an empowerment to act, or
2. As an order or an instruction from a person vested with the "authority" to give such an order (a policeman or a judge), or
3. As a "purchase of service" from a supplier which is no more than a request with a promise of reward attached, or
4. As a request for action because of an obligation owed (child to parent or disciple to his *guru*), or
5. A request with a promise (perhaps an implied promise) of reciprocity (between friends), or
6. As a request for assistance from a family member, friend or "relationship" or "network" partner (which is a combination of an obligation owed and a demand for a discharge of duty), or
7. As a request for a service as a discharge of a duty (student to a teacher, client to lawyer, club member to a club official), or
8. As a request by soliciting a favour (beggar to a rich man, employee to employer or a short person to a tall person)

We live today in a world which is a complex interconnected network of requests and actions. Some of these requests lead to actions. A request – once perceived – may lead to further requests (and counter requests), creating a network of requests and a chain of corresponding actions and reactions. Some of the actions are those desired and intended by the original requestor but many are not.

In appointing a manager this is the bottom line – an assessment of the extent to which the person has or can develop or can learn this potential – the power to mobilise actions.

Between any two people, individual or interpersonal power is the capacity of the one to mobilise actions by the other. It is a composite measure of the competence of one to make a comprehensible request for action and of the driving force behind that request. Interpersonal power, as the ability to mobilise actions, can apply in both directions simultaneously and it should not be mistaken to mean the dominance of the one or the subjugation of the other. A helpless infant can have enormous interpersonal power not only on its mother but on all humans in the vicinity. The power of poverty on the affluent is harnessed by every charitable organisation. It is remarkable for example that the power of poverty radiates and can have wide impact whereas the power of wealth needs a sharp focus to generate actions.

This social power reflects the difference of the states of human condition between the two. This is the difference of condition, such as wealth or authority or knowledge or need or social status, which is analogous to the potential difference of voltage or temperature in the physical world. When allied to the inherent virtues of one person it can be manifested as a motive force of the social interaction; as the force of personality or logic or reason or authority or intellect or any combination of these. It becomes a unique characteristic of the interaction between the two individuals concerned. A manager, of course, needs to deal with many individuals and part of his managerial power, as distinct from interpersonal power, is determined by the extent of his reach. Extent of reach is not the number of individuals he can contact but the number of individuals susceptible to his power to generate actions. Even when dealing with a group of people, the interpersonal power that actually applies is unique to each. For a manager, power then becomes the summation of all the individual interpersonal powers (applying separately or jointly to other individuals within his reach) across the extent of his reach.

$$\text{Managerial power} = \sum \text{interpersonal power across reachable individuals}$$

Whether it is better to have great individual power applying to a few individuals or a lesser power applying to a great many individuals depends on the specific task that the manager is charged with. In large organisations, the number of individuals – excluding one's own subordinates – needed to be reachable by a manager, generally increases as one moves up through the hierarchy. A junior manager may not need to have a very extensive reach. A Production Control Manager may not need as extensive a reach as the Factory manager. Different managerial functions can demand a different extent of reach. The Accounting manager may not need as wide a reach as the Procurement manager.

Most people generally underestimate the level of power they may actually have with another individual. They tend also to underestimate the extent to which their reach actually extends. But there are always cases where some people have an incredibly inflated opinion of their own inherent power and reach. "Know thyself" said the Greeks. It is vitally important that a "good" manager have a reasonably accurate assessment of his own power and, by corollary, of his limitations. Underestimation of one's available power can be paralysing and overestimation can be reckless. But there is no simple instrument such as a potentiometer or a thermometer that can quantify this ability. This potential depends on a combination of the different states of human condition but also on many individual characteristics; judgment, bravery, toughness, integrity, communication skills and an understanding of networks and relationships will all impact the interpersonal power that can be brought to bear.

Much of this ability, this power, can be learned and acquired, and develops with experience. As with most skills, repetition, training and more training does improve the skill. But there is also a part which is unique to the individual – which is determined by his demeanour and his charisma and his character and his genes. Analogies with physics do not work here. This ability to mobilise actions should not be confused with the individuals own competences to carry out actions which themselves would need to be requested; and which would need to be separately mobilised or triggered.

The managerial power to mobilise actions can be compared to – but not equated with – what in the military would be termed "the ability to command". It has long been recognised that individuals vested with the same command authority exhibit varying degrees of ability to utilise this authority. Military academies, staff colleges, psychological profiling, stress testing and testing under simulated emergency conditions are all used to try and identify those suited to command. However, in the managerial context, while "power" does include the potential to command, it has a much broader scope than just "command ability". Most managers must be able to mobilise actions from many who are not under their command. In fact, in the industrial or corporate world the majority of the actions to be mobilised in a particular situation may need to be by people outside the direct chain of command available to a manager. Actions may be needed from government functionaries, superiors, peers, colleagues, suppliers, partners, customers, personal friends, acquaintances and relatives in addition to actions by direct subordinates. Many of these actors may well be under the command of someone else or in a different organisation or part of a competing network. They can even introduce opposing potentials and may decrease the susceptibility of such actors to the manager's requests for actions. Actions – perhaps mainly as reactions – may also be needed from competitors or other players who have no vested interest in fulfilling the manager's objectives. They may even have diametrically opposing objectives yet may still need to be mobilised. A Project manager or a Programme manager may have no direct subordinates under his command at all. It can be observed that a military commander also needs to have this wider managerial power in addition to his command ability. This need is probably greatest during times of peace when objectives are more diffuse, and immediate goals are not as narrow, precise or clear-cut as during times of war.

The assessment of this social power in an individual is inevitably subjective to the assessor. Nevertheless it is an assessment, albeit qualitative, which I would recommend should always be made explicitly. Some objectivity can be included by way of the prospective manager's track record, his grasp of how he may mobilise actions in a hypothetical situation, the extent of his own personal networks, the depth of the relationships in his networks and even well formulated and focused aptitude tests. Personally, I have found the use of hypothetical scenarios during interview sessions and third party assessments of track record – after the interview sessions – the most useful. I have found it fruitful to always include a hypothetical scenario well outside the aspirant's experience and his comfort zone to explore his understanding and visualisation of how actions could be mobilised. I have always found that those who can visualise a course of action – even in a hypothetical situation – can more readily make judgments and embark on courses of action.

From Having "Power" to the "Exercise of Power"

Having the social power to mobilise actions – in the form of his states of human condition and his inherent virtues – is a necessary requirement for a manager to be "good", but it is not a sufficient condition. Can he put the power to use? Can it be converted into the concerted actions of others? This brings us to the second component of our definition. Can the power be exercised? Of course, if power is absent then its exercise becomes moot but, having power does not always lead to its exercise.

"If you do not ask, you do not get" is a maxim which applies. No request made means no power is exercised. The ability to exercise power grows with the exercise itself. The more one has applied or tried to exercise the power, the better the assessment or the self-assessment. A key factor in making an assessment of a prospective manager then becomes one of investigating the frequency and extent to which the aspirant has actually attempted to apply his power and whether he has learnt from his failures.

The exercise of power involves channelling the power by way of requests into actions. Can the requests which mobilise actions be generated with the appropriate people and perceived correctly by them? It consists therefore of the formulation of requests of oneself and of the surrounding environment in such a manner that actions result. Requests which are misunderstood, or fall on deaf ears, or on the wrong ears, or which do not trigger any action, or which lead to actions different to those intended may constitute a failure in the exercise of power rather than a lack of power. A parent who gets no response when ordering a 10 year old to tidy his room probably has the required social power but fails to exercise it. (But, if it was a 16 year old for example, who rejected a parental instruction; it is then more likely to be a case of an insufficient social power with the parent rather than a failing in the exercise of power.) Extending our use of the physics metaphor where we took power to be a Scalar quantity and a magnitude describing a potential to mobilise actions, the "exercise of power" now requires that the power have direction. The "exercise" of power becomes a Vector whereas the power was Scalar. The direction is towards oneself or towards those who have been chosen as being necessary to be mobilised into actions. Just as the magnitude and directions of Vectors can be added together to give a resultant Vector, power exercised in different directions also gives a "resultant" applying to the exercise. Many exercises of power in the same direction are also additive. Choosing the wrong actors or any other misdirection is essentially a failure of the exercise of power. By direction I mean both the path and the destination. For example, requesting a plumber to fix your car – even if he understands the request and is willing to act – could be a case of misdirected power by having an inappropriate destination and could lead to an expensive failure of the exercise of power. Similarly, a memorandum demanding an action, but sent to 20 subordinates could result in nobody being activated. This would also be misdirection since there would be no direction at all and it would be a failure of exercise. A manager who has difficulty to delegate and tries to take on too much himself is also misdirecting his power and failing in the exercise of power. Inevitably the exercise of power is, at the time of action, dependent upon the recipient of the request for action and his perception of the request. In consequence the formulation of a request must be tailored to produce such a perception in the mind of the recipient so as to be at least sufficient to overcome whatever inertia may exist and to initiate the intended action. Different people may well require different requests to bring forth precisely the same resultant action. Identical requests to different people could lead to action in one case and no action in another or elicit completely different actions.

Perhaps Henry II was actually a very clever manager who had intended the elimination of Becket all along, but needed deniability. Perhaps he had calculated precisely and correctly that his rhetorical and apparently directionless question – which could always be repudiated – would, in fact, be taken by the listening knights to be a Royal command and a request for action (as it was)!

It is the manager's judgment – which I deal with separately as a fundamental characteristic – which determines his objectives, his choices regarding the actions to be taken and his choice of people to carry out the chosen actions. It is his judgment which provides the direction for the exercise of power. The directions in which power is exercised need to be correct. Without direction, power is dissipated uselessly. Misdirected power also leads to depletion of the power itself and, if the wrong actions are elicited, to unwanted actions and all their consequences and to "collateral damage". Merely the existence of collateral damage – whether in war or in a managerial situation – is symptomatic to me of misdirected power and synonymous with a failing in the exercise of power. This does not mean that I conclude that misdirection is always unavoidable. What I do contend, however, is that though collateral damage may not be avoidable, it is always a consequence of, and an indicator of, a failing in the exercise of power. It would always have been a more correctly directed and better exercise of power if there had been no collateral damage. Misdirection or collateral damage may be symptomatic of "noise". Just as in physics where it is unfocused, random, and disruptive and hides the true signal, "noise" in the context of managerial actions indicates a lack of direction or misdirection and a failing of exercise. A "noisy" manager is one who creates a high level of collateral damage and disqualifies himself from being a good manager.

Having chosen the complete set of actions to be implemented, and the actors to be put into play, our prospective manager must not only have the requisite social power but also the acumen and competence to formulate and communicate his requests to suit the recipients of the requests and to cause them to perform the desired actions. He needs to have the insight that the very same request can cause different actions from different people. He must be able to determine how his requests must be tailored for different people to elicit the desired actions. This in turn requires true communication skills as opposed to the mere transfer of information (and I treat communication itself separately as being a fundamental characteristic of a "good" manager).

$$\text{Power } (+ \text{ judgment of direction} + \text{communication}) \gg \text{exercise of power}$$

While it is important to distinguish between power and the exercise of power, they are often so closely inter-connected that it is usually practical to try and assess these simultaneously.

Assessment by the Use of Hypothetical Scenarios

To be able to gauge that an individual is capable of exercising power we must be able to assess his skill in eliciting desired actions from various chosen recipients by means of the requests he communicates. The same hypothetical scenarios used to investigate whether he has power can now be extended to test whether he can also exercise power. I have found it convenient to do this by varying, in the hypothetical scenarios, the number or the quality of people available to him, where some are subordinates and others are not. I have found the use of hypothetical scenarios in an interview the most useful technique of getting engaged responses and then making assessments.

I have used general as well as real case studies to develop the hypothetical scenarios. Typical examples of hypothetical scenarios I have used to get aspirants to imagine themselves in are:

- *As a Sales manager when a market collapses or a product becomes obsolete, or*
- *As a Production manager having to manage the fear and opposition when technology and manufacturing are to be transferred from a factory in Europe to a new one in Asia, or*
- *As Harley-Davidson's Marketing manager when Honda introduced their 50 cc mopeds into the US*

I also like to ask aspirants how they would see themselves behave in an emergency situation such as, for example:

- *As the Personnel manager of a company in Kobe when the earthquake hit, or*
- *As the Communications manager for a company when one of its products has failed and has caused a fatal injury, or*
- *As Exxon's Transport manager when the Exxon Valdez spilled its crude oil in Prince William Sound in the Gulf of Alaska, or*
- *As the Manufacturing manager at a location in Europe when a wild-cat strike breaks out over a wage claim*

The important thing, of course, is to design the scenarios to be open-ended and such that there is no right or wrong response. It is the comprehension of the scenario and the breadth of the response and its level of detail which reveals what the aspirant can or cannot visualise. I have found it useful at times to present an incomplete scenario and invite the subject to further develop the scenario itself before addressing the actions that could be contemplated. Such responses can also reveal the in-built self assessment by the applicant of his inherent power to mobilise actions.

Within a 2–3 h interview period I have generally found it possible to present the aspirant with two – sometimes three – hypothetical scenarios to address; one within his area of experience and within his comfort zone, and one or two outside his comfort zone either as scenarios beyond his area of experience or in some emergency situation.

I have also found that getting opinions from third parties and referees is most productive after having first conducted such an interview. This allows the formulation of specific questions based upon his actual performance during the interview. The opinions of his peers can be very frank and forthcoming – though very rarely wholly negative – when sharp, pointed, specific questions can be posed. Questions of a general nature when put to referees or colleagues prior to any interview usually lead to bland, polite and vaguely positive responses which may not be very revealing or useful at all. General references can also be very misleading in cases where the aspirant has actually been asked to resign from his previous position, but is provided with glowing testimonials – perhaps as the price of a "quiet resignation" or to assuage the conscience of his previous superior.

During an interview I have found it helpful to have prepared in advance the two or three hypothetical scenarios within which to place the applicant. Over the years I have learned to allow the aspirant some time – perhaps 15 or 20 min – between presenting him with the scenario and then getting him to describe his behaviour within the scenario. Such exercises can shed light on not only his power and ability to exercise power but also on the other contributing factors such as judgment, strength, communication skills and integrity. My notes from such interviews have then generally been organised into two categories; the first noting my direct assessments of his attributes, and the second recording those specific issues or areas of concern which could be further illuminated by formulating the right questions to his peers and referees.

The Proper Exercise of Power

Al Gini
The central issue of power in leadership is not "Will it be used?", but rather "Will it be used wisely and well?"

There is a large step between being able to exercise power and exercising it properly. Will it be used wisely and well? Power, to be exercised, must have "a particular purpose", an objective. This purpose itself must be a conscious decision, a result of the manager's judgments achieved after an exercise of mind. They may be simple judgments with low consequential risks and perhaps relating to the routine and familiar actions required on most days. They could be very complex, risk-filled judgments, leaping from visions and strategies through strategic objectives to the short term goals to be achieved. Even though the purpose or the objectives may be abundantly clear and well formulated, it is again managerial judgment which is needed to determine the complete set of actions that are "necessary and sufficient" (including reactions and counter-actions) and which could bring about the desired objective. The company of players to implement these actions must be identified and marshalled. Some of the players may need to be empowered. The roles of the various players must be clear, not only to the manager but to the players as well.

The music itself must be written and orchestrated. The consensus needed among the key players, regarding the score to be played and the timing to be used, must be wrought. Where necessary, networks must be activated and relationships brought into play. Communications must be specifically tailored for and directed with precision to the correct players to generate the necessary requests.

At one extreme in the exercise of power is paralysis of action. Such paralysis occurs when the manager in spite of having power and in spite of having made the appropriate analyses finds he is unable to make the final judgment and to make the required choices. To take no action is always a valid option but needs to be a conscious decision, in which case it is not a case of paralysis. At the other extreme we have the manager who rushes to judgment. This can result in a surfeit of actions where many options are addressed simultaneously in the hope that some of the actions will be beneficial. In between these extremes lies the proper exercise of power, wholly dependent upon the manager's judgments and the quality of his judgments.

To achieve his objectives, a manager needs to "conduct" the orchestra of all the different individuals he selects to carry out the "necessary and sufficient" actions. He has to elicit these actions by using a combination of different types of requests – designed specifically to mobilise and motivate the action needed from that particular individual. Different forms of requests are usually available for use with any particular individual. The manager needs to choose the form of request best suited to the individual needed to carry out an action. A manager may as needs dictate order, or threaten, or purchase, or trade, or borrow, or beg, or cajole, or simply request the various players to generate the set of actions that he has determined are required.

(Objectives) + exercise of power + (choice of players + motivation + networks)
$\gg$ proper exercise of power

Power, properly directed through judgment and communication, leads to its exercise by generating actions. To get from the exercise of power to the proper exercise of power needs first the introduction of objectives or a purpose. Additionally it needs the actors to have been chosen and sufficiently motivated for the mobilisation of the selected actions. It is the difference between a football coach instructing the team vaguely to "go out there and do your best" to his engaging in a pre-match team meeting and saying to each player, "go out there and play and play your designated role because that will enable others to play their specific roles and for us to win". The set of actions must be all those that are "necessary" and therefore not be lacking in any way. They must also just be "sufficient" and therefore not exceed the set of required actions. No easy matter!

To assess the ability of a prospective manager to properly exercise power requires the assessor to take a holistic view and to consider all the fundamental attributes making up the individual. His track record, his performance at well structured interviews and the evidence of his peers and referees, are the primary tools available to the assessor. These can go far, but the final judgment is subjective and that of the assessor. It says as much about the assessor as it does about the subject. The subsequent appointment of a manager is itself a managerial task and involves taking risk. But the rewards of making a sound selection and appointing the right person to the right position at the right time are immense.

Consider our appointed manager in a situation of urgency. He gathers together all the relevant information and knowledge, applies his mind (and that of others), makes his judgments and decides on his objective. He makes all the necessary analyses and cross-checks the results against his intuition. He determines the actions necessary to meet his objectives. He chooses just those players needed to generate the complete set of actions and reactions and counter-actions that would be necessary and sufficient to his purpose. He gives the instructions required to his subordinates. He activates individuals from within the networks in his scope of influence and applies his relationships. He motivates all the other players. He then conducts his chosen orchestra. The primary actions are taken and their interactions unfold. Lead players act and set in train further chains of actions. Adverse reactions are pre-empted. Other reactions are anticipated and met by counter-actions. Eventually, as the actions mobilised have their desired effect, the objective is achieved.

"He does the thing".
No missing players. No missed actions.
No extra players. No wasted actions.
No misdirection. No collateral damage.
No dissipation of energy.
No cheers. No jeers.
No fuss, no "muss".
No turbulence.
No noise!
Just the music of the proper exercise of power!

- *Like Matt Busby's majestic Manchester United of the 1960s winning the European Cup in 1968, or*
- *Like the breathtaking speed with which Percy Barnevik merged ASEA of Sweden with BBC of Switzerland and created the new ABB brand, or*
- *Like the controlled and delicate power of Alfred Brendel playing Beethoven's Waldstein Sonata.*

A manager who has succeeded in the proper exercise of power is in no doubt about it when it happens. Just as when the batsman or the golfer knows without question when the ball has been struck by the "sweet spot" on his bat or his driver. For a good manager it should not be too unusual an occurrence. But it is rare enough that when it happens, it is truly memorable.

In the late 1980s and early 1990s I was trying, from ABB in Sweden, to sell a power plant based on a new technology to the Electric Power Development Corporation in Japan for their Wakamatsu site. The power generation industry is extremely conservative and "first-of-a-kind" risks are not popular. The effort to convince the customer to invest in the new technology had been in progress for almost 2 years. The perceived risk for the utility company had been mitigated by the project being designated a National project with approval and funding then being required from the Ministry of Trade and Industry (MITI). But this solution created a new problem for us when it activated a sudden and formidable competition from Hitachi. They invoked the fact that it was to be classified as a National project with Government funds, to advance the view that the power plant supplier therefore needed to be Japanese. Hitachi did not have the required technology but managed to convince the political establishment that they would be able to acquire it. For even the proponents of our technology within EPDC, this was seen as being an unanswerable argument in favour of Hitachi, since Japanese national pride was now at stake. Hitachi even condescended to inviting me to a meeting where they asked me, very politely, not to disturb the status quo and to withdraw our offer, since it was their "turn" to receive an order from EPDC. I managed to remain polite while declining their offer. Our own Japanese VP for Sales felt the case was lost but I was disinclined to give up. With the encouragement of my bosses at the time, Carsten Olesen and Göran Lundberg, we decided to try to change the game. With the help of the Swedish Embassy and under the time pressure of an impending bilateral trade meeting, we succeeded, to get it accepted within the Japanese Foreign Ministry and subsequently within MITI and other Government circles that hurting bilateral relations between Japan and Sweden might result in a bigger national loss of face. Furthermore, we pointed out that permitting an import from Sweden, even for a National project, at a time when the Japanese export surplus was of world-wide concern, could gain them some valuable brownie points. It was perhaps not entirely by design, but we had hit the sweet spot and the opposition melted away. Hitachi eventually withdrew gracefully since it was now in the national interest that they do so, and we signed the contract a few months later. But it was when we changed the game being played and we saw the internal memorandum from MITI acknowledging and adopting our arguments as their own that we knew that we had connected with the "sweet spot".

A few years later I had the unpleasant, but necessary task, of carrying out a drastic downsizing at a boiler manufacturing factory in India. There were three strong unions on the site in Durgapur with reputations for being militant. The factory was located in West Bengal which had a Communist State Government at the time. But by focusing on the employees, on taking care of their interests and on ensuring future employment at the site, we succeeded in getting the State Government to agree, at least, not to oppose the planned reductions. This absence of opposition from the State Government was critical in curtailing the political options available to the unions. But we did not hit the "sweet spot" until we managed to get the unions actively engaged. Though they always remained opposed in principle, they helped us, albeit unofficially, in identifying the individual fears of employees and to accept that their members could be approached with propositions. We needed to reduce our strength to less than 900 people to match our order backlog and preferably to around 600 if the business plan was to be truly viable. In the event a work force of around 1,500 was voluntarily reduced to less than 700.

It was late one evening in Delhi, at an informal and unscheduled meeting with the leaders of two of the three unions that we had come to a practical meeting of minds. The third union also acquiesced a few days later but it is this particular meeting which sticks in my memory as the defining moment and the real "sweet spot" of this exercise.

Within 18 months of the downsizing, the unit which had made losses continuously for over 10 years, had turned around, started winning new orders, and could start recruiting again with a healthy view of the future.

The exercise of power is a manager's stock-in-trade but a "good" manager knows and strives for the music of the proper exercise of power.

Napoleon Bonaparte (1769–1821)
 I love power. But it is as an artist that I love it. I love it as a musician loves his violin, to draw out its sounds and chords and harmonies

Napoleon was no stranger either to power or the proper exercise of power – until finally, corrupted by his own absolute power, he promoted himself to his level of incompetence!

Chapter 3
"A Daniel Come to Judgment"

A *"good"* manager is distinguished by his **judgment** and his willingness to make judgments. A judgment is an exercise of mind to come to an actionable conclusion. The selection of objectives, of the actions needed, of specific actors to be mobilised and their particular actions are all dependent upon the judgment exercised. Conclusions about the goodness or badness of judgements are made long after the judgment itself and only in retrospect. It is the soundness of judgments which must be sought rather than goodness of a future result. This, in turn, requires a quality assurance of the process of coming to judgment which needs to be both rigorous and automatic. But no judgment is without risk. Having a sound judgment must be consummated by the willingness to exercise it.

Infamous Judgments

History is littered with examples of extraordinarily "bad" judgments:

- Virgil in his Aeneid tells us that King Priam of Troy (probably around 12,000 BC) ignored the advice of his priest Laocoön who warned "Do not trust the horse, Trojans! Whatever it is, I fear the Greeks, even bringing gifts". Priam's ego ruled the day and he allowed the Horse within the city walls. History reports that his judgment proved spectacularly catastrophic.
- Construction on the Tower of Pisa began in 1173 but it began to sink after reaching the third floor in 1178. The architect (thought to be Diotisalvi) reportedly defended his design. "It is straight enough" he claimed. But work had to be stopped for about 100 years and the newly rechristened "Leaning Tower" was eventually completed 177 years after construction started.
- In 1876, Western Union's President William Orton declined an offer from Alexander Graham Bell and his financier Gardiner Greene Hubbard, to acquire the rights to the telephone for $100,000 saying "after careful consideration of your invention, while it is a very interesting novelty, we have come to the conclusion that it has no commercial possibilities". At the time Western Union had a monopoly on the telegraph which needed to be defended.

- Lord Kelvin, while President of the Royal Society judged in 1895 that "Heavier-than-air flying machines are impossible."
- In 1962, Dick Rowe of Decca Records concluded that "guitar music is on the way out" when rejecting The Beatles.
- In 1984, ABC-TV declined Bill Cosby's show with the judgment that "the show lacked bite and that viewers wouldn't watch an unrealistic portrayal of blacks as wealthy, well-educated professionals."

While there are many more examples of such "blunders", especially regarding missed opportunities, these stories never actually address whether the judgments made were sound – as sound as they could be, at the time they were made and with the information that was available.

Alfred E Neuman, Mad Magazine
   In retrospect it becomes clear that hindsight is definitely overrated!

The number of opportunities correctly passed over does not usually get recorded or reported. The examples are always cases where history has proved the consequences of the judgments to be "bad". But history does not tell us if the judgments were sound when they were made. We should be a little wary of using hindsight to judge the judgments of the past.

The Nature of Judgments

In the context as I use it here, "judgment" encompasses, but is not limited to, what is variously referred to as decision making, problem definition, problem solving, critical thinking, strategic thinking, goal setting and evaluation of options.

A judgment is the result of an exercise of mind. It is drawn from what is known or assumed or guessed or inferred or deduced to come to a predictive conclusion of what is to be done. I include within the term "judgment" both the process of coming to a "judgment" and the conclusion reached. As an exercise of mind, knowledge, self-knowledge, intelligence, discernment and the elusive quality of wisdom (sapience) are all involved. Judgment therefore includes as the final step what are often termed as "decision making" or "decisions". However, the processes by which judgments are reached are as numerous as there are ways in which the human mind works.

Judgment is a cognitive process. The exercise of mind may be a linear, step-wise process, not dissimilar to the classical scientific method. It contains a number of necessary steps but may not be as clear-cut in differentiating between its steps as a scientific endeavour may be. The process of coming to a judgment first needs the definition of a goal or an objective (implicit or explicit). An objective must include not only a description of the final state to be achieved but also the accompanying Conditions of Satisfaction which when fulfilled confirm that the objective has been achieved. In the context of this objective, the process would lead to a problem statement, followed by the gathering of existing evidence, leading to analyses and resulting in the synthesis of data into a hypothesis or a presentation of actionable options. Then predictions of the consequences of the options would be analysed or further tested by the gathering of new data or evidence, which could then be further analysed and assessed before finally reaching a conclusion about the option to be chosen and how to proceed. There could be many iterations and feedback loops within a largely linear process. Many of the steps could overlap or merge.

The process of judgment could also be non-linear; for example, as an intuitive judgment, often described as a "hunch" or a gut-feeling. This is when the subconscious mind synthesises memory, experience, sensory evidence and knowledge to come to a conclusion. It could also be a conscious but non-linear process; a holistic process where all the steps are taken together or where some run in sequence and some in parallel to each other. It may involve a "lateral thinking" process or a "fuzzy logic" type of approach. It may involve a "hunting" approach where various options are tested in turn with some criterion being used to converge to a final judgment. But, whatever the process, making a judgment means coming to an actionable conclusion.

A judgment in the managerial context is always concerned with a choice about the future – to do one thing rather than another, or to choose one course of action over another, or to choose one person instead of another, or to choose one desired result over another, or to choose one path instead of another. A judgment does not always result in action but always comes to an actionable conclusion. For example, you may judge and conclude that one restaurant has tastier food than another or better service or is preferable for some particular reason. You may actually do nothing following this judgment but the conclusion is actionable in that you could recommend the restaurant to someone else or visit it again or avoid it altogether. This conclusion qualifies as a judgment even if no action actually resulted. In the managerial world, judgments are nearly always required to be made under time pressure and where the resources available are not unlimited.

Even in a court of law, almost every "judgment" has this managerial character. Law courts are essentially reactive rather than proactive as required of a manager. They are activated by a claim of a breach of law and always have the objective of dispensing justice. From what has been in the past, and from what is now, some conclusion is drawn as to what shall be in the future. A judgment by a court may typically be structured as follows: "On the basis of the laws that exist, and because of what has been shown by evidence to have transpired in this case, and noting what has transpired in other similar cases in the past, this court comes to this particular conclusion, and therefore the parties involved shall do as follows...." Courts are vested by society at large with authority. Hence they have the power to mobilise actions, and can levy sanctions to have their rulings implemented. Individuals and managers on the other hand must rely on their own exercise of whatever power that they may have, to convert their judgments into actions. For a manager, his judgment is but one step in the mobilisation of actions to achieve his purpose. Every judgment he makes includes, consciously or unconsciously, a review of the past, a statement about the now and is a forecast into the future. As is the nature of all forecasts, outcomes are uncertain and the actions following a judgment necessarily carry risk.

> William Shakespeare
> A Daniel come to judgment! Yea, a Daniel! O wise young judge, how I do honour thee!

Every individual makes hundreds, if not thousands, of judgments every day. Judgments range in scope from the almost trivial, such as deciding when and where to cross a road or what to have for breakfast, to larger, weightier matters such as buying a house or a car or on deciding to close down a factory or on how to save the world. When a mundane issue is to be addressed or an everyday option is to be chosen, familiarity with the situation and previous experience in similar situations lead to what appear to be instantaneous and intuitive judgments being made which merge seamlessly into the subsequent actions. Many of these "everyday" judgments are at the level of the unconscious and governed by the subconscious mind. But each one of these "trivial" judgments contains all the fundamental characteristics of all judgments:

- An objective with its conditions of satisfaction
- A review of the current status
- A conclusion regarding future action

Judgments at the unconscious level are often a question of habit; where habitual behaviour encompasses both judgment and the subsequent action as a pattern of behaviour. But old habits can be broken and new ones can be formed. Though habits reside in the unconscious, the repetition that leads to habit formation can be done consciously. Current theory, which seems to be supported by evidence in neuroscience, suggests that new habits take 10–21 days of daily repetition to be created and imprinted in the brain. Old habits can be changed but with greater difficulty. Nevertheless, habits as patterns of unconscious judgment and subsequent behaviour, can be created and can be influenced and modified. Of course, they must first be consciously observed to exist if they are to be later modified.

Take the simple case of a person crossing a road. Crossing the road always does have an objective, even if it is never explicitly articulated (and this objective would usually be the arrival at the other side of the road, perhaps as a sub-objective of arriving at a final destination). The subconscious mind makes visual observations followed by an assessment of traffic densities, directions of vehicles, potential crossing places and relative velocities, all at the unconscious level. Previous experiences of crossing the road at this location and at other locations are juxtaposed in the mind together with observations of the current weather conditions and the knowledge of one's own speed of movement. Options are reviewed and risks are assessed, all still at the level of the sub-conscious. Finally the mind reaches the actionable conclusion, say, that crossing the road at just that spot and just after the next car has passed by, will achieve the objective. The subconscious mind finds no unusual circumstance to invalidate previous experience and accepts that the judgment is sound and the risk is acceptable. The mind and body implement the judgment and, without breaking a step, the person marches (or runs if so judged as being necessary) across to the other side of the road. But this entire behaviour (the sequence of judgment followed by the action) is never manifested or even visible in the conscious plane.

Even a complex sequence of judgments involved, for example, in routinely preparing and having breakfast while still not fully awake, may likewise be in the realm of the unconscious. However, similar judgments later in the same day, but now applying to the more serious options presented by the choice of restaurant, the selection of a wine from a wine list and picking what to order from the menu when having lunch, are almost certain to be made consciously.

It is experience, memory and familiarity with a situation which keep judgments in the unconscious plane. But unfamiliar situations, or the level of perceived risk being above some threshold, can trigger the judgment process to shift from the unconscious to the conscious plane. Unusual traffic or weather conditions for example, or an unusual sound which the mind associates with a speeding car, would give a sufficient increase of risk perception to inject consciousness into the judgment of when and where to cross the road.

What is a habit in one person and part of his unconscious behaviour may be a risk-filled and conscious judgment for another. Choosing what to wear and getting dressed in the morning may be a very unremarkable and mundane event which is an unconscious habit for one person. But, for his teenage daughter, it may be a matter fraught with so many potential social risks that it calls for great deliberation and a weighing of many options before making a final decision about what to wear.

In an unfamiliar situation the risk level with each of the available options may be considered so high that the judgment process goes into an interminable analysis loop. Paralysis of analysis may occur and in consequence, no conclusion may be reached and no actions may result.

Once, when visiting the US and on my very first trip to Houston, I decided to walk from my hotel to a restaurant which was only some 500 yards away but was situated on the other side of a busy highway. I could see the restaurant and the objective was very clear but I had never before experienced traffic in Houston. To choose when and where to cross the road without taking unacceptable risk became a conundrum I could not solve. I gave up the effort after being paralysed in indecision at the edge of the road for almost an hour. I no longer attempt to walk in Houston except within a shopping mall!

Take another example. The experienced business traveller glides effortlessly through a busy airport without ever needing to make a conscious judgment. He does not hesitate, may be talking on his cell-phone all the time and he may not even be conscious of how he got from the terminal entrance to finally boarding his aircraft. But he has actually made many, many judgments along the way. Contrast this with the first-time vacation traveller who is hesitant, unsure of which way to go next, constantly checking his tickets and his documents, clutching his bags and carefully reading every message board he comes across. But for him every step represents a situation outside his body of experience. Finding the right check-in counter, checking-in, handling baggage, negotiating passport control, enduring the security checks, finding the right gate and boarding the flight are all unfamiliar steps. At each step he faces a number of options and each set of choices gives rise to a perception of high consequential risk. It is not surprising if he is then occasionally frozen into inaction as he makes his judgments and struggles to avoid being overwhelmed.

Judgment in Managers

One of the primary requirements of a manager, within the time and resource constraints he has, is to make the best judgment possible and not just accept the first possible judgment. In most organisations there is an ingrained methodology for approaching problems which can be a part of the culture and can be stifling. There may well be a particular sequence of setting up problem defining teams and task forces and well-tried criteria for coming to a solution. But, it is a manager's responsibility to look beyond the first solution reached by some "conventional" approach and to look for additional options.

Doug Elliott who was my Professor at Aston University used to say "When you think you have found the solution is the time to start looking for alternatives". He was, at the time, advising his students with regard to scientific inquiry but I believe this holds very true for any manager as well. Another one of his sayings was "Don't make a choice if there is no choice. If you only have one alternative, change one of your assumptions and see what happens".

Especially when under time pressure, the temptation to settle for the first available judgment which promises a feasible course of action can be enormous. To find the balance between challenging all solutions to see if there is a better one but, at the same time, not getting trapped in a paralysis of analysis is a critical challenge for a manager's judgment.

> Herbert Simon, Nobel Laureate in "Research Briefings" (1986)
> The work of managers, of scientists, of engineers, of lawyers – the work that steers the course of society and its economic and government organizations – is largely work of making decisions and solving problems. It is work of choosing issues that require attention, setting goals, finding or designing suitable courses of action, and evaluating and choosing among alternative actions.

A manager needs the ability to make both unconscious and conscious judgments. The first is entirely dependent upon the breadth and depth of his experience. The range of different situations he has confronted in the past and the frequency of occurrence of each situation is what converts his experience into the unconscious behaviour patterns of habit.

The greater the body of his experience, the larger is the variety of judgments which he can handle unconsciously as habitual behaviour. Even processes for handling complex situations can, by repetition, be incorporated into the range of habitual behaviour. For example, the manner of conducting meetings, or of never missing essential agenda points, or of ensuring that feedback is received, or of cross-checking statements, or of testing promises received, can be all handled as a matter of habit. It follows that as experience grows, and the more an individual can accomplish by habit, the greater will be the time he can devote to the conscious judgments he needs to make. He always appears calm and unhurried. The probability of being overwhelmed by the number of judgments to be made in a limited time is drastically reduced. It should be noted that it is only one's own experience which counts at the unconscious level and can be converted into habit. It is not possible to incorporate someone else's experience into our own subconscious judgments, until they become our own experience. A habit can be therefore learned but it cannot be transferred as a fully functioning habit from somebody else. The experience of others is extremely valuable, and drawing on the experience of others is a basic and necessary part of any manager's arsenal, but can only be utilised as contributions to learning in the conscious plane. Only after learning has been accomplished, can repetition then make a regular behaviour pattern into a habit.

A manager will inevitably have some bad habits. That at least is certain. It is extremely difficult to first observe one's own bad habits and then to break or modify them. It is therefore essential that a manager be courageous enough and open enough to give permission to others to observe and comment on his habitual behaviour. If a trusted colleague makes such observations, it triggers the switch bringing the judgment into the conscious. If this is done while still in the midst of such behaviour it becomes a powerful way to make a habit visible and then, if so desired, to enter the painful process of modifying or breaking it.

When assessing the capability of individuals as managers both these areas of conscious and unconscious judgments must be addressed. The ability and willingness to make conscious judgments is essential for a "good" manager but the soundness of his judgments can make or break him as a manager. Assessment of an aspiring manager's judgment must therefore take a view regarding:

- The range of his experience governing his unconscious judgments as habitual behaviour
- The process he follows when making conscious judgments

For the conscious judgments it is further necessary to investigate whether:

1. He knows when to make judgments
2. He is willing and able to make judgments (and therefore expose himself to risk)
3. His judgments are likely to be sound

Judgments do not live in isolation. They are nearly always surrounded by a surfeit of unnecessary information or noise which must be screened away. They do not either live in a simple, linear flow of judgments where one judgment depends upon and neatly flows from the preceding one. An individual is continuously making judgments and may make several judgments simultaneously, some of which may be influenced by the others. These judgments, in turn, will exist in an environment of surrounding judgments made by others and will be influenced and will influence some of these. Some options will be enabled only as a consequence of preceding and surrounding decisions. Whenever a choice is made, some avenues of action will necessarily be closed and some potential benefits of the discarded choices will inevitably be excluded. Sometimes it can be observed that a manager makes a judgment and starts down a particular path, then has regrets about the potential benefits that have been given up and reverses course. No course of action is ever followed through and this vacillation between different courses of action is something very similar to an analysis paralysis.

When to make a judgment is governed by when the first of the necessary and sufficient actions must be implemented. The time constraints faced by a manager are nearly always connected with the time when some objective or part-objective must be achieved. It becomes a part of a manager's judgment then to decide as to when the first action must be started to fit within the deadline. I have found it personally helpful to insist that an objective must always include "a time to complete by" to be of any practical use. If such a deadline does not exist then one must be assumed or imposed. Once a time frame has been specified – and it is always a manager's prerogative to modify this as and when necessary – it becomes a relatively simple matter to work backwards to the time by when the first initiating action must be started. If the starting time turns out to be in the past, hurrying is of little value; the objective is invalid and must be modified. Modifying the objective is always an option and may be achieved by as simple a means as changing the timeline. If no timeline exists and no time line can be created or imposed, then it is a sure sign that it is a judgment that can wait and may even be unnecessary.

Willingness to Make Judgments

Everyone has experienced at some time or other a reluctance to make a judgment or, at the other extreme, jumping too quickly and too often to conclusions. It is not at all uncommon for a manager, on occasion, to have fallen a victim to a "paralysis by analysis" and at the other extreme, to have participated in or experienced an "extinction by instinct".

"Analysis paralysis" occurs when questions lead to analyses which raise new questions which lead to further analyses, *ad infinitum*. The urge to analyse becomes an end in itself and obscures the objectives. Even the smallest detail leads to unending analysis and prevents any conclusion being reached or action being taken. The process of analysis is seen as providing shelter from blame. Initiating a formal analysis becomes the refuge for the insecure manager who has little confidence in his own intuition or his conscious judgments. It can also occur in large organisations, masquerading as a way of handling dissent between individuals or for the resolution of conflicting views. It can be a very effective tool for organisational sabotage disguised as being a constructive way forward. Death by committee is a symptom of analysis paralysis. Referring a question to committees who demand further analyses is also one way of avoiding making a decision, delaying risk and of avoiding blame. Analysis paralysis is often accompanied by a pervasive "CYA" culture. Sometimes a new analysis is called for merely to avoid having to accept or reject the results of the first analysis. In all instances it represents situations where the perceived personal risk of making a judgment is seen to be greater than any benefits accruing if that judgment was followed up by action. Paralysis by analysis can occur with all types of judgments, unconscious or conscious. It is nearly always indicative of a lack of power at the level of the decision making manager. Paralysis can also be caused by trying to spread the responsibility for judgments too widely. A problem shared may well be a problem halved but a judgment shared can become no judgment at all. Ownership of the judgment then becomes obscure and the blame avoidance game begins. The consequences of a paralysis by analysis are serious and far-reaching, not only because the primary objectives remain unfulfilled but also because lost opportunities keep piling up.

At the other extreme, "extinction by instinct" can occur when a manager frequently jumps to conclusions and exhibits a preponderance of "knee-jerk reactions". He tends to react to superficial symptoms rather than addressing any underlying issues. He makes judgments based purely on instinct with little or no analysis and is prone to making new judgments more frequently than necessary. He may rush into decisions because he perceives the risk of taking no decision as being greater than the consequences of a flawed decision. New judgments regularly have to be made to undo the mistakes of previous judgments. All attempts to inject some rationality or to introduce some analysis are summarily rejected. Normal checks and balances no longer apply. Jumping to conclusions can give the appearance of dynamism and energy. Managers trying to impress their superiors are particularly concerned just to be seen to be "doing something". In these situations, others (colleagues, peers and subordinates) can be so overwhelmed by the sheer volume of instinctive and irrational judgments that they no longer provide rational feedback and either leave or become "yes-men". Group-think prevails. Only the "yes-men" dare to speak and dissent is silenced. Mistakes multiply in frequency and amplitude, till extinction is reached. Clearly the decision making manager appears to have great power. But it becomes a catastrophic failure of the exercise of his power.

Unconscious judgments – habitual behaviour or gut-feelings – can also be subject to analysis paralysis or extinction by instinct. Being in the unconscious they are often obscured by a manager's blind spots. But he should be, and needs to be, aware of what he does as habit, and his personal triggers which shift normally habitual behaviour into the conscious plane. He cannot afford to assume that all that he does unconsciously is sound. Not only must he be open to external observers helping to identify his habitual behaviour, but he must also give these observers permission and the "space" to make such observations.

For conscious judgments however, a manager must be able to avoid both paralyses by analysis and extinctions by instinct. He needs to walk the tightrope between these extremes. A "good" manager knows how to mix intuition and formal analysis in his judgment process and to be able to ensure that an actionable conclusion is reached. Sometimes he will need to start with intuition and end by analysis, and sometimes the other way around. He will have the necessary checks and balances in place to avoid too hasty judgments and to avoid paralysis. There is no standard process and the manager must be able to use different mixes of intuition and analyses as varying circumstances dictate. For example if a judgment is likely to have serious consequences, and a deadline is fast approaching, then the manager may have little time for much external advice or much formal analysis and may rely heavily on his own intuition or that of a trusted "expert". If time is available but the consequences can be heavy, he may initiate a very rigorous, analysis based judgment. Or, if the consequences are not as heavy, he may delegate the entire responsibility to a subordinate who he authorises to act, but he may choose the subordinate intuitively.

It is always easier to avoid analysis paralysis than to rectify it. In my experience, once the disease has caught hold, rectification is difficult and painful and time-consuming. It may require surgery to excise some of those who are paralysed. A manager must recognise the symptoms that paralysis is setting in, such as when:

1. Promises start losing their quality, or
2. Excuses and blame start spreading, or
3. CYA memoranda increase, or
4. Committees and task forces are established to define tasks, or
5. Long email chains start circulating to ever-lengthening circulation lists, or
6. Minor deadlines regularly start to slip, or
7. One result only leads to further questions, or
8. Principle actors start to shift responsibility to others

If and when paralysis does occur he needs to know how to address it and be aware of the tools that are available to break out of the vicious cycle which is analysis paralysis. The most effective and often the most practical way is just to change the objectives. He must be able to judge whether and when to break the objective down into smaller objectives, perhaps with shorter deadlines, or to reformulate the matter in hand to smaller bite-size morsels, or to replace an analysis step by an intuitive step. He could, for example, shuffle roles, or initiate a Pareto analysis, or a risk analysis, or arbitrarily discard some of the issues being addressed, or he could inject new experience. And where necessary he must remove or replace some of the actors.

Taking no action is always available as an option and, as a conscious decision, is always permissible, but it should not be mistaken for paralysis. But what is vital for a manager is the willingness and determination to drive the judgment process to reach actionable conclusions. He must take responsibility for the risk exposure that is inevitable. I have found it true that "authority may be given but responsibility must be taken". I do not believe that it is possible to give away responsibility. The "good" manager takes responsibility first and then seeks any missing authority. He must be brave enough to break the log-jam if analysis paralysis sets in, by the judicious use of intuition. He must have the discernment and a methodology to assess risks objectively when situations fall outside the body of his personal experience. He must have the strength and the courage (which are underlying characteristics in their own right and which I will come to later) to be able to utilise the experience of others in forming his own judgments. He must dare to introduce analysis when needed into the judgments of others (including his superiors) and especially if he observes judgments being rushed. And when dealing with superiors he must be able to resist the temptation to become a "yes-man".

A sense of timing is required. A judgment taken earlier than necessary may be based on insufficient information. Waiting for information in the hope of reducing the risk level may lead to judgments being missed or the subsequent actions being rushed. But "just in time" is not a concept which is always best for making judgments (and it is not necessarily best in manufacturing either). Some managers wait with judgments till the last possible moment partly due to their own uncertainties and partly to increase the pressure on others. But as any competent project scheduler will testify, reducing the available time float at any stage of a complex process is a sure way to be late. It is the manager who must take the responsibility for ensuring that judgments get made, at the right time and that actionable conclusions are reached.

Soundness of Judgments

But what constitutes a sound judgment? Will a sound process always lead to a sound judgment? Is it possible to ensure the soundness of unconscious judgments?

One cannot tell if a judgment is "good" until after the objective of the judgment has been achieved. "Good" judgment in this sense means a good result. A "sound" judgment however, implies it was the most proper judgment possible at that point in time, but whether it was the best possible judgment or not will always be uncertain. The soundness of a judgment is not dependent upon the success or failure of the subsequent actions. The quality of the judgment should not be judged solely by the success of the outcome.

Nothing will ever be risk free so it is inevitable that some sound judgments will fail to meet their objectives. Therefore, I restrict myself to the soundness of judgments rather than the goodness of judgments. The "good" manager knows that not all his judgments will be perfect, and he will have the confidence, the bravery and the competence to make mid-course corrections. He will focus on the process of reaching a sound judgment. He will see to it that the environment and mood permit such corrections to be made without loss of ego and loss of face. Of course it will also happen that objectives are achieved in spite of an unsound judgment. But, that would then be something due to luck, and luck represents beneficial circumstances outside one's control and is not amenable to reason.

By ensuring the robustness of the process, I believe it is possible to predicate for the soundest judgment possible, both for conscious and for unconscious judgments.

Even unconscious judgments, which are those incorporated into habit, remain habit because they have a track record of not reaching unsatisfactory outcomes. If habitual behaviour leads to an unsatisfactory outcome it gets tagged with a red flag even in the subconscious which weakens the habit. If sufficiently unsatisfactory the habit is broken and the repeat of similar circumstances triggers the conscious mind immediately. Fortunately, habit forming begins in the conscious and this is where it becomes possible to influence the manner in which the unconscious judgments are made. If a manager makes himself aware of all that he does as habit, it becomes possible to change or modify the habits. For those habits which he deems relevant to his managerial operations, it is possible to incorporate new steps into the habitual behaviour. To observe oneself and one's habitual behaviour is easier said than done. It needs the help and co-operation of external observers, and the "good" manager needs the insight and courage to empower others – to give them permission – to make frank observations of his own behaviour. He can then create new habits from a series of initially conscious and desired steps by constant repetition, again with the aid of external observers and check-lists. It is the observation of a habit which is the key to a subsequent modification. For example, a preferred manner of conducting meetings (a particular routine or a particular sequence of quality checks), or the automatic rephrasing of questions to confirm perceptions, or regularly implementing a feedback loop can be, by repetition, incorporated into the repertoire of "good" habits the manager wishes to inculcate.

Therefore in addition to having a wide experience, the person who is self-aware and more open to receiving advice is more likely to be able to change and modify his habitual behaviour. In terms of assessment, someone who has an awareness of what he does as habit is more likely to make sound unconscious judgments.

For conscious judgments, it is possible to ensure a sound process where the likelihood of a sound judgment is high. Absolute certainty is never possible and is not a useful or practical target. The process itself is not fixed. It may be a rigorous, linear, step-wise approach or it may be a largely intuitive and holistic exercise or it may be any combination. What the manager needs to ensure is that all the critical quality questions have been asked. The main checks he needs to make are:

1. Is the objective clear and measurable? Is it known to all?
2. What is the time frame applying?
3. Has the available data been gathered that is practical to gather within the time and resource constraints applicable?
4. Has all available advice that is practical to get been obtained?
5. Are all practical options, their benefits and their risks on the table?
6. Has what can be analysed been analysed? Are all analyses necessary?
7. Have the consequences of the no action option been assessed?
8. Have the risks and the consequences of failure been assessed?
9. Is there a mitigation plan?
10. Is the action proposed within the capability and the competence of the available resources?
11. Does the proposed course of action "feel" right?

Going through these quality checks does not necessarily have to be time consuming. Sometimes, it can be done with just a few seconds thought and sometimes it may need a very formal exercise with many people involved. For the "good" manager though, going through these check points or quality gates will be a rigorous exercise and one not to be compromised.

The variety of processes that a manager must employ to make judgments mean that it is futile to look for, or establish, a single "sound" process. But it is possible and quite feasible to ensure the quality of whichever process is used. This is, I believe, the key. The quality of a judgment must be secured long before the outcome can be known and the quality of a process to come to a judgment can be secured. The critical check questions described above can be treated as mandatory quality gates. That the judgment process is then actually subjected to these gate checks can, and should be, made as automatic as possible. It is the quality control process which must be incorporated into the subconscious mind of the manager such that it becomes a habit. The "good" manager will have or will form this habit.

A manager's integrity of judgment can face enormous pressures, especially from superiors who have made decisions – usually investment or manpower related decisions – and who are looking for the supporting "evidence" to be supplied by the manager. Such pressures to fabricate the results of analyses and the very premise for a judgment can sometimes come from the manager himself to support an intuitive judgment. To resist such pressures takes courage of course, but it is the managers who have made a habit out of passing all judgments through quality gates who are most likely to be able to resist such pressures.

What Makes for "Bad" Judgments

Rita Mae Brown
Good judgment comes from experience, and often experience comes from bad judgment.

While it may not be possible to ensure that every judgment will have a satisfactory result, a manager must strive to make sound judgments and thereby maximise the probability of getting good results, but he cannot foretell the future. What he can do however, is to avoid some of the features which generally lead to unsound judgments. From my experience I would list the following as areas to watch out for when making judgments:

1. *Keep it simple.* Even if the vision is big, the objectives can be broken down to manageable proportions. Murphy's Law applies and the more that can go wrong will lead to the more that will go wrong. Grandiose plans of action can go grandly wrong.
2. *What not to do is not an objective.* A judgment made solely for avoiding an unwanted result is not a valid judgment. It is a fundamental task of a manager to transform any negative objective such as avoiding a loss or avoiding a delay or avoiding non-compliance, to become a clear objective of what is to be done.
3. *If you don't know where you want to go then it does not matter where you go or if you go at all.* Enthusiasm and energy to get started with actions can sometimes leave a lack of clarity about the objectives of the action and different people may have different views about what is to be achieved. Make sure that

the objectives are clearly formulated and are communicated to, understood and shared by all the players.
4. *Be sure that you will recognise when you have reached your goal.* Ensure that the Conditions of Satisfaction are clear and incorporated into the formulation of the objectives. Success may be dependent upon other surrounding conditions also being met or being avoided. For example, the objective may be to achieve a certain business volume but the surrounding condition could be that the number of employees is not to be increased or that a certain level of profitability must be maintained.
5. *Don't bite off more than you can chew.* Actions planned do not match the resources available (competence, people, time or money). This is common when the expected benefits of the action are so attractive that the actions are started anyway, in the hope that somehow the resources will become available.
6. *A cost benefit analysis regarding a decision is only valid when assessing costs and benefits subsequent to that decision.* Even for a judgment being made in the present it is tempting to include sunk costs of the past (money or people or time) into a cost benefit analysis.
7. *Make sure that all real benefits are taken into account.* Spin-off benefits are sometimes ignored if they are to be accounted for somewhere else or in someone else's balance sheet. This is especially true in large organisations with specialised departments and functions.
8. *Either conduct an analysis without prejudice or don't waste the effort.* Analyses are often initiated even though the result has already been prejudged, perhaps based on intuition or previous experience or the previous experience of others. Time and energy is then wasted in forcing the analysis results to comply with the pre-judgment.
9. *Don't cherry pick analysis results to support your prejudices.* While it is impossible not to have prejudices or views on a matter which is being analysed, it is critical to acknowledge and declare such biases in advance of any analysis. If conducting an analysis then intuition and "gut-feeling" must be declared invalid for assessing the results of such an analysis.
10. *Beware statistics.* A strong correlation is merely a statistical conclusion that a relationship is probable. There is a tendency to assume that a correlation between parameters is evidence of a causal relationship. It is not. It is silent regarding any actual physical or causal relationship between the parameters being correlated. A correlation may indicate a probable relationship but is not evidence of a connection.
11. *Don't deny intuition just because it is intuition. Deny it only with reason.* It is not at all uncommon to hear that some judgment "was made against one's better judgment". There must always be good reason to overrule a "gut feeling" against an option.
12. *Kill the group-think.* Check that the dissident views are not being stifled by group-think. When taking advice make sure that the dissident views are getting through the noise of the "yes-men". If necessary, force some of the "yea-sayers" to find and present the opposing views.

What Makes for "Bad" Judgments

13. *Never be surprised when even the worst case scenario becomes real.* Make sure that a worst case has been analysed, even if only as a thought experiment. But keep the best case scenario in mind to avoid paralysis and to keep depression at bay.
14. *Leave mimicry to chimpanzees and parrots.* Many judgments are made as reactions to the actions of a market leader or actions by competitors. This happens even without any knowledge of the competitor's judgments and objectives which led to those actions in the first place. The objectives for one's own judgments can become very diffuse and in reality, may be no more than to copy the competitor. To do something just because GE or IBM or Toyota or Microsoft did it is insufficient.
15. *Challenge the past.* Past experience and past behaviour can be stifling. While experience is invaluable, time never stands still. Conditions applying to past situations are inevitably changed when facing new and similar scenarios. It is not guaranteed that what worked in the past will work again in the future. It is insufficient to merely repeat a judgment from the past without checking that the previous judgment is still valid.
16. *Throw out the rubbish.* In any situation there is usually a surfeit of unnecessary information and a shortage of relevant information. Always screen and discard unnecessary information and invalid options before making any judgment. If a deadline is first approaching, I have observed that there is a tendency to follow the first well understood, viable option. Other options are discarded due to the over-load of information and due to lack of time and not necessarily because they were less attractive.
17. *The loudest advice or the most recent advice does not have to be the wisest.* With large teams and where many opinions are present, group dynamics do not themselves ensure that only the best opinions survive. There is no natural process by which the best opinion will make itself known.
18. *Avoid inventing judgments to suit the action; let the judgment lead to the actions.* When an analysis indicates that the benefits of a particular, favoured option do not justify the risks or the cost, there can be a tendency to come across additional spin-off benefits or to define new-found objectives to justify the action.
19. *Consensus science is not good science and a judgment by consensus is not always sound judgment.* In large teams, the majority view can be given a lot of weight. But a decision by majority negates the whole purpose of having a manager who takes responsibility for the judgment. A commonality of purpose becomes more and more important as teams get larger, but a communal judgment has no place in management.
20. *Current probabilities about future events are indifferent to past events.* Resist the feeling that chances for the next coin toss or spin of the roulette wheel will change depending on the last coin toss or the last spin. Ten "bad" judgments in a row do not increase the probability of a "good" judgment the next time. But note that the more sound judgments that are made the more likely it is that a sound process will continue.

21. *Integrity is a sink or swim question. You are just as dead drowning by 1 mm as you are drowning by 10 m.* If the judgment makes you uncomfortable regarding your ethics or integrity then it is unsound.

Recognising the Ability

Assessing an individual's readiness to judge and his soundness of judgment is not simple. In addition to track record and history, there are many psychological assessments or decision making ability tests which can be used. However test results should never be considered definitive and should only be used in support of other assessments. In any case, tests must be treated with great caution since they often measure test taking ability rather than the skill being investigated. I am a strong proponent of the importance of track record but am also very sensible to the distortions of hindsight. The results of judgments in the past do not necessarily say much about the soundness of the judgment at the time. However, it is possible to learn much through a well conducted interview process where the focus should be on variety of experience, past judgments, self-awareness and on the process by which judgments are reached.

> Albert Einstein
> Any man who can drive safely while kissing a pretty girl is simply not giving the kiss the attention it deserves.

Investigating the variety of different situations an individual has experienced is important in assessing the likely strength of his habitual behaviour. His exposure to different countries, different cultures and peoples and different social situations can provide some insight. His willingness to take responsibility for his judgments must be tested. If he is not aware of when he has made unsound judgments then it is unlikely that he knows what a sound judgment entails. His involvement in competitive sports and his hobbies can provide a measure of his intrinsic risk taking ability. His awareness of his own habits and behaviour can be inferred by checking how open he is to receiving advice about his own behaviour. His ability to formulate clear objectives and to define the conditions of satisfaction should be tested. To be able to focus on the objective and not be distracted by an over-load of information or having too many options is important.

Responses to simple direct questions can be also very revealing:

1. "Can you describe three bad judgments you have made in the last 12 months?"
2. "Can you describe three good judgments you have made in the last 12 months?"
3. "Can you describe a sound judgment you have made which led to a bad result?"
4. "Do you know when you have made a sound judgment? And how do you know?"
5. "Can you describe some good habits you have and some of your bad habits?"
6. "Can you describe your prejudices and when they may affect your judgment?"

7. "Are you aware of your own weaknesses? And how do you cover for your limitations?"

There is never a guarantee that a sound judgment will give a satisfactory outcome, but I have always preferred to appoint as a manager, someone who I think has sound judgment rather than someone who has a good track record but cannot convince me that his judgment is sound.

Chapter 4
Communication: Hearing What Isn't Said

Communication is the tool that a manager must make use of to mobilise actions from his chosen actors. Communication is a process and not a singular event. It extends from the meaning that he selects and then through all the subsequent steps of converting the meaning into a message which he transmits as information making up a communiqué directed at a particular recipient. The process continues till it is received, interpreted and reconverted into meaning in the recipient's mind. But the process is not complete until the manager gets the feedback confirming that his intended meaning has been successfully transferred. The manager retains responsibility throughout the entire process. Language and culture enable communication and are not barriers. Focusing on the recipient leads naturally to the process required to generate the desired meanings in his mind. Any manager can make himself into a good communicator. Some will have to work harder at it than others. But being aware of the steps contained within a communications process is where the learning starts.

The Elements of Communication

I have often heard the statement "He did not understand what I meant"! But this is just an excuse and, to my mind, an invalid excuse which reflects poorly upon the speaker.

"Information", "message, "communiqué", "meaning" and "communication" are not synonyms. I take these words to have quite distinct definitions:

- Information is anything that can stimulate the senses of an observer.
- A message is a collection of information (stimuli) which is coherent to an observer (who may be the assembler of the stimuli or the receiver) and capable of transmission.
- A communiqué is the message that is transmitted.
- Meaning is the interpretation accorded by a brain (or by a cognitive process) to messages it creates or perceives.
- A communication is the successful transfer of a meaning from one brain to another.

A piece of information such as a letter, or an e-mail, or an advertisement, or a report, or a speech, or a conversation or a broadcast is often described as "a communication". Sometimes just the transfer of information is defined as the process of communication. In my view, this is an incomplete and inadequate definition. For the true communication that must be practiced by a manager, a more rigorous description must be developed. While the study of perception, meaning and communication now spans the fields of management, the arts, sociology, psychology and philosophy we need only to consider communication from the perspective of a practicing manager.

It is perfectly true that merely by being present somewhere and without even saying a single word you are screaming to all within sight "I am here, I am here". You send information merely by being, and even by not being. By not being somewhere you transmit information, intentionally or not, to someone expecting you to be there. But note that there is no information transferred to someone who has no expectation of seeing you there. When a tree falls in a forest a pressure wave is created, but there is no perceived sound unless there is an ear to detect the pressure wave and a brain to interpret it as sound. Even a pressure sensor which may detect the pressure wave does not make the interpretation of sound. For a communication to exist it must first be detected as information and then interpreted as a meaning in the mind of the receiver.

S. F. Scudder
> All living entities communicate.

It follows that Scudder's phrase that "All living entities communicate" in his "The Universal Law of Communication" of 1900 is incomplete. It would be more correct and complete to say that "Every living entity broadcasts information, but any resulting communication resides in the understanding of the receiver". We could perhaps speculate that every living entity needs to communicate but I am less sure that every living entity does communicate. A communication always includes a transfer of information, but while this transfer is necessary, it is insufficient for communication to exist.

Whenever communication is intended, the communiqué is, of course, issued by the communicator but, the final meaning of the communication resides in the mind of the receiver. Where a communication is intended, the responsibility for what has been understood lies always with the communicator, not with the receiver. It is why the statement "He did not understand what I meant!" actually reflects poorly on the speaker. The intending communicator cannot escape from the consequences of what has been finally understood by the receiver. A true communication is only complete when the meaning intended in the mind of the communicator and the meaning understood by the receiver are identical. In between the two lie the following necessary elements:

1. The purpose of the communicator which includes the choice of the recipient
2. Translation of the intended meaning into a message
3. The formulation of the message into a communiqué (where the communiqué is a package of transmittable information)

4. The transfer of information to the chosen recipient
5. The reception of the information
6. The decoding of the information received into a message
7. The interpretation of the received message into a meaning
8. A feedback loop from the receiver to the communicator

All the above steps must exist for a communication to be completed. No individual step is sufficient in itself. The process may well involve iteration based on the feedback. There are many processes, for just the transfer of information, which are, in common parlance, taken to be communications but which are not. A letter or a conversation may be a well directed part of a communication but is not a complete communication in itself.

> Unknown to David Signoff
> The wireless music box has no imaginable commercial value. Who would pay for a message sent to nobody in particular?

A speech to a large audience, or a TV or a radio broadcast is not capable of being directed with precision. These may be part of a communication to some specific listeners but the transfer of information is not a communication by itself. A slide-show or a report or a sound recording or a movie is merely a package of information. Marshall McLuhan in 1964 developed the concept that "the medium is the message". This may well still be the prevailing paradigm today, that the message and the medium it is embedded in are inseparable. Since McLuhan coined the maxim, we have seen the explosive development of media; the fax machine, Intranet and the Internet, e-mail, mobile telephony, text messaging, video conferencing, Internet chat, web conferencing and now tweeting. But, in all cases, the media and the communiqués they carry are just channels with information packages being conveyed, sometimes – but not always – as part of a communication. The choice of medium itself is also part of the information package being transferred.

An intended communication comes into being only when the communicator has some purpose, has chosen his recipient and has a meaning to communicate. Meanings exist in peoples' minds. Messages are composed of packages of information which can be detected by our senses but they are not meanings. Words or pictures or other sensory information may generate meanings in our minds but they do not, in themselves, "mean". The transfer of information, without a purpose, without an intended meaning or without a recipient is not an intended communication as I define it here. The translation of the meaning into a message and coding the message into the information to be transferred is based first on the values, culture, language, history and social context of the communicator. The reverse process at the receiving end is now based on a decoding, and an interpretation based on the values, language, history and social context of the receiver.

The challenge for the communicator is to ensure that the final meaning at the receiving end is what he intends it to be. The feedback loop is vital. It needs to be established by the communicator since it is he who must own the communication process. The communication is not complete till the feedback loop, together with any iteration that it may initiate, provides confirmation that the meaning understood is that which was intended. Without the confirmation provided by the feedback loop, it cannot be known whether a communication has been properly completed or even if any information transfer has taken place at all. The absence of a feedback loop is perhaps the single most common reason for miscommunications.

When the communicator and the receiver share common values and language and social context and have similar histories, then the translation, and coding algorithms employed by the communicator are very close to those for the decoding and interpretation steps at the receiver. They may be so similar that these steps can be entirely implicit and almost invisible. It is the communicator who must determine the differences, if any, applying between himself and the receiver. It is by means of his judgment regarding the decoding and interpretation that will occur at the receiving end that he selects the translation and coding algorithms he needs to use.

The message intended by the communicator is converted into a package of transmittable information to make up the communiqué. The information to be transferred can be in any form or any combination of forms such that it can be detected by the senses of the receiver (verbal, written, visual or tactile). The media to be used for the transfer of the information package may also be any combination of the available means of transmission, as chosen by the communicator. The information package must be suited to the chosen media. The chosen media, in turn, must be capable of being directed at the recipient and overcoming any intervening noise. The information package and the method of transmission must be within the receiving capability of the recipient.

> Peter F. Drucker
> The most important thing in communication is hearing what isn't said

It is the responsibility of the communicator to ensure that unintended information, or information via an unintended transmission medium, is not transmitted. However, the communicator remains responsible for the meanings conveyed, whether intended or not, by the information he consciously or unconsciously broadcasts. It remains the communicator's responsibility to ensure that the information package he transmits is uncorrupted and not drowned by the noise that may exist on its way to the recipient. Note that lack of information is itself information, and may give rise to its own messages which may then be given a meaning in the mind of the receiver. A letter not sent, or a call not made, or a fax not received, or an issue not addressed, fall into this category and can easily generate miscommunication.

Communication for the Manager

For a manager, all his communications, without exception, are to generate some action. Even reporting to a superior, which may well be an action mobilized by the superior, is a managerial communication where the manager is also looking for an action (sometimes implied and sometimes at a later time) from the superior.

It should not be forgotten however, that his role as a "manager" may not extend far beyond the confines of the workplace. It may not necessarily extend to his social activities or to his family life.

Whenever a communication is intended a transfer of information is always required. Not all information transfer however, is as part of an intended communication. A manager needs to be aware that he is constantly radiating information. His mode of listening influences the other party's readiness to listen as well. His body language provides primary information as well as feedback. His attitude, posture, his unconscious gestures all provide information whether intended or not. For a manager, the communication process is never an end in itself. It is merely a tool to be used in the pursuit of his fundamental objectives – the mobilization of actions for a particular purpose. We should distinguish between, first, the quality and capability of the tool itself, and second, the manager's skill at using the tool. The capability of the tool is contained in the rigorousness or the quality of the entire process. This, in turn, requires all the necessary steps to be present and that each step is effective. The skill of the manager lies in the effectiveness with which he implements each step.

A sloppy process, for example with missing steps, or without a clear purpose, or one not properly directed to the receiver, or with poor translations, or with incomplete information, or communiqués which are difficult for the receiver to decipher, all detract from the communication to be achieved. If no feedback loop is available, or if the media required for information transfer are unavailable then the tool itself is poor. But, if the feedback loop exists but is not well utilized, or if an inappropriate medium for information transfer is chosen, or if the meaning received is garbled, then it is the manager's skill which is lacking. In all such cases however, the manager retains the responsibility for the failing in communication. Lack of ability to capture information at the receiver's end does not diminish this responsibility.

> Robert McCloskey
> I know that you believe you understand what you think I said, but I'm not sure you realize that what you heard is not what I meant.

In the quotation from Robert McCloskey above, the "fault" as I see it is not with the receiver, the "you" as it is implied in the quotation, but lies clearly with the speaker, the "I" in the quotation. It has always irked me when I have heard the excuse that somebody has the "wrong perception". My usual response is "And whose fault is that?" The responsibility for a wrong perception lies with the person creating the perception not with the person who passively perceives. The quality of the process and the manager's implementation skills are very closely intertwined. It becomes all the more important that a manager, if he is to have any chance of improvement, be able to distinguish between the process being applied and the skills required.

A common mistake, in my opinion, is the focus that is put on the message or the communiqué or on the medium, rather than on the received meaning. It is all too easy to get diverted by the information package and its contents (reports, pictures, presentations, films, or letters for example) and to lose sight of the recipient. The communiqués can be overwhelmed by all that the communicator wants to say and not based on what the receiver needs to hear. Reports and memoranda often become much too long for the chosen recipient. Material is included just because it exists and looks "nice" and even if it does not contribute to the generation of meaning with the recipient. The communicator can become so enamoured of the "quality" of the information package he has created that he sends it to the whole world to demonstrate his competence and loses track of the original purpose and the intended recipient. It is very easy also to be seduced by the "glamour" or the technology attached to the medium to be used for the information transfer. Video-conferencing or audio-video presentations or net-conferencing or "live streaming" broadcasts are all real examples where I have observed the novelty of the technology and its use can completely drown the communication intended.

When I was an apprentice engineer in the 1960s with GKN at a factory in the British Midlands, information was still being transferred internally by putting documents into metal cylinders which were then pneumatically transported down air-filled pipes to the various factory departments. Needless to say this was a source of great fascination and amusement for all the apprentices. It was great fun to send those canisters whizzing around the factory and we probably used the system in ways never imagined by the designers, but we never really had anything to communicate. In the 1980s, when fax machines first came on to the scene we used to invent documents to be sent around the world just so we could operate the machines.

I wonder sometimes how many of the e-mails and text messages circulating around the world today are actually part of some real communication.

For all managerial communications where the objective is to mobilize action, the focus, I believe, must start and end with the recipient of the communication and the meaning he ascribes to the communication. I have generally found that the best place to start is by focusing not on what I want to say, but on what precisely I want the recipient to do or think when the communication is completed. Categorization by type of information package or type of medium to be used generally provides the wrong focus and can be very misleading. Many times, when I have been asked to review draft speeches or presentations or reports I have been astonished that the communicator has only a very vague notion about the identity of the recipients and what is expected of them. Speeches are all too often prepared to be what the manager wants to say and not on what needs to be heard and by whom. The communications processes to be established and implemented by a manager are, in my view, most correctly grouped according to the type of recipient. As soon as the recipient has been identified and is made the focus, the rest of the process becomes self-evident. It follows very logically to a consideration of the understanding the recipient must reach to undertake the required actions. It feels entirely natural and correct then to tailor the entire communication process to suit the recipient.

I have found it convenient to categorise recipients as follows:

1. Subordinates
2. Peers
3. Superiors

4. Members of personal networks
5. Third parties
   (a) Supportive parties
   (b) Neutral parties
   (c) Opposing parties

Where a manager has direct subordinates they are generally the primary movers for the actions and for the chains of actions to be generated. By their very proximity to the manager they share many values, language, background and the algorithms for the conversion of meanings to information and back to meanings. Information packages can be, and usually are, truncated and verbal "shorthand" is commonly used. Ensuring that there is no chance of any miscommunication at the beginning of the action chain is one of the key responsibilities of the manager. Any mistakes or missteps at the start of an action chain are only magnified by the end of the chain. What distinguishes subordinates especially is that they are a captive audience for the manager. Communications to subordinates inevitably have the character of an instruction or an order. Implicit in such communications is the understanding that complying with the instruction is an obligation. This does ensure that information transfer takes place relatively easily but it does need extra vigilance to ensure that the channels for reception are truly open. It is of no use if a subordinate attends a meeting only because he has to but does not really listen. The closeness of a manager to his subordinates itself can lead to carelessness regarding the feedback loops. Assumptions are far too readily made about what was meant or what was understood without full engagement of the feedbacks. In my experience I have generally found, that with subordinates, emphasis needs to be put on the feedback rather than on the transfer of information. Whether the feedback is obtained verbally or in writing or merely by body language, is not crucial. It is crucial however that understandings are continuously checked, rechecked and reconfirmed, and not just as a one-off event. A manager not only needs to transfer information but must also avoid unintended transmissions of information. In a close-knit group, such as with subordinates, the possibilities of misdirected information transfer and subsequent unintended communications are high and must be explicitly guarded against. It pays to constantly reconfirm – even to the point of irritation – who is doing what and when and why and with whom. In large organizations, the category of subordinates can include all those with a lower hierarchical position than the manager, provided that there is acquiescence from their own line-manager.

By peers, I mean people of a similar standing as the manager but not necessarily falling within the same line of authority as the manager. They may well be in a different organization entirely. Inevitably their actions, or potential actions, are constrained by the lines of authority within which they are constrained to operate. They could be suppliers or customers or partners. They may be managers in other departments in the same organization. They could be government or public officials. Many such people will need to generate actions from time to time at the behest of the manager. When communication is intended, the information packages transferred need to be in a form that is intelligible in the context of their own responsibilities and obligations. Communications to peers cannot therefore be structured as orders except, perhaps, when the recipient belongs to a supplier organization. A higher degree of formality is needed both for information transfer and for applying the feedback loop than with subordinates. Feedback loops cannot be operated continuously but must be used sparingly and with a high degree of specificity. Questions for confirmation of understandings must necessarily be very precise and yet not too onerous to reply to. Using the feedback loops also needs that the feedback channel itself is nurtured.

By superiors, I mean all those within the manager's own organization having a higher hierarchical status. Inevitably and as a simple matter of survival, communications to superiors must take the form of requests and not be perceived as commands. Information packages must be modified – usually shortened – to suit. I have always found that a manager's superiors are a much under-utilised resource. A manager can and should mobilize actions from this very powerful resource group but must achieve this by proper communication. I have generally found superiors – even company CEO's as a junior manager – much more accessible than I initially expected. They are just as prone to appeals to their competence and to their egos as anybody else. The key, of course, lies in ensuring a complete communication (and not just in a bland transfer of information). Feedback loops are much more difficult to establish but are also perfectly feasible. Wherever the quality of the communication is capable of mobilizing some particular action, it is also perfectly able to get a superior to provide feedback. Engaging with and utilizing superiors can be a risky proposition which should not be taken lightly, but it is a necessary skill for a "good" manager. Within the category of "superiors", I also include individuals outside one's own organization but who have the appropriate gravitas as individuals or who have an elevated social or hierarchical status (for example, a professor or somebody deserving of respect or a government minister or even just a relatively elderly person).

The people who are connections within a manager's personal networks form a separate class when considering communications. By personal networks I mean those sets of social connections which have some unique features which in the manager's perception distinguish them from each other. These may be, for example his current golfing partners, or the group of school friends he is regularly in contact with, or a set of his extended family members, or all those within a particular customer organization he has access to and who have access to him. They could be the members of a professional or learned society, or a group of people who follow him on Facebook or members who regularly post to the same Internet forum. As we will see later, the relationships he has with the individuals in his networks will necessarily circumscribe but will also enable the possibilities he has of mobilizing their actions. Actions that may be requested from some network partners may not be feasible with others. A close friend or family member may be willing to accept some requests which, if put to, say, a golfing partner would only damage the relationship. Communications with such network members must take into account the different foundations each network is built on. As with all the categories of recipients, the information packages must be geared to eliciting the desired meaning in the recipients' minds. An additional requirement that appears here is that the communication must not threaten the existence of the network and preferably should confirm and deepen the relationship between network partners.

Third parties are individuals with whom the manager has relatively few interactions, who are outside his own organization, who are not with any directly related organizations (such as with customers or suppliers) and who are outside his personal networks. The manager's knowledge about these parties is necessarily sparse. However, they may be required to be triggered into action, which could be crucial if such an action is part of a desired chain of actions. I have found it useful when interacting with relatively unknown parties to first make an assessment as to whether their own long term goals would render them supportive, neutral or opposed to the goals I was trying to achieve. This is a key enabling assessment. It provides the basis for, and permits the preparation of information packages to suit their perceived inclinations and for the establishment of indirect feedback loops. Feedback loops need to be indirect because not enough may be known about the party to be sure that a direct feedback will be available or feasible. These indirect loops usually involve using others who are in a position to observe the actions undertaken. Establishing the feedback channels as early as possible and preferably even before the information package is transmitted is advisable. People who are needed for the immediate action chain but who are known to be opposed to the manager's long term goals pose a special challenge. They may be rivals in the same organization, or individuals within a customer organization or government representatives or even managers with a competitor. It is vital when embarking on such a communication that the manager be very careful in maintaining his own standards of integrity. (He must of course have his own standards of integrity.) It is all too easy to get sucked into the quicksand of disinformation, manipulation and plain lies.

From Meaning to Message to Communiqué and Back Again

Suppose that you are an observer on a hill and you see a child some distance away playing intently on a railway track and who is unaware that a train is approaching. Your purpose is to prevent an accident. To this end you judge that you cannot communicate with the driver of the train and choose the child as your recipient. You intend to communicate the meaning of "danger" to the child, such that the child acts and moves off the track without delay. You translate this meaning into the message "A train is approaching and you are in its way". You choose the communiqué to be the phrase "Get off the track"; in English and to be transmitted by the medium of your voice – very loudly. But suppose further that you are a visitor in Russia. The child is probably Russian and perhaps, neither speaks nor understands English. You modify your planned communiqué to now consist of a scream, without any words, but now augmented by the visual signal of you pointing and waving towards the train. You scream and you point and you wave. The child hears you scream, looks at you, and then looks towards where you are pointing, sees the train and receives the information. In its mind it hears the words "Get off the track, quickly" but of course in Russian. The meaning of the danger is perfectly understood in its mind, exactly as you intended. The child is moved to action and jumps off the track to safety, as you intended. You receive visual feedback and confirmation that the communication was received and led to the desired action.

If you had consulted your pocket dictionary and tried to translate your words into Russian, you would have been too late. If you had only waved, no matter how vigorously, you would not have caught the child's attention. If you had chosen any other medium than your voice no information transfer may have taken place. If you had not shouted loud enough your information would have been sent but not received. If you had screamed without pointing, the child's attention would have been captured but the only action may have been just to look at you.

In the event, all the necessary and sufficient steps for a true communication were fulfilled successfully. You had a purpose and an intended action. You had a chosen recipient; you translated your meaning into a message and put it into the form of a communiqué which you modified and then transmitted. The transmission was well directed and overcame any intervening noise. The information was received and converted into a perceived message and this led to an understanding in the recipient's mind which led to action. The feedback confirmed that the meaning understood was the one you intended.

A manager's life is usually a little more complex. He rarely has to deal with just one recipient (though it could be argued that even when making a speech to a few hundred people he actually only ever deals with single recipients, but simultaneously with many such). The meanings he needs to convey are not usually so straightforward or unambiguous. In the industrial or commercial world, meanings come not only in all the various shades of grey but they also appear in every conceivable nuance of colour. The actions to be mobilised may involve a long chain of actions. The messages he needs to formulate to convey his meanings may involve long and complex reasoning and argumentation. The information packages he must use may involve speech, documents, sounds, and various audio-visual materials. He must choose from a variety of available transmission media to transfer the communiqués. He must perhaps use a multiplicity of transmission methods to convey different parts of the communiqué. If the transmission of information involves translation or the use of interpreters then he must ensure the correctness and the integrity of the transmission. He must arrange for feedback and choose the appropriate channels also from a variety of available ways.

But no matter how involved the communication is to be, the same simple steps of the communication process are involved. Even the most complex and intricate managerial communication, to an array of recipients scattered across the world, is exactly the same, in principle, as shouting at that child and pointing at that train.

Cross-Cultural Communications

In today's world, cultural differences appear not just across country boundaries but even within the same organisation and between peoples in the same country. Today's mobility means that managers of all nationalities and all backgrounds can be found anywhere across the globe. I find the Japanese concept that all communications consist of two parts to be universally applicable and a particularly practical and useful concept. The concept distinguishes between what lies on the surface (*tatemae*) which is the formal façade, and the true voice (*honne*) which lies underneath. Sometimes the two modes may be very clearly separated as they are in Japan. For example, this is well illustrated by the formal mode (façade) used when in the workplace and the informal mode which prevails in the karaoke bar. But any Japanese manager also knows that he does not have the entire picture until he has heard the true voice and put it in the context defined and bounded by the formal façade. Usually however, separation of the two modes is not as clear-cut as in Japan. Often the communicator will switch, sometimes continuously, from one mode to the other. The façade and the true voice may, from time to time, be seen and heard simultaneously. It is always the recipient who has to distinguish between the two. The other side of the coin is that the communicator must be able to discern which of his communiqués will be taken to be "on the surface" and which will be perceived as being his "true voice". This poses its own challenges in formulating messages, preparing the information packages and choosing the medium for information transfer.

The true voice (*honne*), in any culture and in any language, is usually characterised by a level of informality, but it should not be confused with other informal information exchange processes. The true voice needs the framework of the formal façade to be properly put into context. Gossip or small talk around the coffee table is unlikely to be taken very seriously and is not usually used for the true voice. Information obtained through the grapevine for example – which exists in every organisation – may be much more than just rumour and gossip, but is not the true voice of a communication since it has no formal context within which it can exist. It should be noted that the grapevine is a valid and feasible medium for information transfer but it carries large risks of misinterpretation and of misdirection.

There is probably some deep-seated human need to have special places or situations "designated" for the "true voice" to be heard. Most countries seem to have some specific social situations where this happens; the golf course in the US, the Club (or the pub) in the UK, the sauna in Finland, the dinner followed by the karaoke bar in Japan, the 3-h lunch in Madrid, the wedding reception in India, the café in Paris or the gym in Germany. (In Germany, it used to be the *bierkeller* but I can attest to the fact that it has now moved to the gym!) A manager does not need to be a social scientist but he needs to be aware that such places exist and where they are and how they are used. Sometimes casual conversations in such situations are misinterpreted to be highly significant when they are not, because they do not come within the framework and context supplied by the formal façade.

The fundamental steps of the communication process are universally applicable. Communication across different recipients, cultural variations, language differences, country boundaries and different organisational structures all require exactly the same process. If the chosen recipient is made the focus and the starting point of the process, then the cultural and other perceived barriers are, in fact, converted into the mere practicalities of ensuring that the sequence of steps from meaning to communiqués and back to meanings are implemented correctly. Seemingly abstract challenges without a clear line of attack can be converted into a series of practical tasks. Cultural and language differences are too often, in my opinion, portrayed as barriers and used as an excuse for miscommunication. The failing is actually in the manager's communication process or his skill in implementing it.

During the late 1980s and early 1990s at ABB a number of acquisitions were being considered in Eastern Europe and I was a member of some of the teams looking at these. První Brněnská (First Brno) was one such company under consideration and was fully acquired by ABB in 1993. During the acquisition process many presentations and meetings were held with and for First Brno managers and executives to promote the benefits of being a part of the ABB Group. The presentations were often financial in nature and had been prepared very carefully, but the feedback was not confirming to us that real communication was taking place. We had missed the fact that after 40 years in a communist environment, the very concept of making a profit was considered immoral. Most of the managers were deeply uncomfortable with the idea of becoming part of an "immoral activity pandering to the greed of the owners". The communications process remained stalled till we began addressing the philosophical concepts of profit and morality and not just the financial and accounting methodology involved. There have been changes of ownership since, with Alstom and Siemens also acquiring parts of the business from ABB at the same site in Brno, but the site as a whole is highly successful and extremely profitable today.

In 2003, Alstom sold its Industrial Power Generation business to Siemens. Siemens was set up and operated with a great deal of central control from headquarters. However the business acquired from Alstom was highly decentralised with manufacturing and engineering spread around the world. This acquisition proved highly successful for Siemens and the key success factor in my opinion was Frank Stieler's ability to communicate both to superiors on the one hand and to peers and subordinates on the other. In one direction he had to communicate the need for introducing a degree of decentralisation to the Siemens Board. In the other he had to communicate and establish a decentralised structure – which was foreign to the employees coming from Siemens – while incorporating a system of checks and balances unfamiliar to the employees coming from Alstom. It was a complex balancing act but the success of the communications is what avoided anarchy and which led to a tripling of volume.

Culture and language and social history are actually the tools that make communication possible, not the barriers to communication. It is the fact that animals do not have any well-developed language that makes it difficult for us to communicate with them, not that we do not know their language. It is not necessary for the manager himself to be an expert in the language or the culture or in social science but he must know when and how these tools are to be used. "There are managers who see a challenge in every task and those who merely see a task in every challenge". The "good" manager sees communication across differences of culture and language and history and social background merely as a task.

The Feedback Loop

Perhaps the most difficult steps to be performed, but the most critical, are establishing and utilising feedback loops. Very often this is not addressed explicitly at all and is left to chance or to the unconscious. Habitual behaviour in the form of observing the recipient's body language, or the automatic rephrasing of questions, or formulation of the message into different communiqués, or repetition by using different media, are all ways in which we unconsciously implement feedback loops.

It is my thesis – and a practice that I have tried to follow – that a manager needs to address feedback explicitly and very early on in the communication process. As soon as a recipient is identified he needs to pose the questions:

1. How will I know what was understood by the recipient?
2. What are the channels for finding out?

He then needs to establish and put into practice a methodology for finding answers. He needs to be aware of what he does in this regard as a matter of habit and then to modify or strengthen these habits as a conscious decision. If he finds that he relies too much on assumptions rather than on evidence, he needs to break or modify some "bad" habits.

Feedback can be obtained directly or indirectly. Direct feedback is fast and generally reliable with recipients who are close. With distant recipients, there is a risk that the direct feedback is actually a new communication, now directed at the manager and having its own agenda for actions. For example, getting a direct feedback from a customer about one aspect of a service provided may actually just lead to his disguised request to obtain some further service. Many Purchasing managers first find all the possible complaints they can bring to the table about a particular supplier before entering into a discussion about a new purchase. It is always healthy to have more than one feedback channel and preferably at least one which is through an "independent" observer. Multiple feedback loops can of course lead to conflicting information and then the manager's judgment has to come into play.

Paradoxically, assumptions about understandings and consequent miscommunications are more likely with people close to the manager. While such miscommunication may not happen very often, it may be very disruptive when it comes as a surprise.

When I was first appointed as the manager of a sales department, I quickly realised that the salesmen's own feedback after a customer visit (inevitably positive – what else?) was not totally reliable. The feedback, when available directly from the customer, usually had some hidden agenda and could also be misleading. I found that the use of independent observers, when they could be arranged, was a powerful complement to the other feedback loops. I started a process where a salesman's reports were not acceptable till they were backed up by "independent" evidence. Insisting that the salesmen find me independent observers to verify their efforts was not at all popular to begin with but was extremely effective – in many ways – once the routine was established. The accuracy of the feedback improved greatly, but more importantly, the quality of our own communications process itself was lifted to a new level.

As a generalisation, I have found that the closer the recipient, the more important it is to explicitly ensure proper feedback. For more distant recipients, their understandings are less likely to be taken for granted but it then becomes critical to ensure that the communiqués formulated are actually intelligible. With distant recipients, I have always found it mandatory to establish more than one feedback loop, operating independently and in parallel, usually by finding parties who are in a position to observe the recipient and his actions. It is especially useful when the recipient has many differences of social context or language or culture and it becomes vital to interpret and distinguish correctly between the façade and the true voice. Observers who can provide feedback are always around – but it may take some effort to find them and mobilise them.

When I was stationed in Delhi I had the use of a company car and chauffeur. It was not long before I was also utilising the city-wide chauffeurs' network to get confirmation and feedback regarding which competitor had been calling on my customer and when and who the customer had visited! It goes without saying that all my movements were also being reported to others through the chauffeurs' network.

Conversations for Communication

William Shakespeare
Give every man your ear, but few thy voice

A conversation between two people, usually supported by some documents (such as reports, memoranda or e-mail correspondence), is probably the most commonly used medium for transferring information within a communication process. Informal transfer of information nearly always take place in face-to-face conversations or, sometimes, in telephone conversations or e-mail exchanges provided they build on relationships already established with the help of face-to-face conversations. It is my empirical conclusion that physical proximity – "the meeting between four eyes" – is a key enabler for real exchange of information in these conversations. A manager needs to be constantly listening for the "true voice" and needs to be adept at conversations for transferring information as well as for getting feedback.

At the place of work, conversations occupy the majority of a manager's time. With superiors, colleagues and subordinates, unplanned, informal conversations take place frequently. The high frequency itself allows such conversations to be very brief, but the shared context allows the density of information transfer to be very high. The certainty that further such conversations will take place also contributes to a sharp focus on the subject and the elimination of information extraneous to the subject in hand. Very often greetings and closing remarks and goodbyes and the like are dispensed with in these brief conversations. Scheduled, formal meetings are in effect no more than planned and structured conversations, but are very important since these are where the formal mode of information transfer prevails. Such meetings may involve many participants or could involve just two people. The informal conversations take place within the context and the bounds set by the formal transfers of information and there is usually no difficulty in finding the opportunities for the informal conversations. I believe that the informal conversations alone would not be anywhere as effective without the framework provided by the transfer of information at the formal meetings. The scheduled formal meetings, even if very few, are vital.

Outside of the workplace the opportunities for having these informal conversations is limited; by geography, by time constraints and the availability of the required participants. Here the manager must resort to informal conversations which must be planned in advance and well prepared. The manager must choose the timing and content of the informal information transfers such that they fall within the schedule and framework of formal meetings in order to give the right context to the informal conversations when they do occur. In most cases it is possible to arrange for an informal meeting once a formal meeting has been scheduled. It is essential in such conversations that inhibitions are lowered so that the "true voice" can be heard. It is precisely for this reason that the location chosen is often a restaurant or a golf course or a pub. These are primarily places having a social purpose and provide a relaxed, non-threatening atmosphere which helps remove or reduce inhibitions. These situations – provided everybody remains largely sober – then provide the opportunity for the physical proximity and the face-to-face meetings where the true voice can be heard.

But language and culture and behaviour are intertwined. Care must be taken especially in informal, cross-cultural conversations to ensure that misunderstandings are avoided. The Sapir–Whorf Hypothesis proposes that languages affect the world-view such that speakers of different languages perceive others differently and they behave differently because of it. In other words language determines thought and differences in language mean differences of thought. This hypothesis is rather too extreme for me but no doubt has large elements of truth.

The Finns (rather than the Eskimos of urban legend) have – out of necessity – developed more than 40 words to describe different kinds of snow and ice. The Sami language spoken in Lapland is said to have even more. But in the heat and dust of India, Hindi has only one word (barrf) which is used – without distinction – for ice, hail, frost, snow, sleet, glaciers, ice cream, ice cubes or icebergs. It would be pointless to expect the "true voice" to emerge in an informal conversation with an Indian manager about the suitability of different kinds of snow for skiing!

The subject of informal conversations would be incomplete without mentioning the "grapevine". There is no organisation of any size (and the critical threshold is probably about ten people) which does not have a grapevine. Information flows through the grapevine as a series of informal conversations but these are conversations which do not necessarily have the context provided by a formal mode of information exchange. It was once thought that the grapevine was just a source of damaging rumours and gossip and something to be suppressed. This view has changed and it is generally recognised that grapevines do serve needs regarding the health of the organisation. Testing has shown that information flowing through a grapevine is remarkably accurate, sometimes embellished as all stories are, but with a nucleus of highly accurate information. Some estimates suggest that over 80% of grapevine information is accurate. It has become apparent that grapevine information does not originate from gossip. It can sometimes lead to some gossip but grapevine information usually originates from a first-hand witness to some event or from a person who saw some document or heard some information. Initially it radiates outwards from the witness but very soon starts radiating also from the first receivers. The 20% or so of the information which is not strictly accurate is usually made up of embellishments to the story. It is in this portion that gossip creeps in. The information flow is extremely fast. It is not constrained by the hierarchical structures of the organisation and has no respect for geography or department boundaries. It follows the overlaps and interconnections of the social and personal networks of the members of the organisation. Nowadays, grapevines are seen to be, on balance, beneficial for the health of organisations by providing an early warning system, improving efficiency, creating group cohesion and for sharing and shaping a culture. The grapevine also seems to provide some kind of a necessary safety valve for any organisation. I have observed that larger or more rigid organisations seem to have more wide-spread and active grapevines. My working hypothesis is that grapevines are actually created by the organisation itself, acting like an organism, to protect its own health.

Attempts have been made to use the grapevine intentionally to float "trial balloons" or to sensitise an organisation to bad news. Deliberately exaggerated rumours of drastic downsizing or fears of closure have often been intentionally propagated on grapevines in the hope that the less unpleasant reality will be better accepted when it comes. These attempts have often backfired because the information has been distorted along the way and has reached unintended recipients. The grapevine, in my experience, due to the sheer speed of propagation of information is not controllable or predictable, either regarding content or to direction. A manager must listen and listen carefully to the grapevine but I believe it should be used primarily as a means of "listening" to the "voice of the organisation" and not to communicate to the organisation. He should preferably be a part of the grapevine himself, which then gives him the opportunity of improving information accuracy from within. But, he should be much more wary of trying to use it intentionally as a medium for a communication.

Identifying a Good Communicator

Some people are naturally good communicators and others have to work at it. But the skills can all be learned. The key judgment to be made is whether, consciously or unconsciously, the communicator fulfils the various steps of the

Identifying a Good Communicator

true communication process. In a short or limited interaction with an individual it is difficult to observe the entire process he may be implementing. Nevertheless it is possible to observe some of the characteristics which are usually exhibited by good communicators and thereafter make a judgment.

In formal conversations such as in an interview, good communicators will:

1. Show a quiet confidence
2. Exhibit the body language which indicates that they are listening carefully
3. Show that their words are chosen carefully and that their messages are considered opinions
4. Be fluent in their delivery but pause deliberately in conversations to pick up feedback
5. Repeat their messages in different words but will not be repetitive in their language
6. Use non-verbal language (gestures or body language) to support their points
7. Ask for clarifications of meaning even if you are deliberately vague – "Did you mean that.......?"
8. Generally pose open rather than closed questions
9. Provide feedback without prompting
10. Readily explain their opinion when faced with an open question
11. Demonstrate curiosity and interest
12. Be able to describe how he gets or can get feedback in different situations
13. Not be easily shocked or intimidated or unbalanced by an outrageous suggestion (for example, "I don't think you have the knowledge for this job" or "We really should not have invited you for this interview")
14. Try and find common ground if presented with an extreme scenario but will not be provoked to respond emotionally
15. Not volunteer the information but will not be afraid to explain his fundamental values in practical terms if asked directly
16. Show that he is trying to see things from your view point
17. Be curious and ask reasonable questions about you and the surrounding environment
18. Try, from time to time, to shift the conversation into an informal mode

Any manager can make himself into a good communicator. Some will have to work harder at it than others. But being aware of the steps contained within a communications process is where the learning starts.

Chapter 5
Inescapable Networks and Relationships of Mutuality

Networks and relationships are a fundamental asset that a manager can bring to bear in the mobilisation of his desired actions. Networks have their own purposes but the flow of goods, services, advice and emotions between network partners provides a special resource in the mobilisation of actions when the actions fulfil both the objectives of the manager and the purposes of the network. There may well be an upper limit to the number of stable and meaningful relationships any individual can have and this demands that a good manager choose his networks and develop his relationships within them with care. "Escalation of Engagement" is the technique that a manager must master.

Networks for a Manager

A manager must mobilise the actions he desires from subordinates, peers, superiors, other associates, acquaintances and even from strangers. Networks are particular associations of individuals and organisations, each with its own particular purpose. Where a manager is a member of a network, his relationships to other members governs the flow of goods, services, advice and emotion to and from such members. The breadth of a manager's networks and his relationships within them are a fundamental asset he brings to bear in his ability to mobilise actions. But networks and relationships can be managed consciously. The good manager participates in networks and develops his relationships judiciously and intentionally.

The Nature of Networks

The Geneva bible of 1560 has "And thou shall make unto it a grate like networke of brass" (Exodus 27, 4). In the 1600s the word "network" was used to describe the mesh like structure of plants and animals. By the eighteenth century the weaving and textile trades were referring to net-like structures as "networks". The industrial growth of the nineteenth century saw the word being applied to describe inter-connected canals and the growth of railway links and then to the spread of electrical distribution lines.

In the twentieth century, usage spread rapidly to radio broadcasting, sociology, computer science, biology, medicine, physics, traffic systems, telecommunication and science in general. From being a static, physical description of a reticulated or net-like structure the word "network" today represents a dynamic structure, with interconnected and communicating junctions. The manner in which networks of interconnected nodes function led to new areas of scientific inquiry and "network theory" and "network analysis" have now become specialised branches of mathematics and of engineering, with applications in many of the applied sciences.

"Social networks" were first labelled as such in the 1940s and their study has become an important subject in sociology. Since the 1990s, the development of personal computers, the Internet, wireless data transmission and broadband – in that order – has seen the exponential growth of social networking sites.

> Kevin Kelly
> A brain is a society of very small, simple modules that cannot be said to be thinking, that are not smart in themselves. But when you have a network of them together, out of that arises a kind of smartness.

I confine myself here to observations and perceptions regarding the characteristics and use of personal, social networks that are, or may be, relevant for a manager. To define and clarify some of the basics, I resort again to analogies from the physical world.

An electrical conductor (a wire) or a fluid conductor (a pipe) or a data link can connect respectively, two electrical junctions or two fluid reservoirs or two computers. If three or more nodes (junctions) are connected by wires and each node is connected to at least two others, an electrical network comes into being. Similarly, if three or more nodes (reservoirs) are connected by pipes and each reservoir is connected to at least two others, a fluid network (usually hydraulic or pneumatic) comes into existence. If three or more computers are connected by data transfer links and each computer is connected to at least two others, a computer network comes into being. Any node which has only one connector attached becomes merely an adjunct to that connected node and does not contribute uniquely to the network.

The mere existence of junctions or reservoirs or computers does not make a network. The network is only constituted when the connections between the nodes are established such that each node has connections to at least two others. Both nodal connections must permit the flow of the same "thing". (A trivial observation perhaps, but a node cannot qualify as part of a network even if it has two connectors but one connector is electrical and the other is a fluid connector. Two connections carrying the same "thing" between the same two nodes also do not qualify.) Once a network is constituted, it may still do nothing. It may merely exist indefinitely in a dormant state with no detectable activity or flow. A network of reservoirs needs to be energised by means of a volume and a head of some fluid, or by an inflow of fluid from outside the network, before any flows occur within the network and any levels in the reservoirs change. If computers are connected but do not exchange any data then the computer network exists, but remains dormant until it is energised for or by the flow of some data. Nevertheless, it is perfectly feasible for a network to exist in a dormant state without any flows occurring.

Any network – unless it was constituted entirely by chance – usually has some purpose. Even those created by chance follow the physical laws of nature and come into existence as a consequence of driving forces which are a purpose unto themselves. Even a natural network of rivers and lakes created by the force of gravity could be said to have the "purpose" of transmitting water to the sea. Whether an energised network can achieve its purpose is a different issue and depends upon its capability. The purpose of a network may change with time. Networks already existing, whether constituted by natural forces or by chance or for some other purpose, can be co-opted to fulfil a new purpose, either to replace the original purpose, or to create an additional purpose which is discovered to be within the capability of the network. For example, an irrigation network established to regulate water flows could be used, in addition, to regulate reservoir levels when floods pose a danger. A network of animal movement paths in the jungle could be used instead by predators for hunting or, in today's world, for conducting an animal census. A computer network set up for say, gathering weather information from many remote locations could be used additionally for disseminating quite unrelated information to the computers at those locations. A network of vendors created for the supply of some goods or services could be converted into a network of potential customers for some other goods or services.

The actual flow between any two nodes depends on their relative states. If there is some kind of an enabling potential difference between them then a flow will occur. For electric current to flow a voltage difference is required between the two nodes. For a fluid to flow a pressure difference is required between two reservoirs or junctions. For data to flow between computers an enabling "potential" must be created by appropriate software. Generally the flow can be in either direction provided the potential difference "points" to the receiving node. In some networks there is no storage capacity at the nodes and the inflow to the network must equal the outflow from the network. Within the network the flow must then always be in flux but note that very high internal flows can still occur even if there is no inflow or outflow. In many networks, where a flow is due to a potential difference, the flow itself acts to reduce that potential difference. Flow between reservoirs tends to reduce the difference of levels and the flow of an electric current tends to reduce the voltage difference, unless the potential difference is maintained by an inflow to the first node. If there is no place for the flow to go, the enabling potential difference equalises between the nodes and the flow stops. Potential differences always drive towards a point of equilibrium. In other networks the nodes themselves may provide some storage capacity as with water levels in an interconnected reservoir network, but here too the flows cease if the enabling potentials are equalised.

Networks, the analysis of networks, the use of mathematics to model networks, the design of networks and the prediction of the behaviour of constructed networks are expanding fields of study. Analysis of networks in the natural world, such as the coordinated and synchronised behaviour of ants and bees for example, is being transferred to the design of computer networks. Network theory is being used to analyse cancer cells and their behaviour. The most complex, constructed networks are probably those trying to create artificial intelligence where the goal is to try and reach the complexity and power of the neural network in the human brain. When networks are imbued with a purpose, they can seem to be self-correcting and self-healing and even seem to have some of the characteristics of a living organism. Living organisms themselves are sometimes analysed as networks of cells. As a minimum the purpose of a network is just to establish the capability of the flow of some "thing" between the nodes. The flow may be of something material (such as electrons or water) or something abstract (such as information or advice or an emotion).

Human Networks and Personal Networks

There are over six billion people in a world that is constantly getting "smaller". Most are interconnected with others in various social groups. The main characteristic of the world getting "smaller" is that the separation distance (not spatial distance *per se* but the time to reach or connect with another person) is getting smaller. The potential to associate and connect with more and more people is increasing. The so-called small world hypothesis postulates that just "six degrees of separation" are sufficient for any human to connect with any other human. This is not proven and is probably not a law, but it does seem that not too many degrees of separation are needed to achieve a very wide reach. Studies indicate, for example, that between five and seven degrees of separation are sufficient for connecting any two people who have access to e-mail.

> Martin Luther King, Jr.
> All men are caught in an inescapable network of mutuality.

Human networks are perforce social networks and share many features with inanimate networks. Just as with physical networks, it takes at least three humans to create a network. Each human node must be connected to at least two others to be a unique network participant. The connectors in human networks are often abstract and there are many different types of connectors. The connections can be, for example, of friendship; of shared interests or beliefs; for pooling of resources, knowledge or experience; of kinship, of shared activities or for some mutual benefit including financial benefit. Whatever the connector is, it must foster a flow of some "thing" or "things" of value between the human nodes. In any particular network the connectors must transmit the same flow of "things". If a network involves multiple types of connectors (of kinship and say golf as a special interest) then each node must have two connectors of each type. Therefore a relative who was not also a golfer would not then be a member of this particular network. The flow could be tangible and consist of information or of goods or a service or advice or an action.

In a car pooling network for example or in a baby-sitting club, it is a service and actions which flow between members. Advice and experience could be exchanged to the mutual benefit of the participants in a technical Internet forum. It could also be a flow of intangible qualities that are valued by the humans in the network. It could be a flow of emotional support or empathy or sympathy or encouragement in a network of family relations or a network of friends, or it could be political support in a community wide network.

As in physical networks, the actual flow between any two nodes depends on their relative states. An enabling potential difference must exist for a flow. The "things" that flow (information or a service or advice or an action or an emotion) defines the kind of potential difference needed to set the flow in motion and in which direction. This potential difference between two individuals is then what I refer to as the "relationship" between the two. I believe the analogy with inanimate flows holds insofar as the relative magnitude of the relationship directs the direction and the magnitude of the flow. However this analogy should not be taken too much further.

A major difference between inanimate networks and social networks is that human nodes are aware of the purpose of the network and that they are participants within the network. In fact, the network effectively does not exist for humans if they are not aware that they are part of the network. The purpose of the network may be perceived only as an implicitly understood purpose. For example, the purpose of a family network may never be explicitly articulated, but the social and cultural background provides a common perception, among the family members, as to the purpose of the "family". Unlike voltage or a fluid pressure, but similar to computers, relationships can give rise to flows in both directions simultaneously. Instead of a flow reducing the driving potential difference as in most natural networks, a flow in a social network can both strengthen the relationship and even expand the carrying capacity of the connector.

In social networks the participating nodes range from individuals and families up to organisations and even nations. Networks can connect to other networks through shared nodes to create new networks. It is not necessary that all the nodes involved in a particular network be identical but they do need to be reasonably similar. It would be quite surprising for individuals to participate as nodes for example, in a network of nations. But individuals and small organisations can well be part of the same network and large multi-national corporations can be in the same network as government institutions or even nations. Trade associations are networks involving enterprises of varying sizes in some related branch of business. (It could however, be argued however, that even networks of nations or large institutional organisations can ultimately be broken down to networks of individuals and the relationships between them).

Social networks thus represent definable, interconnected groups of people having some expected beneficial flow between the participants. There may be no other purpose than the flow itself (provision of information or a service) or there may be a declared goal for the network to achieve (particular election results for a political support network or fund-raising to support a city orchestra or the improvement of the level of skill among members in a "squash ladder"). Social networks in practice consist of groups of individuals, in a beneficial association, sharing some common but identifying features, such as functions (professional associations) or cultural tastes (a drama group) or political views or having attended the same school (alumni associations). Rules, often unwritten, do apply as to qualifying for membership in a network. Some of the membership rules can vary from being very loose, evolving and dynamic as for an Internet forum, to being highly specialised, unchanging and very strict as for, say, the Royal Society. Membership rules in kinship networks are immutable. Membership numbers in some networks can be largely static but in others the number of members and the purpose of the network can be continuously changing. Small, closely knit groups are usually highly specialised, maintain a strict partition between themselves and the "outside" world and provide a relatively narrow range of benefits but the values of the benefit flows can be very high. Connections between individuals are usually very strong in such networks and typical examples could be a Masonic lodge or an exclusive country club or a street gang. Large, open networks with many weak connections have a changing and fluctuating membership. However they can bring to bear a very wide range of experience and knowledge and can provide benefits over many fields but where the value of the benefits flowing is relatively low. A technical Internet forum or a rambling association or a football supporters club could be examples.

In management and in the business world, the terms "networks" and "networking" and "relationship" are used frequently but not always very clearly or precisely. There is often a wide divergence in perceptions of what these terms mean. It is often overlooked that the network by itself is static. The purpose of the network must be driven by one or more of its members and the network itself must be energised by the prevailing relationships. The "relationship" (the driving potential) causes the flows within – and always confined to – the network. The flow can itself alter the relationship – and not only in the direction of reducing the driving force. The flow of service can create new channels for new flows just as the lack of a flow can "kill" a channel. It is not always clear whether what is being discussed is:

1. The static network (the infrastructure), or
2. The relationship potential (the driving force), or
3. The resulting flow

$$A\ network + a\ relationship = a\ flow$$

Having a great many acquaintances is often assumed to be a sign of having a wide or a strong network. But the key features which distinguish an acquaintance from a network partner is first whether a relationship exists between them which would lead to flow and second whether a grouping of such connections can be said to have some purpose which would bring a network into existence. In any organisation, a manager will just by virtue of his work responsibilities, have a number of connections not only with his subordinates but also with peers and superiors. The strength of his relationships with these connections, and especially those who may be only peripherally connected with his work, will be proportional to the effort spent in building and maintaining these relationships. The important point is then the number of meaningful relationships a manager has and not just the number of acquaintances.

The concept of having key account managers (KAMs) is common in many industries but there is often confusion as to their role and their responsibilities with regard to creating networks and developing relationships. I have experienced incompetent KAMs who have believed that their network consisted of the internal telephone directory of their customer. Others have believed that having an e-mail address and sending the occasional congratulatory e-mail constituted a relationship. But I have also had the pleasure of working with some superb KAMs, who had active networks spanning many hierarchical levels within the customer organisation and who were themselves perceived as being a very valuable partner by their customers. One who was a key account manager for a global oil company explained to me once that as he got older his real challenge was not maintaining relations with those of his own age or older but with younger, up-and-coming managers. As an "outsider" representing a supplier organisation his task was to select a few who he thought would go far and with whom he initiated and developed relationships. He was playing the role of "teacher" to two who were aspiring golfers and had developed genuine friendships with a number of others. The reach of his networks was truly impressive and his network partners ranged from the level of Board Members and down to one member of the customer's graduate trainee programme.

It was once thought that an individual could maintain stable relationships with no more than about 150 other individuals as being a cognitive limit (the so-called Dunbar Number). However, it is now considered that this maximum limit is more likely to be around 230–300 people. In any case it does seem clear that an individual will have stable social relationships with, at most, about 200–300 others. If there is such a limit – and it seems intuitively likely that there is – then it is clearly important that a manager be selective in how many networks he participates in and the people he chooses to maintain stable relationships with. More important than numbers however, when considering a manager's capabilities, are the number of networks he participates in, the reach and scope of the networks and his relationship with others in his networks.

The inherent strength of a network should be distinguished from the strength of individual connections. There could be weak connections within a very strong network or vice versa. The number of nodes, the number of inter-connections, redundancy (meaning the possibility of alternative routes if one connection is broken) and the strength of the connections, all contribute to the overall strength of the network. Small, closed networks with specialised membership rules are extremely vulnerable to the loss of even a few members either because they dip below some critical mass or because there is insufficient redundancy. Stringent membership requirements and a closed nature of a network usually give rise to strong connections, but it can be difficult for broken connections to heal by the influx of new nodes or remade connections. Such networks are characterised by having some key members without whom the networks could collapse. Cliques forming in the workplace or street gangs are examples of such networks. Large, open networks have a high degree of redundancy and can constantly replace nodes or renew broken connections. No single member then has a monopoly on connections such that the network is jeopardised without him. However, such open networks do tend to have, on average, weaker connections between the nodes.

Any particular individual is a member of a number of such social networks. With the individual as the focus, the community given by the membership of all the networks he participates in are his personal networks. In some of his personal networks he will be a part of the nucleus providing the vital connection for other members and a major contributor to the strength of the network. In others he will be a peripheral member where the strength or integrity of the network is not strongly dependent upon his membership or that of his connections. It is the extent (number and reach) of his personal networks and his relationships with others in his networks which together determine the value of his personal networks to him as an individual and in his role as a manager.

Relationships

A relationship, in my opinion, can be said to exist between two individuals as soon as one associates with the other. It would be an academic exercise in semantics to debate what precisely an association between individuals means and when a relationship can be defined to have started. It is more relevant and useful for our purposes to consider the depth and strength of relationships.

> Antoine de Saint-Exupéry
> Man is a knot into which relationships are tied.

In physics, driving potentials are exclusively related to a particular kind of flow. Voltage difference drives current exclusively, pressure difference drives fluid flow and a temperature difference gives heat flow. A "relationship" between any two individuals, on the other hand, is not exclusively tied to just one kind of the various flows that can take place between people. It is a representation of the driving force which leads to any or all of the "social flows" between them. Thus the relationship is exclusive and unique to a particular pair of individuals rather than being exclusively connected to one particular type of flow. It can give rise to flows of information or advice or a service or an emotion or goods or actions or any combinations of these. The types of flow generated vary from one pair of individuals to the next. Relationships vary over time and can give different flows at different times between the same pair of individuals.

When dealing earlier with communication I chose a categorisation based on the type of recipient as being the most appropriate for providing a means of attaining the quality of communication needed by a manager. When dealing with relationships a similar classification by type of individual pairs is possible. I find this more tractable than trying to group the immense variety of types of social flow that are possible.

Purely for convenience, I choose the following categories and believe that the bulk of an individual's stable relationships will be covered under:

1. Pairings based on kinship
   (a) Parent–child
   (b) Immediate family (siblings, grand-children, grand-parents, uncles, aunts, nephews and nieces)
   (c) Extended family
2. Friendship pairs
   (a) Intimate friends
   (b) Multiple common interest friends
   (c) Single interest friends
   (d) Acquaintances
3. Peer to peer pairs
4. Teacher–student (including coach–player, guide–traveller, sensei–kohai or guru–chela pairings)
5. Superior–subordinate (including master–servant, senior–junior, higher caste–lower caste, employer–employee or boss–worker pairings)
6. With persons of status or authority (judges, police, doctors, nurses, public figures or well known personalities)

Types of relationships and the flows they generate are not exclusive to any particular pairing. Clearly some flows are more likely with some pairings than with others. Many relationship induced flows are governed by perceptions of duties, rights, obligations and debt in the relationship. Duties and rights are often linked and it is sometimes claimed that a right for someone creates a duty for someone else. But this is, I think, a laziness of thought.

For the sake of clarity, I shall use "fulfilment of duty" to mean the repayment of a debt created by an acknowledged "obligation". It seems obvious to me that an individual's duty must be acknowledged by the individual to be perceived as a duty and cannot be imposed. An obligation or debt may be created for, or imposed on, an individual but whether it is converted to a duty or not is solely his call. Doing one's duty is then to fulfil an acknowledged obligation. When I borrow money from the bank I have an obligation, imposed by contract, to repay. But it is I who must acknowledge my duty to the bank and repay the loan. An employee's duty to his employer is because of the contractual obligation that he has. A parent's duty to a child follows the parent's self-generated sense of obligation. Society may create a pressure on the parent to have such an obligation, but the duty felt by the parent to the child (as opposed to any duty felt to the surrounding society) is ultimately self-generated. The child's duty to a parent also then flows from the self-generated obligation felt by the child. A teacher's duty to his student may originate in the contractual obligation he may have to his employer but ultimately flows from what he perceives as his own obligations to his student. He may perceive an immense duty to a very talented youngster and virtually none towards a more indifferent student. In simple terms a duty does not exist until an individual perceives that he has the duty.

I take a "right" to be a privilege or a permit or a licence to act. A "right" must therefore be granted by someone with the authority to do so. In real life, "rights" are often granted by people and organisations that have insufficient authority to do so. The rights "to pursue happiness" or to "speak freely" are granted by most societies to the individual. But nobody is guaranteed happiness or free speech. Whether a right is exercised or not is the individual's call, subject to his capability. Society may have granted me the right to vote or the right to health care but it remains up to me to exercise these rights. A lioness (or a mother) takes care of her cub (or her child) because she, somehow feels an instinctive duty to do so; probably based on a complex mix of survival instinct, maternal love and biological needs and not because some authority granted the cub (or the child) the right to be taken care of.

It is a manager's employment contract and his appointment as a manager by an employer which grants him certain rights of action. It is his call whether the rights are exercised. Equally he may have contractual obligations which he acknowledges, thereby creating duties for himself. But it is not his contract which creates any duties for his subordinates. Their duties do not flow directly from the rights granted to him. It is his subordinates' own contracts of employment with the same employer, which impose obligations on them and thereby creates their duty to follow the manager's instructions. But this is their duty to the employer and to the manager only as a representative of the employer. The simple logic is that a contract between two parties cannot bind a third party unless the third party becomes a party to the same contract.

However, an obligation can be partially transferred to a network partner if the relationship is close enough. A close friend when I was a student, once lent me his car to pick my mother up from the airport. But he might well have refused lending me his car, without in any way damaging our relationship, if I had needed the car merely to go out on a date. The fact that we both perceived picking up my mother as my obligation and my duty has an obvious impact. Our relationship was clearly strong enough to lead to some transfer of my obligations to him, but only as his obligation to assist me (but not, I think, as his obligation to pick my mother up). My going out on a date, on the other hand, would not have been seen as a duty and would not have transferred to him any perception of an obligation to assist. And if I had been trying to borrow the car from just any acquaintance it is unlikely that I would have succeeded in either case.

Relationship flows can also be due to abstract feelings and emotions. Liking, love, dislike or hate in a relationship are all potentials which generate their own flows between network partners. These flows may consist variously of information exchange, or the provision of goods and services, or the generation of actions, or an empathic transfer of emotion or any combination of these. Similarly, curiosity, greed, the search for knowledge, the desire to assist, philanthropy, altruism or selfishness are also all relationship qualities which give rise to such flows.

A.A. Milne
  Piglet sidled up to Pooh from behind. "Pooh!" he whispered. "Yes, Piglet?" "Nothing," said Piglet, taking Pooh's paw. "I just wanted to be sure of you."

Classification into the different pairings is only a convenient way of observing how relationships may be initiated and how they can be developed. All the various flows can occur between all the pair-types. The social context, culture, language and history surrounding a pair determine the perceptions of duty and obligations and rights which prevail. In Asia (Japan, China, Korea, India . . .) nuances of duty, honour, service, obligations and debt are reflected in the complexity of relations between castes, sub-castes, priests, disciples, royalty, family, slaves, friends, teachers and students. Concepts of duty (*giri* in Japan or *dharma* in India) are no doubt changing but are ingrained and govern the relationship flows that occur. These, in turn, map the available paths by which a relationship may be developed.

The duties and obligations of teachers and students is a particular potent relationship and apply to the roles and not just those formally designated to be teachers or students. A teacher–student pairing anywhere in the world could develop to be a peer-to-peer connection and even to become a relationship between intimate friends as the relationship deepens. However the manner in which this could develop in Japan is quite different to the manner in which it could happen in Europe. In my experience it is far more likely for a student in Europe or the US to become his professor's collaborator and see their relationship develop to be a peer-to-peer relationship than in Japan or India. In Japan or India the *sensei–kohai* or the *guru–chela* relationships do not transform into a peer-to-peer relationship very often. The skill of the student and the respect accorded to him by the teacher may increase over the years but the role of teacher always remains with the teacher. In all countries though, the roles of teacher or student could be taken by any two people and the roles are not restricted by age or gender or formal designations. The subsequent relationships then follow the assumed roles.

A network pairing with a person of authority can develop, or be developed, to become a pairing of peers. Senior bureaucrats or civil servants who are involved in licensing or permitting processes are often in positions of great authority in relation to corporations and business enterprises. The manner in which senior, retired civil servants become senior managers in the corporate world in Japan (*amakudari* – descent from heaven) is not so different to the manner in which senior government appointees in the US Administration become lobbyists for corporations in Washington when their appointments have run their term, or when Finance Ministry officials anywhere become bank directors when they retire. In all these cases, a relationship originally between a person in authority and those he has authority over, changes to become a peer-to-peer or even an employee–employer relationship, when the term of authority is over. The value of a retired bureaucrat or government official lies almost entirely in the personal networks he has developed over his career. Similarly, many senior military officers – whether in North America or Europe or in Asia – change from being a customer during their military careers to becoming an employee of corporations involved in the supply of military equipment when they retire.

The manner in which single-interest friends develop their relationship by the inclusion of additional common interests is much the same all over the world. Golfing buddies can become family friends and an Internet forum partner can become an employer not only in all countries but across country boundaries. I have not observed any great differences either in the number of friends considered intimate and the level of intimacy enjoyed in different countries. But the flows applying between intimate friends are constrained by the social context and the surrounding culture and these do differ from country to country. The extended family in India is a caste-based community (where members are distantly related and all belong to the same sub-caste), and exhibits much deeper relationships than generally seen in other countries. Such communities may consist of a few hundred or even a few thousand people and the relationships (which include duty and obligation) are almost as deep and as strong that would normally only be found within an immediate family circle. Historically these were social groups which became trading groups and traders who leveraged their strong internal relationships as they spread in and outside of India, and these networks remain strong. Membership of an expatriate group starts only because of common nationality and language but can then develop rapidly to encompass much deeper relationships.

Many relationship flows include actions. A relationship between two people in a network therefore includes, but has a much wider scope than, just the inter-personal power for the mobilisation of actions. Clearly, a manager has the potential to use his networks and his relationships to members of his networks to mobilise actions. Any empowerment of his partners for the mobilisation of their actions, then also depends upon the manager having an understanding of the personal networks that they have and the relationships that they enjoy.

The development of, and the ability to develop, relationships with network partners then becomes an important part of a manager's portfolio. Even if some of these are not directly in pursuit of his managerial role, the strength of his relationships in his personal networks is an integral part of his personality and his ability to mobilise actions. I call the manner of development of relationships the "escalation of engagement".

Escalation of Engagement

It is not always necessary or desirable to have strong relationships with every member of one's social networks. The manner in which an individual, or more particularly a manager, initiates and develops relationships are relevant to his capabilities. In fact, one key judgment to be exercised by every manager is to choose which relationships are to be cultivated and which need not. If human capacity is limited to having not more than about 200–300 significant social relationships then it becomes important to choose judiciously. Where he judges them to be beneficial to his managerial role, the network and his relationships do provide an asset in his balance sheet. Relationships are always mutual and while they can be stronger in one direction than another, they cannot be one-sided. To initiate and then gradually engage with another individual so as to develop and deepen a relationship is a skill. This is dependent not only upon the "chemistry" applying between the two but also on the manager's actions, conscious or otherwise, to actively develop the connection. "Chemistry" here is a label which covers all the multitude of relevant factors, but which are not so well understood, as to why some people "hit it off" and others do not.

A relationship is dynamic and varies with time. It escalates as the mutual engagement increases and goes through distinct steps; from "initiation" or "association" to "acquaintance" to "friendship" to "bonding". The progression of the relationship is nearly always accompanied by a deepening of trust. Increasing trust is, in turn, accompanied by an increase in the level of risk that each is willing to take. The network flows expand and escalate as a relationship deepens, from information and advice to actions and eventually to emotions. The relationship may stop and remain stable at any stage or could lie dormant at any level. It may at any time retract, or may proceed to a termination or be reactivated. At the deepest level of bonding, the pair is no longer seen by the outside world as separate nodes but as a single unit. In the network sense, the two nodes then merge into one.

Initiating a relationship happens usually by chance but often by choice. Kinship pairings based on birth do not require initiation and cannot be chosen, but relationships with kin can, like any other relationship, be weak or strong and are amenable to cultivation and development. Kinship by marriage can extend an individual's family network but is mostly by the choices of others. However, people do try and create or modify the extent of kinship networks by arranging marriages. Arranged marriages are as old as the institution itself and are resorted to for a variety of reasons. It could be for a perceived genetic protection of the "breed"; for a parent to fulfil a duty; for the growth or protection of family assets; for the creation or protection of dynasties; or simply for continuing or extending the family network. Culture and social background do influence the perceptions of duty and obligations which apply between family members and these can vary somewhat across countries. But the actual relationship between any two family members can be anywhere within the whole range of possible relationships and overrides cultural expectations.

Only a small portion of casual meetings develop into relationships and only some of the developed relations will be within a network. When people are sought out as an intended network partner, it is then the initiator who must take risk first to overcome the barriers of trust. Very often the risk taken consists of disclosure of information or by exposure to the rejection of an offer or an invitation. If such risk is taken judiciously then, in my perception, there is a good probability that a connection will be established. But trust and risk-taking must be reciprocated for the relationship to develop further. An introduction to a friend of a friend is a powerful and effective initiator of a relationship. Here the interlocutor effectively plays the role of a "guarantor" to both, similar to the traditional role of the "match-maker". This overcomes some of the initial trust barriers and can be a very sound basis for further engagement.

When I first started working as a salesman in ABB, I was appointed to take responsibility for sales to Japan. My manager asked me how I would go about initiating a relationship with a particular senior manager in a customer organisation. The prospective customer was a Japanese utility company. I recall making long lists of all the various offers I could potentially make to, let me call him, Nishimura-san. I had never met Nishimura-san who was hierarchically very much senior to me, but who had consented to see me because of my background in research. But my manager, who was a wily old fox, just shook his head and said "Don't make any offers. Try asking for a favour". And that is what I did. At our first meeting in his office, Nishimura-san talked about personal matters (my person, not his), education systems, family, Swedish winters and sports; everything except the sales opportunity that was my primary goal. That evening at dinner, I took the chance, exposed my ignorance, showed my interest and requested Nishimura-san – as a student might request a teacher – to explain the intricacies of a Sumo-basho that was ongoing at that time. He did me the favour. Over the years, in between actually doing some business together, he accompanied me to two bashos and he continued explaining Sumo to me for the next 18 years. The relationship grew and lasted till he retired as Executive Vice President of the utility. It persisted long after I had moved away from sales and had shifted through three different countries.

Asking for a favour is an acknowledgement of "inferiority", invites rejection and is risky. Even if granted, the favour always puts you into debt. It is similar to a show of submission by a wolf to the pack leader which always risks rejection. But it can be a very powerful way of starting a relationship.

Over the years I have found that asking for a favour has a much higher internal perception of risk than there actually is. It is the acknowledgement of insufficiency that is most difficult and I suppose that it is the suppression of ego that is the cause. But I have found people – and even total strangers – to be remarkably receptive to providing a favour when it is well within their competence and carries no risk. I suppose that it is the ego boost that comes from doing a favour that is the cause.

Having initiated a relationship, it is the escalation of the level of engagement which determines whether it proceeds to the acquaintance phase and on to friendship. Engagement here means one or both parties taking additional risk, making new commitments and extending flows of information, goods, services, actions or of some intangible abstract quantity (such as support, advice, sympathy or empathy). As engagement levels increase, the levels of mutual trust increase and the perceived levels of risk decrease. Acquaintances can develop to the next stage to be friends with whom beneficial interaction takes place. Regular interaction is characterised by regular flows which are perceived to be mutually beneficial and where both parties have an interest in the flow, and therefore the relationship, continuing. Most relationships will probably stabilise and continue indefinitely at this level. The relationship will still continue to grow, but slowly, and the connection will now be characterised by high levels of trust and perceptions of mutual reliability. A very few relationships will develop into a full-fledged bonding where now mutual trust moves into the area of mutual dependence. However, this much deeper relationship is not without risk. Bonding with the friend of a friend can lead to rivalry and competition. Breaking of bonds once they have been forged can be traumatic and disruptive. Termination of the relationship is difficult. Within networks, a bonded pair can appear as a single, very strong node with many interconnections. The break-up of a bonded pair can lead to one of the nodes being excluded from the network.

The choosing of network partners and then developing relationships is of importance to all individuals but it is a vital skill for a manager. He must assess not only the personality types of others but put them into the context of his own. He must choose his tactics of escalation to suit. He could choose to gradually increase from small engagements in one area to include other areas; or to increase successively from smaller to larger engagements in the same area; or to use a "big bang" approach with a single overwhelming engagement. The primary tool in applying such tactics is communication. A step change in the relationship and level of engagement occurs when the parties shift from just a formal mode of communication to include the informal mode in which they expose their "true voices".

Escalation of engagement is also the manager's primary tool with team building among his subordinates. An effective way is by increasing his own level of engagement with each team member individually and, by way of example, encouraging similar escalations by the team members among themselves. This is where he can enable and encourage engagements to enter into new areas by organising for example, social, cultural or sports events involving not only team members but also their families. To build the team it is necessary to build trust, to reduce inhibitions and to get the members speaking informally in their "true voices". Expanding the fields available for escalation of engagement is especially critical in multi-national or multi-cultural teams, where the common ground with familiar reference points must be identified to allow penetration of the surface differences.

It is not uncommon for sales managers to exhort their salesmen to "suck the customer in" to increased levels of commitments. This is nothing more than an escalation of engagement. Corporations often have programmes for increasing the engagement of employees. All instances of escalation of engagement can be perceived as being manipulative but there is a clear line between proper escalation of engagement and what I would consider to be manipulation. Manipulation is, I believe, when trust is built up with the intention of later misusing or betraying that trust. But there is a simple way for a manager to check. If the escalations he plans to take violate either his own values or his personal integrity, then he has entered the area of manipulation.

Relationships Across Cultures

I believe strongly that the universal drivers of human behaviour lie deeper than language and culture. This seems to be supported by research which has found there are at least several key dimensions of interpersonal behaviour that are common across cultures. The same variables have been found to apply across many cultures and are referred to as "psychological universals".

Even though the underlying drivers may be universal, language and culture are inseparable and shroud the "psychological universals". This does not mean that a manager must be an expert in the language and culture of all countries that he deals with or of all the people he interacts with. What it does mean is that he must be aware of the differences of surface veneer due to language and cultural differences. The awareness must be sufficient so as to be able to penetrate below this surface to reach the universal drivers.

He must know that the various ways in which English words are used in different parts of the world, especially spoken English, are not always obvious and can easily deceive. The differences between UK and US English are well known. But English as used in India or Australia or South Africa or Malaysia have their own unique characteristics. Other speakers of English often use UK or US English depending upon how they were taught the language. It then becomes important to know whether the Russian banker that a manager may be interacting with, was taught US or UK English. Written English is generally more formal and more uniform but can often contain literal translations from another language. But the words used in the literal translation are silent regarding the cultural and social context from which they came. Many people are uncomfortable with spoken English and prefer written exchanges. The manager must be able to judge when he needs to look beyond the words he hears or reads and check the context in which they originated. He does not need to be an expert on Korean culture, but if he is to deal with Korea or Koreans, he should be aware that most Koreans are uncomfortable when they do not know the hierarchical status of people they are dealing with. He does not need to know all the different forms of low, middle or high speech and all the niceties of the various grammatical forms, but he should know that such forms exist and that they signify many gradations of civility among Koreans. He should know when it is necessary to check and get below the surface.

If he is dealing in Japan or with Japanese he needs to know that concepts of duty (*giri*) and obligation are much wider in scope and much more nuanced than in Europe. Similar Confucian concepts of duty apply in Korea and China. He does not need to be an expert but he should certainly be aware when his relationship partners are experiencing the call of duty and when they are not. He needs to know if and when they perceive that he has obligations towards them. The culture of shame that is supposed to prevail in Japan is often grossly misconstrued. Such feelings of shame are restricted to when someone perceives that he may appear in a bad light in front of the group of people he respects socially. This is *seken-tei* where *seken* is the social group one regularly associates with or looks up to. It is highly unlikely that a non-Japanese manager would be seen by his Japanese network partner to be one of the *seken*. He needs to know that his partner is unlikely to suffer any feelings of shame towards him. On the other hand, he also needs to know and build on the certainty that his Japanese partner will not risk shame in front of his *seken*, by subjecting him to anything which would not appear proper to them.

Fortunately, the specialised languages of the professions (science or medicine or engineering or law or finance) are usually based on common, and universal, principles and concepts. The same technical or specialised words are often used in many languages. They provide a "live" dictionary – a Rosetta stone – for a manager. This dictionary creates the common reference points to be able to check and ensure that the correct meanings are actually attributed to the language used.

Even the different cultures and language (jargon) that can exist in different departments of the same organisation (say between a manufacturing department and finance) must be penetrated when building networks and relationships. Again, the critical part is to be aware that the differences exist, to respect the differences, to identify them when they appear and not necessarily to be familiar with the details of the other language or culture. Expert help can always be marshalled provided the manager knows when to call for it. In large organisations there is a tendency for specialised and functional departments or product divisions to live within their own "silos". Sometimes the fences around such silos within the same organisation can become very high. One of the characteristics of the "good" manager will be the time he invests in building networks across such silo boundaries and who has the insight that all his network partners are then available in time of need.

I learnt much from Eduardo Angelo, one of my Brazilian colleagues who had the uncanny knack – I think in his sub-conscious – to focus on the individual rather than on the country or organisation he belonged to or what labels he may have been stamped with. His network partners ranged from politicians to bankers to sugarcane cutters and he taught me the importance of showing trust. No doubt he courted personal rejection but this gave him the ability to converse with anybody at any hierarchical level and not to be inhibited or intimidated by titles and designations and pompousness of any sort.

The starting point for a good manager must be to reject the view that any surface layer of culture or language is impenetrable. In my opinion this is a fundamental attitude that he must have. He must begin by taking the attitude that communication, or network building, or relationship development, or the mobilisation of actions, across a cultural or linguistic boundary is perfectly feasible and just another task. By focusing on the individuals involved and scrupulously avoiding generalisations and stereotypes, a manager can ensure both the correctness of his communications and the interpretation of communications received. This, in turn, allows the proper escalation of engagements in building up mutually beneficial relationships.

Human networks today span continents and countries effortlessly and can encompass millions of nodes (Facebook for example). Choosing the right networks to participate in is a necessary skill for a manager. But it is insufficient until he also masters the art of choosing and developing his relationships within the networks.

Chapter 6
The Strength of Ten

No manager operates without stresses of all kinds. He is continuously subjected to physical, mental, psychological and emotional stresses. They may be cyclic or prolonged or sporadic or intermittent. It is his ability to withstand stress and continue operating without breaking down which we can call his **strength of character.** *Every individual can be said to have a variety of "character traits" or attributes which together make up his "character". The manner in which these traits combine within the individual give his "strength of character". An individual's strength is always present and is brought to bear automatically whenever stress is encountered. It cannot be turned "on" or "off" at will or to suit changing circumstances but it is never absent. It is unique to the individual and different individuals will be more or less suitable for the particular stresses encountered. Strength carries no connotations of inherent goodness or badness but whether it is wholly or partially sufficient or suitable depends on the particular individual and the specific stresses experienced. But strength is not invisible or unchanging or unchangeable. It can be discerned, assessed and developed.*

The Materials Analogy

The strength of a material is a measure of its ability to withstand stress without failure by fracture or by rupture.

The strength of character of a person is a measure of his ability to withstand the stresses he encounters without failure by "breaking down".

Napoleon Hill
    Character is to man what carbon is to steel

It is remarkable that so many of the terms used in materials science to describe the strength of materials are also applicable to human character. *Strong, tough, resilient, brittle, malleable, tempered, hard, stiff, yield, stress, strain, deformation, ductile, elastic, rigid, fracture, fatigued* and *twisted* are all words which have very precise meanings when applied to the properties and behaviour of materials. They are also all words which can be used – with very similar meanings – in describing facets of human character.

Stress in materials science is measured in units of the force applied per unit area of the material. Stress may be *tensile* (longitudinal pulling) or *compressive* (longitudinal squeezing) or it may be *shear* (sideways) or it may be *torsion* (twisting). The *strength* of a material is determined by its microstructure and defined as the magnitude of the stress that must be applied for the material to fail by *fracture* or by *rupture*. As the applied stress is increased, all materials *deform* and the extent of deformation is called *strain*. The deformation is initially reversible and the material returns to its original dimensions when the stress is removed. Reversible deformations are known as *elastic deformations*. At a particular level of stress, *cracks* can develop in the material microstructure such that deformation becomes irreversible and the material is said to *yield*. This stress level is called the *yield strength*. In crystalline materials, cracks are called *dislocations* and represent a displacement of one of the regular planes in a crystal structure. Irreversible deformations at stresses beyond the yield stress are said to be *plastic deformations*. In some other materials failure can occur without any significant yield deformation. This is the failure by fracture of a *brittle* material. Even in materials that do yield, increasing the stress beyond the yield strength eventually leads in all cases to fracture. The stress at fracture is called the *ultimate strength* of the material. Strength and *toughness* are different but related characteristics in materials science. Toughness is a measure of the energy that can be absorbed before fracture occurs. At any given level of stress, the more a material deforms without rupturing, the greater the energy absorbed. A brittle material may have high strength but deforms little and is not tough. A strong and tough material is one which has a high stress level for fracture and exhibits high deformation at high stress levels before fracture. A *ductile* material has the ability to deform without fracture under a tensile (pulling) stress, such as when drawing a metal ingot into wire. A *malleable* material can be extensively reshaped without fracture under a compressive (squeezing) stress for example when metal is pressed to make sheets or plates. Repeated application and release of stress can lead to *fatigue* and initiates cracks. Propagation of cracks through the material can lead to a fracture or a failure of the material to perform its intended purpose. Some materials experience a very slow permanent deformation over time, called *creep*, especially at elevated temperatures, even when stresses are below the yield strength.

The development of new materials tailored to have desired properties is what has made the modern world possible. Materials science has progressed as other sciences have developed and their application has placed new demands for desired material properties. Developments in materials have in turn enabled new applications and inventions. Alloys, super-alloys, plastics, semi-conductors, composites, ceramics and carbon fibres are all examples of materials created in response to desired properties and which have, in turn, led to the invention, manufacture and use of new artefacts. Selection of a material, based on its properties, as being suitable for a particular application, is a fundamental judgment at the design stage in all the applied sciences.

There seem to be many parallels between the properties of inanimate materials and the components of human character. A person's strength of character is similarly dependent upon his microstructure and is also a measure of his breaking stress. Toughness in a person, just as in materials, is not synonymous with strength but it is a related characteristic. It represents a person's ability to absorb a great volume of stress or repeated applications of stress where he may yield to some extent, but does not break. As with a material, his resilience marks his ability to absorb setbacks and to recover his equanimity. He can also be subject to repeated stress cycles or difficult working conditions for prolonged periods leading to fatigue or creep where a gradual onset of small failings can lead to a total failure. Stubbornness in character has great similarity to brittleness in a material. The microstructure of the manager's character, just like that of a material, can be changed by tempering or hardening or some other strengthening processes. Some managers are strong in tension and resist being pulled along by the latest fashion. Others are strong in compression and can withstand the weight of many trying to squeeze them into a particular shape. Just as material properties make them suitable for particular applications, the different characters of managers make them suitable for particular environments or particular tasks.

Properties of materials are amenable to precise tests and the results of the tests, which can be expressed mathematically, apply universally to all materials having the same composition and microstructure. Human characteristics are subject to much greater variation, are not as easily measurable and cannot be as readily predicted. Tests for the ultimate strength of a material are carried out by stressing a standard piece of the material to the point of destruction and the test pieces themselves are thereafter rendered useless. The strength of human character however, is not amenable to similar testing and does not allow of the same quantitative and mathematical approach. The science of materials though, is illustrative of, and does provide some very valuable insights regarding, human character, but it must be emphasized that it is only an analogy. Analogies serve very well for getting clarity in a new area of study by comparison with a familiar area, but there are many aspects of human character which are quite unlike material properties and the analogy no longer applies. Unlike materials, even conflicting character traits can co-exist in a person and the same trait can be manifested differently in different circumstances or at different times. A material is either brittle or it is ductile, but never both. But human character, for example, may be brittle and uncompromising in regard to integrity but flexible with regard to fallibility, both at the same time. A particular manager may be malleable and yielding with his superior while being hard or inflexible with a subordinate. A manager may exhibit different, and even diametrically opposite, character traits to the same person but at different times. Strength of character is not an independent trait in itself but is a composite of many different features.

Character Traits

Any property or attribute that could be considered to be descriptive of, or causative of, a person's behaviour can be taken to be a character trait. Observers of character in another person may vary in what they consider to be significant traits and such subjective observations are not to be equated with the objectivity available from a materials test. I use "character traits" to describe the separate "attributes" a person has, but where no judgment is implied as to the desirability or otherwise of that particular trait. I believe this provides much more clarity than the use of the words "qualities" or "strengths" or "virtues" for these individual properties since these words impute a universal desirability of that particular property. In any language, the words "quality" or "virtue" or "strength" contain a pre-emptive judgment of being "good". But pursuing my materials analogy, I take a character trait of a human, like a fundamental property of a material, to be neither good nor bad. It merely is.

In the 1930s, psychologists studying character and personality found that the English language had over 17,000 words related to human personality, and of these over 4,000 adjectives related to human personality which could all be considered to be character traits. I take character traits to be descriptions of the fundamental components of character. They are however labels and these labels describe similar observable features in the behaviour of different people. However, I do not mean to suggest that any label is identical in its manifestations internally within a person. Just as I cannot tell whether my internal perception of the colour "red" is the same as that of some other person, I cannot tell if "honesty" creates identical neural and physiological patterns within different people. But "honesty" in different people is manifested by the same observable behaviour patterns.

I suggest the following groups of attributes, in no particular order, as examples of such traits:

- Openness, wisdom, intelligence, transparency, quest for knowledge, curiosity, ingenuity
- Conscientiousness, self-awareness, social responsibility, sense of relationships
- Values and a value system, integrity, rectitude, honesty, acquisitiveness, philanthropy
- Extroversion, pragmatism, confidence, perseverance, quest for excellence, optimism, industriousness
- Discernment, risk perception, risk taking ability, prudence, fortitude, neuroticism
- Judgment, justice, objectivity, even-handedness, diligence, reasonableness
- Appreciation, loyalty, faith, generosity, altruism, humour, agreeableness

The sheer number of character traits that exist is so large and the manner in which all the individual traits combine within a person is so complex that it is impractical to try and assess these individually or to formulate some universally applicable theory of how character traits are constituted within a person, or how they combine to make up character. There has been much study and a great deal of empirical data has been collected by psychologists and sociologists in recent years.

There have been many attempts to cluster character traits, to discern the underlying patterns connecting them to behaviour and to devise general theories and corresponding tests. The list of traits I give above is arbitrary and just one such example of a clustering.

As yet, there are no general theories which can link all these observations and which apply across all cultures. There seems to be some tentative agreement among psychologists however, that the main clusters of character traits are dependant almost equally on heredity and on environment. Where measurements have been made they seem to indicate the importance of heredity to lie between 40 and 60%. If anything the estimates of heredity may be slightly over-stated since it may also include the results of very early learning in an infant's environment. There are no traits that can be considered to be exclusively due to heredity or to learning and it does not seem possible to separately identify hereditary traits from learned traits. Character traits in a person are not unchanging or constant through a life-time. They can be shown to change with time and with learning and with circumstance and this seems to apply to all character traits. Age, experience, maturity family size, birth order and sex also seem to have some impact on the mix of traits existing and on the development and rate of development of these traits. Nevertheless, all the traits can be learned and are therefore capable of being developed intentionally. The main clusters of character traits seem to be reproduced across different cultures and languages and countries, but their importance or their rate of development may vary from culture to culture.

Traits are merely descriptors of the different facets of a person.

Strength of Character

Positive psychology is a term coined by Maslow in 1954 but is a relatively new branch of psychology and is concerned specifically with the study and development of the strengths and virtues of human character, rather than being focused on the treatment of mental illness as aberrations of the mental state. There is even a handbook and classification of "Character Strengths and Virtues". The engineer's approach that I take, is based on my everyday observations, is probably much influenced by positive psychology and is a practical way for a manager to deal with character.

Every individual can be said to have a variety of "character traits" or attributes which together make up his "character". It is not necessary to assume that all character traits are present in all persons or that any particular traits are necessary and indispensible to have character. To have a character does not mean that a person may not have an over-abundance of one trait or too little of another or an abundance of traits. But whatever traits a person possesses will go to making up his character and to establishing whatever strength of character he has. This also suggests however, that for character to change, one or more character traits must change.

The description I like best is one that could be said to be based on function:
"Strength of character is a measure of the internal resources a person can call on, entirely from within himself:

1. to resist the stresses of a given situation,
2. to provide direction, and
3. to generate the impetus for his behaviour and his actions"

Strength of character thus provides a person's moral shield based on his own moral values, his internal compass as well as his call to action. It is what he brings to bear in all the situations he faces. When facing stress or a difficult situation, strength of character governs his behaviour and his actions and is either sufficient or suitable for the situation or it is not. But it is what it is, and comes into play as it is. It is not, and cannot be, varied at will to suit a particular situation or level of stress. When faced with a particularly stressful situation, a person cannot choose to "use a little more strength of character", just as when faced with an easy situation he cannot choose to "use a little less strength of character". Strength of character is more like the skin a person is encased in and not a suit of clothes that can be worn when necessary and returned to storage if not needed. He carries it around with him and he uses what he has.

> Alfred Lord Tennyson
> My strength is as the strength of ten because my heart is pure.

There is no simple scale or meter by which to take the measure of this intensely individual strength of character. It can only be discerned in the context of his actions and behaviour in stressful or difficult situations. It may then be judged, by an external observer, to be low or to be high, or to be sufficient or insufficient, or good or bad in the context of the difficult situation being faced. If the situation being faced is not particularly difficult or stressful, then a person's actions and behaviour are well within his capabilities and do not reveal very much about his strength of character.

Strength of character is not unchanging but it changes slowly; perhaps more rapidly during childhood and only very gradually in adulthood. It can change over time as a person learns or develops and as the component character traits change. A person's physical characteristics (tall or short, strong or weak, sick or fit) do not correlate directly with strength of character. But they do determine the self-image a mind has of itself and can, in that way, influence some of the character traits and thereby the strength of character. But, ultimately, a person's character traits and therefore his character at any particular time emanate solely from his mind. Following this thought leads to the conclusion that the strength of character itself reflects the person's own values and his sense of right or wrong but no trait, by itself, can be considered to be imbued with some absolute goodness or badness. It is the actions and behaviour of the person which can lead to a judgment by an observer about the suitability or sufficiency or capacity of his strength of character. A criminal may have as strong or as weak a character as a philanthropist. It is purpose and not character *per se* which distinguish them. The criminal may, in his own judgment or in that of his peers, consider his strength of character sufficient and "good" for his own purpose. But society, when it labels him a "weak character", judges not his character but his purpose. Some other society may label him a hero and consider him a "strong character". Purpose may be a consequence of character but does not determine strength of character. Robin Hood was a thief to the Sherriff of Nottingham but a folk hero to the oppressed peasants, but his inherent strength of character was exactly the same in both perceptions. The scale, if any single scale exists at all, for strength of character cannot, I think, be one-dimensional or linear. But clearly, in our use of language we perceive and think about "strength of character" primarily along just the "strong–weak" dimension. Other adjectives (thin, thick, bright or dull for example) are rarely used. Even the one-dimensional "good–bad" axis seems to be reserved in our use of language for describing "character" rather than for "strength of character". When we make a judgment in some particular situation that one person has a "stronger" character than another, we usually mean that his strength of character is more suitable for the prevailing stresses and difficulties of that particular situation.

I summarise therefore that:

1. A person's various character traits are what are inherent in him, which
2. When combined together give the quality we label "character", and
3. The capacity of this character to resist stress while directing his actions is what we term his "strength of character"

Since character traits themselves can vary with time and circumstance, the "strength of character" is then a composite property describing the current status of those combined traits. But any judgment about the suitability or capacity or sufficiency of that strength of character can only be made against the backdrop of the prevailing circumstances in which the actions and behaviour of that person are manifested.

Strength of character is not to be confused with personality nor is it directly correlated with physical strength. But it uniquely marks our behaviour and our actions and our interactions with others while under stress. It is not virtue as the Stoics claimed and completely impervious to all emotional influence. It is not some absolute morality but does reflect the moral stance represented by the person's values. It is not merely being one or more of the character traits, be it "honest" or "brave" or any one of the other 4,000 adjectives that could be character traits. Having strength is what enables us to handle stress and setbacks and difficult situations without panic or anxiety attacks or losing self-control or becoming irrational or being overwhelmed. It enables us to hold our values uncompromised and intact. Our strength of character is what enables us to behave and act consistently with our own self-image of ourselves and to maintain integrity and direction and purpose. It does seem to be something that can be learned and which develops with usage and experience and time.

In spite of the enormous complexity of the subject, it is perfectly feasible to consider character and strength of character in a limited and practical manner. In the managerial world, what needs to be considered, for or by a manager, is not some absolute number as a measure of his strength of character, or to correctly place his psychological profile in the grand scheme of all possible human profiles, but merely to judge whether the strength of character that he has, or that he can develop, matches or will match his purposes. For any given purpose it is perfectly possible to identify the most important character traits that are desirable. The stresses and setbacks that are likely in striving for that particular purpose can also be anticipated. For example, in a situation of a market downturn and drastic restructuring we can anticipate the difficulties and stresses that would be faced by a Personnel manager as he negotiates with trades union and employees in shutting down a factory location. Or, in a period of expansion we can forecast the character traits that would be needed by a Factory manager in getting a new production line into operation against some very testing deadlines. Identifying and assessing these traits together with a judgment of the suitability of the strength of character to meet the anticipated stresses and potential setbacks is not an intractable problem. To make such relatively limited assessments of strength of character is then not only perfectly feasible but, in my opinion, absolutely essential for a manager or a prospective manager. But it must always be borne in mind that a person's strength of character is something within him and any observer's judgment about his strength neither adds nor detracts to his capacity to handle stress.

Stress and Strength

In any particular application, a material may be suitable or it may not. A pedestrian footbridge for example, could be built from a variety of metals or wood or reinforced plastics or ropes. But cardboard or linen or paper would fail under the applied stresses, would not be strong enough and therefore would not be suitable. Among the many materials that are suitable, some would be more suitable than others and the degree of suitability would depend upon other criteria. Every criterion for selection can always be taken to be a stress criterion. These could be stresses due to time available or money available or construction workers available or susceptibility to corrosion or tendency to warp in wet weather or resistance to high winds. The relevant criteria taken together would make one material more suitable than all the others. It could well be, in this case, that wood was the most suitable material, best capable of resisting all the stresses taken together, even though steel might have the highest absolute strength and the greatest load bearing capacity.

Similarly, in any particular managerial situation, it is the totality of the prevailing stresses which distinguishes between the suitability of various strengths of character of people in that situation. The most suitable manager to resist the prevailing stresses in a particular situation may not be the most suitable in some other situation where the stresses were different. Suitability of a person carries no connotations about the goodness of that person. However the selection of an unsuitable person for some purpose does carry a connotation about the judgment of the selector. A Project manager may well require just as much strength of character as, say, a Managing Director, but the stresses encountered and the strengths required are not the same. This requires that we consider the kinds of stress that a manager may be subject to.

Stresses in materials are those experienced internally within the microstructure of the material and arise from external forces such as tension, compression, shear, torsion or bending. Forces can also be created by the external environment and can then be experienced as stresses. Surrounding conditions such as temperature or pressure or dynamic or cycling conditions or chemical reactions at the surface of the material could be external factors causing stresses in the material.

Impulses causing stresses in humans, called stressors, are mental, emotional or physical. Mental stress originates typically from uncertainty, fear, threat perceptions, anxiety and depression. Physical stress such as due to over-exertion or overwork or tiredness or sickness or pain leads also to mental stress. All negative emotions, and even positive emotions when they are in excess, can lead to mental stress. Any cognitive conflict between a person's value system on the one hand, and behaviour or actions that he encounters or feels constrained to take on the other, can lead to feelings of self-betrayal, inadequacy and uncertainty resulting in immense mental stress. Strength of character is the shield against the mental stresses a person is subjected to. If this strength is not equal to the task and the stresses overcome the available capacity for resistance, then human breakdown starts to occur. Small cracks or tears appear in the fabric of the person and can propagate through the entire fabric, eventually causing failure. Variations in strength of character mean that some people can resist certain types of stress better than others. Some people can resist many different types of stress simultaneously. Human breakdowns – the cracks and tears in the human fabric – usually manifest themselves as panic or flight or anxiety attacks or irrational behaviour or paralysis of thought and action. If unchecked, these cracks and tears propagate under continuing or increased stress and lead eventually to total failure or a "burn-out". The difference between brittle materials which fracture suddenly without much deformation, as opposed to tough materials which yield and can undergo considerable plastic deformation before failure, also shows up with people. A tough person may absorb a large number of small breakdowns and still be able to continue functioning, whereas a stubborn person may be able to withstand a high level of stress but can collapse suddenly soon after some threshold is reached.

I was in ABB's Kobe office with two of my colleagues from Sweden on the evening of 16 January. One, let me call him Sven, was in his late thirties and the other, let me call him Gustav, was then in his late twenties. We were frantically preparing the final contract for the Karita power plant which was to be signed with Ishikawajima-Harima Heavy Industries in Tokyo on 17 January. It was getting late, all the contract appendices had not been proof-read, and photo-copiers were running hot. We were not quite finished and we had appointments at our Tokyo office early on the 17th. I decided that the appointment had to be kept and I would therefore leave on the last Shinkansen for Tokyo that evening. Sven and Gustav would complete the documents and travel up to Tokyo the next morning to reach by noon and in time for the contract signing. I just made the last train to Tokyo out of Shin-Kobe station and checked in to the Imperial Hotel in Tokyo some time after midnight.

At 5:46 the next morning I was startled out of bed on the 20th floor of the Imperial Hotel in Tokyo by an enormous thump. All the room lights had turned on. The bedside radio and the TV had turned themselves on and were blaring out emergency warnings. As I struggled to get out of bed and make sense of what was happening, the pictures on the wall were swaying ominously. From the window I could see that all traffic on Hibiya Dori had come to a stop. People were standing still or moving very slowly. As I struggled for my balance I realised that the pictures on the wall were actually quite still; it was the building that was swaying.

After over 300 years of relative calm, a still-sleeping Kobe had been slammed by the full force of the Great Hanshin earthquake of 1995. The epicentre was just off the Kobe coast on Awaji Island. Over 6,000 people perished. The next few hours were chaotic in the Tokyo office as we tried to make contact with our colleagues and friends in Kobe. All road and rail connections into Kobe were cut. Our attempts to hire a helicopter were futile since air space had been closed to non-essential traffic, relief had priority, and every news agency in the world was queuing to get their cameras into the air. The frenzied mood in the Tokyo office turned silent and eerie and fatalistic. The TV images were dark and ominous. There was little commentary. People spoke in whispers. Telephone connection was impossible since all available direct lines from Tokyo were reserved for the relief agencies. We could not make contact and there was nothing we could do. In Kobe, fires starting breaking out and by late evening all the TV pictures were of the horror of Kobe burning. Towards midnight, amazingly, the mood lifted. Contact had been made. Through our Hong Kong office and some unlikely mobile phone networks we were back in touch with the Kobe office. Teams of our colleagues from across Japan had started gathering supplies and planning routes on the back roads in to Kobe. Some had already set out with digging equipment and medical supplies. We started getting reports from friends and relatives and colleagues. Roads and highways were either damaged or clogged. Some of our colleagues in Kobe led by the ABB Country Manager Bo Dankis had taken to their motor-bikes to check-up on friends and relatives. Tension was relieved by what little action that could be taken. After a few hours but about 18 h after the quake struck, I managed to have a brief conversation with Gustav. Both he and Sven were physically unhurt. Their hotel had partially collapsed but they had managed to break open their hotel room doors and extricate themselves from the listing building. It had taken them all day to walk the 6 km from the centre of Kobe, through all the rubble and the still collapsing buildings in Sannomiya, to our offices on Port Island. The one bridge from the mainland to Port Island was damaged and closed to cars, but fortunately still standing and still open to pedestrians. But Sven was apparently deeply traumatised and had virtually frozen. He had to be coaxed to move and had to be led all the way. His mood was fluctuating wildly between deep depressions on the one hand and a great rage on the other. One minute he would be despairing of all hope and in the next he would be railing against the injustice of it all. Gustav was the epitome of calm. He had taken charge and had found some water and blankets. He had reported in at our offices which was relatively undamaged and had become the contact hub for all our employees. He had found two camp beds at the Portopia Hotel near our offices. He was assisting at the emergency food station set up at the hotel. He was investigating all that was happening around him while taking continuous care of Sven. He was, I learned later, keeping the spirits up of all those near him and was actively considering options for how to proceed. All the piers and jetties on Port Island were damaged. The KCAT – Kobe City Air Terminal – was badly damaged and out of action and no boats could berth. But 2 days later they managed, along with many others, to clamber onto a private boat to travel across Osaka Bay to Kansai Airport (off Osaka), which was back in operation by then. Then they found place on a Lufthansa flight to Frankfurt. We met them there and escorted them on to Copenhagen and then home to Norrköping.

Their families were waiting as were the medical check-ups. There followed a period of rest and specialised counselling for them both. They had tremendous support from all their colleagues and within 2 weeks they were both back at work. All seemed to be well and they were on the road to recovery. But now comes the curious part. Three months later, I accompanied Sven on a trip back to Kobe to show our solidarity with Kobe and to meet and thank the many Japanese colleagues and friends who had all been through the same trauma and had been so caring and helpful during that period. Sven revisited the site of the hotel he had stayed at – which no longer existed – met some of the hotel staff, received all his carefully stored belongings which had been abandoned at the hotel and managed to recover his balance completely. This was in spite of having come so close to breaking point which had shown up at the time as a paralysis. As he put it himself; "If Gustav had not forced me out, I would probably have stayed put in the hotel till it collapsed". But Gustav did not accompany us back to Kobe. He, who had been so calm and cool and rational and optimistic, who had taken the lead, was not able to even contemplate travelling with us back to Kobe. He would avoid any discussion about Japan, let alone any discussion about Kobe or his experiences there. About 15 months later, Gustav had still not returned to Kobe, would still not talk about Japan, would leave the room if the earthquake was mentioned and eventually left the company to move into a different field.

Did Gustav or Sven then have the greater strength of character?

The question is, to my way of thinking, improper and has no answer. Different situations call for different strengths. Could they have come through the situation if they had not had the differences in their characters? My materials' science analogy does not provide me with any answers either. In fact, the materials analogy clearly does not work. But it does give me a way of looking at what transpired. Gustav clearly had the much higher ultimate stress but the long term strain on his character was of the irreversible kind even though his yield point for immediate action had clearly not been breached; he underwent a form of "plastic deformation" in the language of materials science. Sven, on the other hand, had the lower yield point and actually ceased functioning for a while. But even though his yield point had been exceeded, the long term strain he experienced was of the reversible kind – an "elastic deformation". Gustav clearly had a measure of brittleness which prevented the strain from reversing and Sven had a kind of toughness or resilience which kicked in long after the event.

But the other question that comes to mind and for which I also have no answer is "And how would I have reacted if I had not taken the last train out of Kobe?"

A person perceives stress when he feels an imbalance between the demands upon him and the resources available within him. He feels he cannot or may not be able to cope. Studies suggest that perceptions of stress in the work-place have increased sharply over recent years. The frequency of burnout has also increased over recent decades. Stress is a major reason attributed to people leaving an organization. In the work place, stresses are typically caused by deadlines, high workload, feelings of isolation, lack of useful work, personal rivalries, personal ambition, oppressive management control, lack of management support, micro-control by managers, business or organization changes, poor results, lack of competence, lack of control, bullying and the working environment. These are just examples of the everyday stresses that a manager must face while carrying out his basic function of mobilizing actions towards his purpose. Part of his tasks includes the management of stress to maximise his effectiveness and that of his colleagues. This in turn consists of ameliorating the external conditions that may cause stress and of actions to increase the capacity of people to withstand stress. Inevitably, the latter consists of measures to develop and build strength of character.

Ameliorating the surrounding conditions to reduce stress impulses may seem obvious but need first to be observed and then acted upon by a manager. Improving the working environment sounds trivial but can have a profound impact. This may be by, for example, the introduction of open-plan office layouts or improving ventilation or introducing sound-proofing. Introduction of planning and time management techniques, introducing flex-time or allowing working from home can all improve the perception of control and reduce stress points.

Stress by itself is not always a bad thing and is actually desirable at non-damaging levels. Effectiveness of both physical and mental activity can be much increased under stress provided that the stress lies within the capacity – the strength of character – of the person concerned. In my analogy with materials, the yield stress is what should not be exceeded, so that any deformation remains elastic deformation and reversible. Irreversible damage to the microstructure, of materials or of humans, usually begins only when this stress has been exceeded.

Friedrich Nietzsche
What does not destroy me makes me stronger.

A good manager knows the value of maintaining pressure, but a pressure which is not destructive, on him or on others. He also knows that performing under stress, close to the limit but without sustaining permanent damage, increases the intensity of feelings when targets are achieved. In something akin to the "work hardening" of a material, experience under pressure leads to an increase in the level of stress that can be tolerated without damage in the future.

Developing Strength of Character

Strength of character can be developed either by addressing the component character traits or by improving the primary functions. The difference is like that of just treating the high blood sugar level in a diabetic or altering his entire life-style. In practice it is probably necessary to do both. The number of character traits is far too many, and the individual variations between people are too large, to be able to deal with more than just a few. However the traits considered most important to meet anticipated stress situations can be selected and then addressed individually. The functional approach takes a more holistic view and addresses the composite result but the individual effect on each component character trait may not then be visible.

> Marcus Aurelius
> You have power over your mind – not outside events. Realize this, and you will find strength.

In either approach, the starting point is to establish what needs to be improved and developed. This can, in its simplest form, be based entirely on perceptions. A manager may perceive that integrity or openness or risk-perception or self-awareness are traits that if developed would be helpful in better coping with stress in the work-place, with himself or with an individual subordinate or with a group of people. Or he may just feel that the general ability to withstand stress must be developed. At the other extreme, comprehensive stress testing or psychological profiling could be carried out and used as the basis of a development programme. Here too, programmes of development could be designed to meet common areas of perceived weakness in a group or could be tailored to meet the perceived needs of a particular individual.

Having identified the individual character traits that need to be developed the manager needs to put in place a programme to address these, either for himself or for others. The focus is always on the individual trait and whatever the consequences may be for character or strength of character become by-products of the trait development. This could be seen as "improving the quality of the bricks and assuming that the quality of the house will automatically improve". In my experience this is an effective approach primarily because the focus is clear and the concepts are not too complex or diffuse to be grasped. Testing for individual traits is also easier to arrange and the results of such tests are fairly unambiguous. Such testing usually takes the form of questionnaires sometimes together with interview sessions. I have generally utilised specialists with psychological training to ensure objectivity and consistency in the results. In the work-place, the traits that I have usually found to be necessary, needing development and which can be addressed practically have been reasonableness, integrity or ethics, transparency, self-confidence, self-awareness, risk taking, prudence and sense of relationships. Many other traits could also be addressed. Such development programmes are often perceived merely as programmes to improve necessary skills and are consequently approached with enthusiasm. Character building programmes on the other hand, can be perceived as being presumptuous and trespassing into an individual's personal space. This can create a resistance which can defeat the objective of the programme.

Training and development programmes need the active engagement of participants to be effective. It is well worth the effort to spend a little time in designing programmes to ensure that the relevance of the programme is visible to the participants. Creating appropriate development programmes depends to a great deal upon the character trait being addressed. It is not always necessary to use specialists to conduct any programme, but having some specialists at least to design the programme is advisable. For example, transparency or openness can be addressed in group sessions with simulated scenarios and role play. The usefulness of such sessions I find is strongly dependent upon the skill of the moderator. Integrity and ethics can also be addressed in a similar way but here some form of academic training regarding the difficult concepts involved is also necessary. Risk taking and prudence and diligence courses and seminars are usually perceived as being very relevant and participants are usually very engaged. Developing relationship and communication skills is not only for sales people and can be of great benefit in virtually every field. Purely from observation, I would conclude that character trait building programmes do develop those particular traits and I have no doubt that they are beneficial. That they develop strength of character is also clear but to what extent is not so easy to observe.

The other approach – which should be seen as being more of a complement rather than as an alternative to developing selected character traits – is to address observed shortfalls in one or more of the three main "functions" of strength of character:

1. Resistance to stress (the shield)
2. Determining direction (the internal compass)
3. Impetus to act (internal motivation)

This is an approach I have found more suited to an individual rather than a group.

On two occasions I have used such programmes for individuals who reached or were very close to burnout. In one case it was a Project manager in Sweden responsible for an R & D programme and a site. He was overwhelmed by a combination of funding difficulties, accidents at site, shortage of skilled personnel and unexpectedly poor test results of the R & D programme. This was a case of physical and mental exhaustion. In another case my Chief Accounting manager in India developed a form of paranoia which led to a paralysis of action. It happened when the number of his inexperienced subordinates had increased, the quality of the accounts had deteriorated and many mistakes were being discovered. But that analysis only came long after the event. In both cases, the individual programmes implemented became effectively rehabilitation programmes, extending over many months rather than being pro-active programmes. The programmes were eventually successful but slow, and I shall always regret that the signs of impending burnout were not picked up at a much earlier stage.

Developing Strength of Character

However, I have also utilised such individually tailored programmes for young managers identified as being of great promise. Much effort is needed for testing and assessment and for designing a programme to suit. This inevitably leads to limitations on the number of managers that can be accommodated in such programmes. Nevertheless, the possibility to conduct such programmes has been one of the most rewarding aspects of working in large multi-national organisations where the need has been recognised and where the resources were made available. The Top Talent programme at Siemens is one such example. It has been intellectually challenging to devise programmes to suit talented young managers from Japan or India or Brazil or Europe. It is difficult and far too early to conclude that these programmes were decisive or successful, but I am sure they made a positive contribution, and it has been gratifying to watch these young managers grow and fulfil their promise.

Keeping the pressure up is a well tried and tested method for a manager to increase the effectiveness of his troupe. But pressure tactics must be well thought through and properly applied. To apply pressure without any assessment of the resistance capacity of the subject – his strength of character – is both stupid and irresponsible. Without also having a plan for helping the subjects to build up their stress resistance, pressure tactics are short-sighted and no credit to a manager. Applying pressure properly should not be confused with harassment or causing irritation or embarrassment or bullying. All pressure will inevitably cause some fear, some perceptions of threat or some anxiety. A good manager will have made some plans for how to counter or remove these if they progress from being motivating factors to being destructive or disruptive. I have found that just making sure that a system of support is available and visible sharply increases the tolerance to stress. I have found pressure to be most effective when it has been even-handed, has created a group resolve and has provided the motivation for people to stretch themselves. If pressure is perceived as being victimisation or discrimination then it becomes destructive. Deadlines and time pressures are very real in the work-place and usually do not need to be engineered. But where they exist the manager must take the opportunity and utilise them to increase the effectiveness of his team. It has generally been more productive to focus on an opportunity rather than a threat ("we can keep our jobs if we do ...." rather than "we will lose our jobs if we do not. ..."), but the pressure that is effective for one person may not be sufficient for another and may be destructive for someone else.

A great deal of development of strengths of character can be achieved by way of example. Values are best transferred by living them, and not by making slide presentations. Transparency and openness flows through an organisation if it is first exercised from the top. Making reliable promises becomes a habit for all if the manager's promises are always reliable, if he makes only considered commitments, if he gives early warning when he cannot meet dates and if he always does what he says he will do. By bringing clarity to what he values and especially perhaps to what he does not, the manager inculcates behaviour patterns and, in time, these can become ingrained in habit and in the strength of character of the practitioners. If mistakes are clearly and openly corrected and successes rewarded, then some of his values become visible and can be emulated. If the manager shows that he values the quest for knowledge or the appreciation of music or rewards industriousness, then the ripples spread. He must demonstrate by example how to take responsibility and what it means to be accountable. Most importantly the manager must provide space for the strength of character of his subordinates to grow. He needs to give permission for people to say "No" when necessary and to encourage creative dissent. He needs to discourage the "yea-sayers" who have not exercised their minds. Observing and emulating the behaviour of those one looks up to is perhaps the single most important contributor to the development of strength of character. The manager's responsibility to demonstrate strength of character as a role model for those who look up to him is heavy.

Strength of character is not one-dimensional, cannot be measured in numbers and is not easily assessed. But it must not be ignored.

Chapter 7
The Red Badge of Courage

Courage is the subordination of fear to purpose. A manager is perforce required to take risk. Every judgment or selection or decision he takes results in actions with an uncertain outcome. The presence of risk and the uncertainty about results inevitably give rise to apprehensions and fears. It is a manager's task to subordinate such fears and continue with judiciously chosen actions towards his objectives. Extending his capability for taking actions and stretching the envelope of actions available to him are key elements of his core competence. It is his courage which enables him to operate in new and untried areas which are outside his comfort zone and thereby generate a steady stream of brave actions. A manager can create a "courage space" around himself and as this expands and grows and meets other spaces of courage a "culture of courage" can develop within an organisation.

Of Bravery and Courage

In the style of E. Belfort Bax in his book "Courage" in 1890, I take courage to be: "*the subordination of fear to purpose*".

In modern usage, the words courage and bravery are almost synonymous and are very often used interchangeably. Historically however, "brave" contains the hint of a display or a show. "Courage" in origin, is of the heart and the spirit. I find that I do use the words with a slight distinction between them. I use "courage" more often to be the general capability and I take "bravery" as being associated more with actions and the carrying out of particular events.

Mark Twain
> Courage is resistance to fear, mastery of fear – not absence of fear.

The distinction then becomes that having courage leads to brave actions but one brave action does not always mean the existence of courage. Courage therefore represents the capacity for a steady stream of brave, purposeful actions and I find this a useful distinction for corporate and industrial life.

Courage is also often described as "doing the right thing", but in such a formulation "right" can only mean consistent with the individual's own values.

Of course, what the individual considers as being "right" may not be in agreement with what an observer considers "right". Furthermore, many actions, which are no doubt "right", may not involve any significant level of threat or fear for the actor and such actions cannot, I think, then be considered to be brave or to require any bravery. To an observer, such actions are then completely silent regarding the need or use of bravery or courage.

Bravery or courage, in my usage, implies no moral judgment and contains no inherent goodness or badness. The fear that always accompanies bravery or courage is in the mind. It is the mind's emotional response to a threat perception, while anxiety is the response to a possible future threat. It is inevitably caused by an uncertainty of outcome of the actions intended or expected, and is always due to a threat of physical or mental stress or pain. Levels of fear range from very mild as apprehension and increasing in strength through worry and fear to the overpowering levels of terror and dread. Courage can then be impacted, through the level of fear, by morality or goodness, but only insofar as a person's mental stress and fear is influenced by his own moral values and judgments. Of course the thresholds of what would be perceived as stress or pain can vary greatly and depends upon the individual. In many cases the level of fear is linked, quite rationally, to the level of perceived risk but this is not always so. Fears are emotional responses and can often be irrational. Some actions which carry little actual risk may generate great fears. All the many phobias which people are subject to, fear of heights or spiders or open air for example may bear little relation to actual risks. For someone suffering from agoraphobia, the act of going into the garden may be an extremely brave action.

Without fear being present, bravery and courage do not appear on stage. Fear is a survival instinct and any species without fear, if ever they existed, are by now certainly all extinct. As an emotional reaction to a perceived threat fear is particular to the individual and varies from one individual to the next. Courage, being the subordination of fear to purposeful action, is equally particular to the individual. The absence of fear in some situation does not mean that a person has no courage, but it does mean that bravery or courage need not be invoked and have no role to play in that particular situation. Courage is inherent in the individual and comes into play as soon as fear is present. Courage, like character, is not like a jacket, stored away in a cupboard, and taken out and worn only when the weather is inclement. It comes into play automatically when triggered by a threshold level of fear. But though its use is automatic and unconscious, courage as a capacity can be consciously built up.

> Lewis Carroll
> Tweedledum in "Alice Through a Looking Glass!"
> "I'm very brave generally", he went on in a low voice: "only today I happen to have a headache".

False courage is behaviour masquerading as courage. It is when fear is pretended so that actions may seem to be brave, but actually are not. "Liquid" courage or "Dutch" courage probably originates from the practice of serving rum to sailors before a naval engagement. Current usage is when an alcoholic haze is induced intentionally to dull the senses and minimize perceptions of fear. This then allows actions to be performed which otherwise would not be. To show fear is often considered a sign of weakness, especially in the military, and people go to great lengths to conceal their fears. "Bravado" is when a false front is used to deceive an observer by masking the fear being felt, but the concealment does not in itself reduce the fear. A display of bravado therefore does not necessarily disqualify or negate actions from being courageous or brave. A "brave display" is a usage closer to the origins of the word and it is concerned primarily with appearance and show, and the use of the word contains no commentary on bravery or courage. The purpose of the display is just the show itself, and the actions involved may or may not be brave. For example the entire ceremony of the "Trooping of the Colour" is a brave display. But some of the participants may have great fears about their own skills for the show and their actions may then require a measure of bravery. A "bravo" is used to describe a political assassin performing his business but again the word itself does not contain any meanings of fear or bravery. So a bravo may act surreptitiously or openly and perhaps even with bravado but not necessarily without bravery. Assassins and terrorists are often labelled as "cowards" but here the word is used to explicitly reject and oppose their being considered heroes or martyrs within their own social circles. In such cases the word "coward" is used as a commentary on purpose and has little to do with fear or its subordination.

On the battlefield, medals are awarded for "bravery", for "courage", for "valour" and for "gallantry" but battlefield honours are rarely – if ever – given for being a "hero". It is my perception though, that the military itself does not much care for the label of "hero", or for naming people as "heroes". However, governments, politicians, the movies, children, comic books and media adore "heroes". National honours, in the form of people being canonised as "Heroes of the Republic" or "Heroes of something or the other", are fairly common. Fortunately there are, as yet, no super-hero medals and super-heroes are still confined to comic books and movies. It has always struck me that super-heroes must be particularly devoid of courage since their fantastic abilities must mean that they have little opportunity to feel any fear. But I too relished the Superman and Batman and Spiderman comics as a child and can escape into the movies even now! In Greek and Hindu mythology and the Norse sagas of old, our heroes usually waste no time in declaring themselves to be heroes and this is fortunate since it helps the reader to distinguish between the good guys and the bad guys.

In Stephen Crane's "The Red Badge of Courage", written long after but about the American Civil War, the Youth who has never seen action, both pities and envies wounded soldiers he comes across, and pines to have a wound of his own as a "red badge" which visibly attests to his courage. He craves the badge to prove to himself and to others that that he does indeed have courage. However, I shall leave aside the medals and the badges, and the gallant and dashing heroes with their daring deeds, and super-heroes vanquishing dastardly super-villains. Instead, I shall concentrate on the much less glamorous world of quiet, every-day courage, the courage of pushing oneself outside one's comfort zone, of doing what must be done, not without fear and sometimes while hiding the fear, but always in spite of the fear.

I have heard it said that courage lies in confronting fear or defeating fear but this, I think, misses the central point. The manager must focus on his actions not on his fears. He must carry out whatever purposeful action has been decided, even though fear exists, not where the defeating of the fear becomes the primary focus and where the action becomes secondary or merely a by-product. The fundamental characteristic of courage is that the purpose and the required actions remain central and fear is then the constraint which must be subordinated.

A brave action by one person who perceives fear in a particular situation may not be particularly brave for someone else who does not perceive the same level of fear. Whenever an outcome is uncertain there is risk. The level and type of risk, if realised, may or may not lead to a perception of threat and the accompanying fear that that entails. The distinction between a brave person and a foolhardy one then becomes one of discernment and judgment of risk and not the level of fear or the level of risk. Both may perceive threat and experience fear. The brave action is one where the risk and the probability of a satisfactory outcome have been judged prior to any action. Whether the judgment is sound or poor is also irrelevant to bravery. Bravery is unconnected with the level of risk but requires that the risk has actually been weighed. Risks may be high or low with either brave or reckless actions. A foolhardy action is not necessarily without fear; it is one devoid of judgment. It is the absence of judgment or ignoring judgment or wilful misjudgement and not the perceived level of risk which injects the "fool" into the foolhardy.

Aristotle considered courage to be the median position of a human virtue measured on a scale ranging from cowardice – as a deficit of courage – at one end to foolhardiness or recklessness – as an over-abundance of courage – at the other. This is not, I think, a valid scale because all these three descriptions of the human condition do not lie in the same linear dimension. Courage and cowardice lie on a line linking fear and action. At one end, for courage, action subordinates fear whereas at the other end, for cowardice, fear dominates action. Courage and foolhardiness are linked on a quite different line, that of judgment. At one end, the foolhardy action ignores, or has no judgment of risk and at the other end a courageous action has weighed the risk and decided to continue.

> Margaret Truman
> Courage is rarely reckless or foolish ... courage usually involves a highly realistic estimate of the odds that must be faced.

Where the outcome is certain then there is no risk to be perceived and therefore there can be no call on bravery. There may be fear associated with the consequences of a certain outcome and courage may well be required to deal with the consequences, but not for the immediate action itself. If there is a lack of ability to perceive the risk that exists, then this is a lack of discernment bordering on stupidity and there is again, no context for referring to bravery or courage. The outcome of any action is independent of the bravery of the actor involved. A brave person does not always succeed. A foolhardy person, if lucky, may enjoy a favourable outcome but remains a foolhardy person. And there is always the additional fear that an action with a low probability of success earns the label of "brave" when it is successful, while a failed action – even though it had a high probability of success – will lead to the label of being a "fool".

Brave actions should not be confused with those of thrill-seekers who undertake actions only to experience the "high" of the body's physiological response to fear. The seeking of "thrills" is commonplace across all ages and all cultures and can appear in riding a roller coaster or in stealing a car for a joyride or on the floor of the stock exchange. These actions have no other purpose than to experience the increased heart beat and the adrenaline rush, and this desire for the thrill of excitement should not be mistaken for courage.

Heroic and courageous actions occur not only on the battlefield but also in civil life; such as rushing into a burning building to save someone or diving into a river to rescue a drowning person or standing up to a much bigger bully to protect a friend. These are all examples of extraordinary actions of the moment which are almost at the level of instinctive reactions. They are relatively rare events and are not part of the common events of everyday life in a work-place. But, while these acts of heroism would usually require bravery, heroism is not itself a necessary quality for having courage or being a good manager. Many managers, no doubt, have heroic qualities, but what I seek to describe here is the quiet, steady, unobtrusive, every-day kind of courage which does not have to be of the heroic kind and is rarely spectacular.

Courage is not to be confused with endurance since endurance deals with a fear already realized; pain, suffering, discomfort, stress, abuse, rejection and negative emotions are all matters which require courage when they threaten and, must be endured if they are realized. The fear of the continuation of something already being endured could also demand courage. But I take the quality which enables something to be endured as fortitude, though courage may well have preceded the endurance. For example a person who is sick or in pain or under some emotional stress, but still continues with some necessary actions – but not those causing his distress – shows fortitude rather than courage. But when you ask a child to grit his teeth and smile through his very first, terrifying experience of an injection, you are asking him for bravery not fortitude.

As in all actions, where uncertain outcomes are subject to probability and risk, failures will occur. If brave actions are taken, frequently and regularly, by a good manager with sound judgment then, on balance, there will be a preponderance of satisfactory outcomes. For a manager therefore, what is needed is not the occasional, isolated and unique example of bravery but a steady stream of brave actions constantly breaking new ground. They do not have to be spectacular or heroic. A good manager, in my opinion, has and must have courage. It is this capacity which then enables him to maintain a steady stream of actions which challenge his comfort zone; which are judiciously chosen but are in the space where apprehension and fear exist and therefore require bravery. Courage is desirable in a manager, not for the sake of achieving some absolute virtue or as a moral imperative but for purely practical reasons of effectiveness and for enhancing the capacity to manage. Brave actions which succeed necessarily test and extend one's limits. Future uncertainty is thereby reduced and the threshold at which fear is perceived is raised. Confidence increases. The same action or similar actions are performed with less fear, more skill and much faster the next time around. The bar can be raised for the next jump and previously unthinkable actions become feasible and can be contemplated. The envelope of actions available – actions which that manager considers feasible – is thus stretched in multiple dimensions. The more often such actions are taken the faster the envelope of available actions expands. Even brave actions which fail can be a constructive learning experience in that they reveal, by the manner of their failing, precisely where limitations lie.

> William Shakespeare
> Courage mounteth with occasion.

The steady implementation of brave actions by a manager leads to a better knowledge of his own limits and an increased confidence in the quality of his judgments. This leads to an increase of his power and, in short, an increase of his capacity as a manager. His "fear of fear itself" reduces and his courage increases and paradoxically, he needs it less. A manager demonstrates his courage continuously by his actions and it is the steadiness and regularity with which he subordinates his fears to his actions which make him the role model for those around him; he needs no label or badge or medal for that.

Courage Across Cultures

Philosophy often distinguishes, or tries to, between moral courage and physical courage and civil courage and intellectual courage. Moral courage is measured against the individual's own values and beliefs. Sometimes it becomes duty imposed and demanded of its members by religions. Civil courage is measured against the touchstone of what civil society expects from a good citizen and civil duties are sometimes even enshrined in the legislation of some countries. Physical and intellectual courage are not usually demanded by law but are often expected by particular societies. These distinctions may well be applicable in explaining the various circumstances which give rise to different kinds of fears and individual motivations. But every kind of courage, at the deepest level of the individual and his actions, always reduce to being some fear having to be subordinated to some action. In considering the courage needed for a good manager I do not try to make these rather difficult labelling distinctions or to try and comprehend the origins of fear. Instead I focus on the actions involved and the fears to be subordinated.

The phenomenon of fear and therefore courage transcend language or culture. But courage is expressed and can only be observed in the colours and context that language and culture provide. This can lead to the conclusion that courage itself can vary in different countries and different cultures, but I have not found that there is any fundamental difference in the substance of the courageous actions required of a manager whether in Europe or Asia or the US. However the language used to speak about, and the metaphors used to describe, courage can be very different.

The courage of the *sakura* (cherry blossom) is the traditional metaphor in Japan for the concepts of *Bushido* and the courage of the *samurai*. The courage of the tiger or the eagle or the elephant and its place in *Dharma* may be the governing metaphors in India. Greek mythology and the Norse Sagas have direct descendants in medieval chivalry and gallantry. Even today, heraldic animals (lions and bears for example) and bright primary colours may be used as the metaphors for courage in Europe. Descriptions of courage and bravery often use military analogies and terminology. All the religions focus on moral courage and "big" moral issues and the ideals of courage as displayed in the extreme cases of martyrdom and sainthood. The comparisons usually tend to be with the heroic brand of courage rather than with what I consider the "every-day" manifestations of courage.

The observation of bravery is dependent upon the observer's perception of what causes, or should justly cause, fear. Here differences of language and culture do have an impact. Perceptions of physical threat and fears of physical discomfort and pain may be much the same across the world but what constitutes a moral or civil or social stress may be markedly different across countries and cultures. Breaking off a business relationship does not induce any great fear and is done without much collateral damage in the US or in Europe. In Asia, such an action may demand very high levels of courage. The person who has to break off a relationship may experience great trepidation as to how to go about doing it and a dread of the social and civil consequences. A manager in Europe may be afraid of losing his identity and of not being given due credit as an individual in a team, whereas his counterpart in Korea may be much more afraid of being seen as egoistic and disruptive of the group harmony. The everyday fears of an Indian manager of inadvertently infringing against religious or caste taboos are incomprehensible, even in other parts of Asia. Fears of attracting individual blame and sanction are much higher in Europe and the US than within the group cultures of Japan or Korea. A whistleblower in the US may fear legal or financial consequences and a whistleblower in India may fear for his life, but a whistleblower in Japan fears for his very soul. Fears of not following the correct form and of then losing honour or face in Asia are very real, but are of little consequence in Europe. Culture and language thus influence what the individual perceives as fear. This fear is, in turn, a constraint or a barrier to his actions. Whatever the level of innate courage that may be available to the individual determines the extent to which his actions can subordinate these fears and overcome these barriers. Culture and language can therefore be said to influence the situations where there is a need for courage but they do not determine the level of courage which exists in the individual.

In the work place the prevailing organisational culture can have a profound impact on the employee's desire to be courageous. Many organisations have what can be called a culture of courage, where stretching the envelope becomes the norm and not the exception, and where mistakes are allowed but strongly linked to learning.

If blame and punishment predominate in an organisation then the perceptions of fear are enhanced and any actions carrying risk are discouraged and less likely to be undertaken. Aversion to risk subordinates everything else. In large bureaucratic organisations where the culture can be to avoid blame and where performance based rewards are limited, it is the following of established processes which becomes predominant, and this leaves little space for doing anything that is without precedent. Very hierarchical or tightly controlled functional organisations limit the spread of information between hierarchic levels and across functions. Demarcation between departments can be very sharp and such non-transparency is often to be found in "family-run" organisations or where secrecy is considered of great importance. In the case of Enron and more recently with Satyam Computers for example, it was the need for keeping wrong-doings secret within the organisation, apart from the abject lack of courage, which was one of the contributors to their downfall. In such organisations, deviations from very strictly defined areas of operation become very difficult and require great courage if barriers are to be breached.

Companies with open cultures can encourage new areas of actions and are more innovative and have a higher tolerance for risk taking. But they can have a higher incidence of mistakes which must then be compensated for by speed of correction and by speed of learning. Open cultures are not necessarily cultures of courage. In large open organisations spanning many locations and perhaps also many countries, sub-cultures develop. The sub-cultures vary and can themselves cover the whole range of possible cultures. New cultural interfaces are established and can be the source of new conflicts. If strong role models are not present then an open culture can easily slip into becoming a reckless one with little responsibility being taken and no accountability. In such an environment there is little learning from mistakes and the incidence of error can increase uncontrollably to the point of catastrophe.

Irrespective of the type of organisation he finds himself in, the good manager will inevitably influence the prevailing culture and it will require courage to do so. To take risk judiciously and openly discuss and face potential negative outcomes dispassionately is possible, desirable and essential, and it can be done no matter what organisational culture prevails.

Courage in the Work Place

The work-place is not unlike a battlefield in some respects though some clear distinctions do apply. As in the workplace, many of a soldier's actions are in response to orders. But on the battlefield, the sanctions for not following orders are more directly life threatening than in the work-place. Consequently, a soldier on a battlefield may face a greater threat for not following an order than the action itself. He does not usually have the choice of rejecting a course of action which has been ordered. Similarly, to show fear or to show dissent on the battlefield is tantamount to treason or cowardice and the extreme threats that they signify. In the business world life-threatening situations are less common but job-threatening situations are never far away (but the threat of unemployment is a particular threat that a soldier rarely experiences). With the greater levels of fear involved, disobeying an order on a battlefield demands much greater courage than in the work-place!

Heroic actions may be less common but can also be found in the work-place. To take great personal risk on behalf of one's subordinates, or to put one's job on the line for a matter of principle, or to invite ridicule and abuse in implementing "unpopular" actions could also qualify as being heroic. "Whistleblower" legislation which has been introduced in many countries actually functions by trying to eliminate the need for heroism. Such legislation usually introduces protection for the individual and thereby tries to reduce the threat-perception and the fear of the whistleblower. The concept is that with less courage being required, an individual is more likely to reveal information about illegal practices. However, whistleblowers in the past were not protected by any legislation, and have sometimes been quite heroic when they have jeopardized their jobs and their well-being in pursuing what they felt was right.

While courage exists in the individual, it is only bravery that can be observed and that only through his actions. Courage can only be inferred by observing a multiplicity of brave actions. Bravery lies in the eyes of the beholder and depends upon his perception of the fear inherent in the action. This immediately creates the possibility of a mismatch between the bravery actually involved and what has been observed. This mismatch is very common in the work-place, especially with skilled, experienced and competent people who may assume a much lower perception of fear and risk that a less skilled or younger person may actually feel. For a manager who must mobilize actions and therefore must assess the behaviour of others, it becomes vitally important to be able to discern the level of fear being experienced by the actor, and not to merely project or transpose his own fear perceptions onto the person who is to carry out the action.

During my tenure heading the Alstom Group in India, I had the task of merging some of our companies into a listed company. The majority ownership of one of the companies to be merged had been acquired from the Government of India about 5 years earlier. It had originally been a private company which had gone bankrupt and had ended up in Government ownership. At the time of reconstruction (similar to that after a Chapter 11 filing in the US) the outstanding loans from the State Bank of India (itself a nationalised bank) had been written down and converted to equity. Unfortunately, someone at the Bank had blundered and had neglected to record the transaction. The transfer to equity and the write down had been missed and the original loan was still on the Bank's books. Since a merger is a court-appointed process, the SBI opposed the merger in the Bombay High Court contending that the original loan (about five Million Dollars at the time of the bankruptcy) still needed to be repaid. The High Court approved the merger anyway and the SBI appealed – twice; first to a single judge bench and then when they lost again to the full Court of Appeal. The Government of India was not formally a party to the case except as another minority shareholder. When this appeal too was lost, the SBI took the matter to the Supreme Court of India. During this process, I first had a great deal of pressure from Government civil servants, advisors and even some lawyers on the side-lines, that I needed to settle this out of court since it was futile to challenge the Government or the largest bank in India which also happened to belong to the Government. One approach had been made to our lawyers offering to be a go-between for a settlement but that had sounded to me like an attempt at extortion and I ignored it. The case seemed to me to be so clear-cut and the court judgments till then had backed my perception that I instructed our Supreme Court lawyers to continue. I then started receiving calls from our Headquarters in Paris questioning whether this was the right approach and whether it was not better to give in. Nick Salmon, my boss in Paris and my Board of Directors however, backed me to the hilt. One reason for my position was my perception that I understood how the bureaucratic mind in the SBI functioned. I concluded, after some analysis, that the SBI manager currently responsible for the loan on their books – but who had not been responsible for the original mistake – was pursuing a process just to ensure that he could not be blamed and to ensure that he had covered every available option. I was a little more apprehensive about the impartiality of the Courts but had judged that our case was unlikely to have political overtones. In the event this was the correct decision and the Supreme Court took about 5 s to throw the SBI appeal out of court. The Appeals court had earlier passed strictures on the SBI for wasting the Court's time and these were effectively endorsed by the Supreme Court. The unfortunate SBI manager failed even to avoid blame and was posted to a remote and not very comfortable location. I was told later by many that it had been extremely brave, firstly to take on the SBI (and by proxy the Government) and secondly to resist the pressure from Headquarters, but the strange thing is that I have no perception or memory of any exercise of bravery. Even now, in retrospect, I have no sense of any bravery being involved – only of a strictly rational and rather obvious decision. No doubt I had apprehensions about the outcome, but after weighing all the options the defence of our position up to the Supreme Court seemed the right and proper thing to do. Perhaps the decision was tinged with a certain amount of intellectual arrogance towards all the bystanders proffering advice but who had not truly familiarised themselves with the facts of the case.

When the SBI lost their second appeal one of our senior managers resigned and left the company. It was many years later that I came to know, entirely by accident, that he had offered to help the SBI manager for a percentage of the settlement as a consideration. At some point he had lost his nerve, his fears had prevailed and he botched the entire extortion attempt!

My point is that bravery is never perceived internally. The individual can only feel fear and can either let the fear determine his actions or he can make his judgments and take his actions in spite of the fear. It is in operating outside the comfort zone that courage comes alive.

Courage is needed by managers across all functions and across all hierarchical levels in an organisation. Perceptions of fear can be generated by even the most routine of activities; meeting new people, doing a new task for the first time, anticipating that something will go wrong, apprehension about available competence, waiting for someone else's judgment or actions and uncertainty of any kind can give rise to apprehension and anxiety and fear. Even the most simple of tasks can arouse fear when surrounded by uncertainty.

When I was first living in Japan and learning the language, I recall the terror that welled up in me whenever the telephone rang and there was no one else in the room to answer it!

Many of the situations requiring courage are connected with people interactions. Conflicts are feared and very often avoided rather than resolved. People in conflict with each other are bypassed to avoid becoming involved. Giving objective, negative feedback is notoriously weak in all organisations at all levels. Criticising performance or competence shortfalls arouse feelings of angst. Giving praise seems to be very difficult for some because they fear being seen as "soft" or "weak". Necessary discussions with superiors are often put off in case the superior opens some other unknown and dangerous subject. Early warnings are not given because "it is not my business". Unpleasant tasks – such as firing someone or telling someone he has made a mistake or rejecting a salary claim – are evaded and passed on to others rather than addressed directly. Some people find it extremely difficult to say "No" especially to superiors. Requests for actions are not rejected as they should be because that might admit to a lack of competence or time.

Since culture and language influence the perception of fear in an observer they also determine the bravery and courage that is perceived by an external observer. Furthermore it is only an observer – not the actor himself – who usually needs to comment on, or put a label to, the bravery of an action. What a manager needs is therefore not to label himself as a brave person, but just to focus on the subordination of his fears to his actions, by constantly moving his actions to the limits of his comfort zone. This brings about an exercise of his intrinsic level of courage which, by being regularly employed, leads to a "culture of courage" in his sphere of influence.

Creating a Culture of Courage

There was a story told after Hurricane Katrina hit New Orleans in 2005, that a manager of one of the pumping stations could have channelled water from one area of the city to another which would have reduced some of the damage caused. However the decision to make such a diversion of water was vested in his superior and explicitly excluded from his authority. Of course, in the prevailing chaos, his superior could not be contacted. In the event, he did not dare to exceed his authority and the water was not diverted. It is not possible to say how much extra damage or loss of life this decision caused, but his decision certainly did not reduce the damage sustained.

Clearly the organisational environment did not encourage anyone to take on extra responsibility and perhaps penalised breaches of designated authority. In any case the fear he perceived for exceeding his authority must have been significantly greater than any fear or discomfort he may have felt for the consequences of his inaction. Effectively the manager had no incentive to leave his zone of comfort. Whether this story is true or not, it provides an example of an organisation which allowed no space for a culture of courage and in fact, one which positively discriminated against courage being expressed.

The opportunities for a manager to show courage are continuous and endless. His actions can create the space around him such that his subordinates (and why not also his peers and his superiors?) feel it necessary and beneficial to emulate his approach. The space around him reflects his courage, and if it grows and meets and meshes with other similar spaces a culture of courage can be established. A critical number of such role models are needed to ensure the spread of such a culture throughout an organisation. An individual manager can always maintain the immediate space around him and to a large extent also in the hierarchy below him, but for the courage space to spread across an organisation he needs like-minded peers maintaining similar spaces of courage. The courage space around a manager is not only one within which courage is enabled, it also provides an extension to the shield provided by his strength of character.

There are some general behavioural characteristics which distinguish courageous managers, all of which help to develop a courage space. To intervene in conflicts between others is seen as threatening by most people and not only in the work place. Large modern cities have witnessed the growth of the phenomenon of the apathetic bystanders who perceive many fears, and do not intervene even when they see horrendous crimes being committed in front of them on the street. Apathetic bystanders are also present in the work place where intervention and conflict resolution is often seen as a hazardous action. Conflicts between people are among the most disruptive and energy sapping happenings in a work-place. Once a conflict occurs the protagonists have an additional fear of being, or being seen as, the loser in any settlement, which then further discourages any resolution among them. The immediate surroundings can become polarised and the conflict can escalate to others. Where he observes a conflict the courageous manager addresses it immediately. If addressed early, the urge to compromise can be activated by assisting the parties to see the others point of view, and the conflict can be amicably resolved while it is still small. A manager may well encourage, and should encourage, healthy rivalry but he then needs to be extremely watchful that this does not cross the line to become conflict. When any conflict appears he ensures that the parties are made aware that their conflict has been observed, and that a resolution is awaited. He makes himself available for conflict resolution perhaps as a mediator. If he has developed the reputation of being rigorous and just, his role as a mediator is not just acceptable but can be actively desired by the warring parties. Among subordinates, a manager has the appointed authority to play the arbitrator. But the result of any arbitration can often be resented, especially by a losing party. Instead of proceeding immediately to arbitration, a manager can, by means of his authority, use the threat of arbitration to encourage an "out of court" settlement. But he is always prepared, though only when absolutely necessary, to act as judge and jury and force a resolution. But the bottom line is that whether he uses diplomacy or persuasion or coercion or his final authority, he does not allow conflicts to fester. The manner in which conflicts are made transparent and the speed with which they get resolved is one of the hallmark signatures of a culture of courage.

The courageous manager handles the unpleasant situations and the tough conversations first, not last. His criticisms are timely and fair and objective.

Subordinates know that they will get unpleasant news directly from him and not by rumour or through the grapevine. They know that when they are told off it will be personally and directly and not by an email or a surrogate messenger. They have trust that criticism will be just and are confident that such criticisms will not be in front of an audience of their subordinates or peers. Consciously or unconsciously, the manager creates the atmosphere and environment in which the courage of his subordinates can be given full exposure. He protects his subordinates from the criticism of superiors but ensures that praise for a subordinate is reported upwards. He looks for learning opportunities for his subordinates to challenge their skills and their envelopes of action. He trusts their judgments and demonstrates thereby that he is willing to take risk. He permits mistakes provided that the learning from the mistakes is always explicit. The culture of courage is a learning culture. The fear of making mistakes is drastically reduced in an environment where every mistake is seen as something to be observed, corrected and learned from, and not only as a reason for blame. The learning culture itself leads to much improved early warnings. When the fear of making a mistake is reduced, warnings of mistakes happening or about to happen come very early indeed. The manager has the spin-off benefit of getting very few unpleasant surprises.

The courage space is also characterised by a very high level of trust. It takes courage to trust but the reward is the trust that returns. The manager builds not only a bilateral trust between him and others but is as concerned about the multi-lateral trust among the others. The starting point is with the bilateral exchanges of trust which he must initiate and then extend to become multi-lateral. This does not happen without his taking risk; small risks to begin with but steadily growing as trust is reciprocated. The actions required are not rocket science but they must be systematic and measured. By keeping promises, by providing the freedom to question, by listening, by being prepared to be convinced by argument and to change as a consequence and by demonstrating transparency are all examples of courageous actions that lead to the development of trust.

He challenges and stimulates the vision of his subordinates by clarifying and interpreting the larger organisational visions in his own personal terms such that they can relate their own endeavours to the larger whole. He encourages their manifestations of courage by providing the back-up and security needed for them to overcome their barriers of fear. He does not allow people to sit quietly within their comfort zones but instead looks to provoke them to enlarge their envelopes of action. He looks for opportunities to delegate his responsibilities and expand theirs. I see empowerment not just as the giving of authority but as that which enables the taking of responsibility. When empowered subordinates voluntarily offer and take over some of the manager's responsibilities, and he lets them do so because there are other responsibilities he would, in turn, like to take on, then the culture of courage has become real.

As he trusts them more, his expectations of his subordinates increase. He shows appreciation often, even if glowing praise may be sparing. But praise is never absent and therefore it is valued all the more. His promises are reliable and when there is any risk that they may not be fulfilled, it is he who provides early warning and renegotiates them, such that a promise is never allowed to be broken. He pushes himself and his limits. He takes risk judiciously and his criteria for taking risk are transparent. He avoids the overstating of achievements or the "low-balling" of forecasts just to make his performance seem better than it is. He does not hide his fears and demonstrates that they are merely the constraints to be overcome, but not the focus of, his actions. He does not exaggerate his fears or use them as an excuse for actions not taken.

Perhaps the most effective way for a manager to develop the culture of courage is by actually putting his authority as a superior "at risk" while subordinating his fear of a loss of his authority. This could be done for example, by:

1. Permitting open discussion of his decisions, or
2. By acknowledging a previous mistake, or
3. By giving subordinates the "space" to voice their opinions, or
4. By permitting free access of his subordinates to his superiors, or
5. Delegating his duties to some of his subordinates especially in front of superiors, or
6. By ensuring that subordinates get full exposure for creditable actions, and
7. By shielding them from attack when mistakes are made

A good manager who has the courage to put his authority "at risk" will still maintain his respect and his authority and he will enable and embolden those around him to stretch their abilities and develop towards their full potential.

Courage with Peers and Superiors

The innate courage that is in any individual does not change merely because the audience for his actions has changed. Nevertheless, there is a difference in the type of actions that fall within the feasible envelope for a manager depending upon whether he is dealing with subordinates or with superiors. With subordinates, a manager starts with an inbuilt, vested authority which obviously keeps his level of fear relatively low when contemplating actions. Where his superiors are his audience, the authority shifts to them. This leads to different and increased risk and fear perceptions for the manager when contemplating actions.

Where there is full compliance with a superior's opinions or judgment there is little extra to fear. Additional risk is created by having to dissent when necessary and yet comply with the authority of a superior. To voice dissent – which is truly felt and not just for the purpose of showing dissent – against the opinion of a superior or the majority of one's peers is not easy, but it is a requirement for a manager who is employed primarily for the exercise of his own mind (and not just to be a "yes-man"). It is always incumbent on a manager to respect and not to undermine the authority of his superiors. This is in the nature of a civil duty to his employer. The manager must perhaps enforce decisions or implement actions that he does not agree with. The courageous manager is one who privately voices his dissent to his superior and yet fully implements the actions required by a valid, superior authority. The courage lies in ensuring that his dissent is properly registered, without heat and without insolence and in a creative manner. This is where the good manager takes the opportunity to propose alternatives to the actions he disagrees with. In all my experience it has never been difficult for me as a superior to listen to suggestions from a subordinate for doing things better, but has always been irritating and vexing to hear only about what cannot be done.

It was in 1978, in England, in a contract research organisation that I was first appointed a "manager" when my boss Raymond Hoy advised me "There are always at least ten thousand and one reasons why something cannot be done. What I need from you is not a reason why not to do something but to tell me how it can be done or done better".

If a manager has performed with credibility and integrity and professionalism, surrounded by his own courage space, there is no superior of any worth who will not at least listen if he proposes improved alternatives. In the extreme case, a matter of dissent may touch upon a fundamental value, where dissent must then become a "resigning issue". A manager must always have his own core personal values as his reference and his touchstone. He must in his own mind have a clear picture of where his values are untouchable and inviolable. This is the core of his integrity, which cannot change from day to day, or to suit the latest orders from his superior. His identity lies in his integrity and must remain intact. This, perforce, must result in the preparedness – at some personal threshold – to resign rather than to carry out an action which he believes is wrong. However, there is a vast range of courageous actions which can be taken short of resigning provided that the actions involved do not enter into the realms of recklessness. They can be as simple as convincing a superior that he has overlooked some information, all the way up to a full-frontal confrontation on a matter of important principle – but not one of integrity. There are times when confrontation is needed, but when it is chosen it must be in the belief that it is the "right and proper" thing to do. It is only to an observer that it will appear as a brave action. Where a confrontation is chosen as the way to go, the good manager enters into it well prepared and with all the arguments, documents and evidence needed to convince the superior. He must also have a clear view as to how the confrontation end-game is to play out. And if his view does not prevail then he must be ready for the resignation which may be the unavoidable ending.

I believe that the use of a threat to resign to win some concession is nothing but a form of blackmail. Whenever I have received such conditional resignations, I have had no hesitation in immediately accepting them and have rarely entertained any further discussion. I have experienced this a few times and only in one instance have I accepted a withdrawal of the resignation after an unconditional apology. Curiously, when there have been no conditions attached to a request to resign, I have found that I have been very prepared to have a discussion and explore compromise solutions, but never when under a threat or if I judged it to be an attempt at blackmail. I am convinced that it is never possible to negotiate with a "gun to one's head".

To show dissent with peers or superiors always carries a fear of the outcome – and the courage comes in continuing anyway. The courage involved in maintaining personal integrity and yet fulfilling the requirements of authority is dealt with extensively in the concept of *Bushido*, where courage is inextricably linked with the fulfilment of duty and obligation (*giri*). The fulfilment of duty and obligation, including duty owed to a superior, then becomes an integral and a fundamental part of the individual's values. But not every individual will take the same extreme position of a *Samurai* warrior who subordinates – to the point of suicide – all other obligations to the duty owed to a feudal lord.

> George Bernard Shaw
> When a stupid man is doing something he is ashamed of, he always declares that it is his duty.

But supposed duty, can also be used an excuse to avoid courageous actions. Moral duty can be claimed to justify intellectual cowardice or a civil duty to a superior can be claimed to rationalise fudging of values. A duty to follow a process can be claimed to avoid taking unprecedented actions. Civil duty to the well-being of the organisation can be used to justify an erosion of standards of integrity. Shady practices may be rationalised as being necessary to protect jobs. A duty to the majority can be used to justify or excuse an oppression of a minority. These are all issues of courage, where avoidance of blame is preferred to the risk inherent in the exercise of some courage in doing what is right. But a manager who does not or will not stand up and show dissent when it is truly felt is one who fears to exercise his mind. If actions are subordinated to fears then courage has left the room and we enter into the land of the Wizard of Oz.

> **From The Wizard of Oz**
> **Cowardly Lion**: What makes a king out of a slave?
> Courage!
> What makes the flag on the mast to wave?
> Courage!
> What makes the elephant charge his tusk
> in the misty mist, or the dusky dusk?
> What makes the muskrat guard his musk?
> Courage!
> What makes the Sphinx the seventh wonder?
> Courage!
> What makes the dawn come up like thunder?
> Courage!
> What makes the Hottentot so hot?
> What puts the "ape" in apricot?
> What have they got that I ain't got?
> **Chorus:** Courage!

A manager does not explicitly try to be brave. But as he regularly and judiciously acts within those spaces where he has apprehensions and fears he inevitably subordinates his fears to his purposeful actions. He exercises his courage.

Chapter 8
"Praise Loudly, Blame Softly": The Art of Motivation

*A manager's own motivation and his **ability to motivate** his chosen actors is what provide force to the actions he mobilises. When exercised properly, this force manifests itself as enthusiasm or inspiration or impetus or commitment on the part of his chosen actors. Proper motivation however, walks a tightrope between manipulation and bribery on the one hand and the unleashing of unfettered greed on the other. To walk this thin line the manager must practice what is an art rather than a science but he must have some familiarity with the state of the science and of theories of motivation. He must utilise the psychology of needs and deficiencies and to do this he must be able to assess the factors which represent needs and desires for his actors. In practice he needs to address the rewards and penalties he can apply to achieve the force of motivation in his chosen players.*

Of Carrots and Sticks

In human behaviour, motivation can be considered to be a force. It is brought to bear when performing actions. Where actions have no purpose motivation is undefined. Where there is purpose I take it to be without doubt that the purpose is better served when the required actions are carried out by people who are motivated rather than by people who are indifferent.

The motivated state can then be described as that biological, emotional or cognitive condition which generates a force – variously called incentive, enthusiasm, inspiration, drive, desire, impetus or commitment – which can be applied to a person's actions. The difference between a motivated person and an unmotivated person lies in the force they bring to bear when performing the same action. It follows that motivation is that particular force within a person which infuses dynamism into his actions or his behaviour towards a particular purpose. The art of motivation then lies in the manner of generating such a force of engagement in people when acting towards a particular purpose. It is the influencing of human desires and drives by addressing their needs and deficiencies such that they have a vested interest in achieving the purpose.

A "carrot on a stick" is an idiom which refers to inducing an action for a reward which is out of reach and never attained. This expression originates in inducing a donkey to move a cart and the implication is that the donkey is too stupid to realize that the reward always remains unattainable. The more usual idiom today is of a "carrot *and* a stick" and refers to the simultaneous application of a promised reward and a threat of a penalty. The "carrot and stick" expression in current usage involves the simultaneous application of both incentives and penalties in the modern workplace and no longer carries the same connotation of stupidity.

> Catherine the Great of Russia
> I praise loudly, I blame softly

Let us take rewards to be anything that satisfies and penalties to be anything that dissatisfies. But it must be emphasized that satisfaction and dissatisfaction are then not the opposites of each other. They are then on two entirely different scales, each starting from zero, but where the two scales are not diametrically opposed. An absence of penalty (which is not to be confused with the absence of an expected penalty) gives zero dissatisfaction but provides nothing directly on the satisfaction scale. An absence of reward (which is not to be confused with a deficiency of an expected reward), provides zero satisfaction but also provides nothing directly on the dissatisfaction scale. It is because they are not necessarily directly opposed to each other that satisfactions and dissatisfactions can simultaneously coexist.

Given that reward is just a promise of a future state of satisfaction and a penalty is a threat of a future state of dissatisfaction, I now define motivation to be the force giving an acceleration which results in a velocity to reach or avoid those future states. Motivation, in this approach, always boils down to one of two drives; the drive for satisfaction or the drive to avoid dissatisfaction; the drive for a reward or the drive to avoid a penalty. I use "drive" rather than "desire" because the desire for something may not lead to any action and could be lacking in drive, whereas I take "drive" to be the initiator of purposeful actions and which automatically includes any preceding desire. A desire is a potential for a force but motivation is the force itself. Just as in the physical sciences, motivation as a driving force is due to a difference of potential. A promised state – a reward or a penalty – is what I call a "motivator" but the magnitude of any resultant force – any motivation – depends upon the difference between the promised state and the current state. Motivators may be direct or indirect. A monetary reward is nearly always doubly indirect. First the reward materializes after some unrelated action is achieved by the subject. The subject then translates the monetary reward into some change of state for himself that would then be enabled and which would need some further action on his part to be achieved. For example, a manager may be rewarded with a cash bonus for achieving a particular financial target due to his actions at work, which he then uses to buy a new car which changes his state of satisfaction. The motivation for his actions in the workplace actually results from his desire for a new car.

Many different drives can exist simultaneously within an individual and cover many different states of satisfaction or dissatisfaction. One drive may influence another. Motivations may reinforce some drives or may oppose others. But, in its most basic form, each motivation – each drive – remains just a matter of responding to a carrot or a stick.

I find that the advantage with this definition is that motivation is then not in itself very complicated. It is the force experienced by an individual consequent to his desire to move from his current state to a different state of satisfaction or dissatisfaction. What are infinitely more complicated however, are the causes of human satisfaction and dissatisfaction, and the enormous variation in what different people consider satisfying or dissatisfying. I use the terms "satisfaction" and "dissatisfaction" in their widest possible meanings. Satisfaction then is a consequence of anything an individual perceives as being beneficial or desirable relative to his present state. Similarly dissatisfaction is a consequence of anything that an individual perceives as being detrimental or undesirable. At any given instant, the current state of satisfaction or dissatisfaction determines what a person may consider beneficial or detrimental. The same action could be the response to either a drive to gain satisfaction or one to avoid dissatisfaction. Depending upon the current state, the same action may simultaneously address both dissatisfaction and a satisfaction.

For example, the action of eating may be motivated by the need to remove hunger as dissatisfaction or it may be motivated by the satisfaction inherent in appreciating good food. However, someone suffering from acute hunger pangs will use eating to remove this undesirable state first and will not, at least initially, be motivated to eat as the act of a connoisseur of food. If the hunger is not acute and the person is not sated, which is the normal state of affairs at most meal times, the act of eating can simultaneously address both the level of hunger and the desire to appreciate the food. When following a diet, the act of eating some particular food could still be to address hunger but additionally could now be to address a matter of health. Similarly, eating at a wedding banquet, or at a particular restaurant, or in the company of a particular set of friends, or just having popcorn at the movies can have additional motives to just the avoidance of hunger.

It is a universal and well established observation that when some dissatisfaction is acute, all other drives and actions are subordinated to the alleviation of the acute dissatisfaction. Extreme physical or mental stress or extreme discomfort – be it with the surrounding company or with the level of salary or the exposure to weather or having a splitting headache – all lead to the drive to alleviate that particular, intolerable dissatisfaction and that becomes the dominant motivation. All other drives are put on hold. When a number of dissatisfactions are present simultaneously, the most acute takes precedence. It can also be observed that the drives towards levels of satisfaction only begin to take effect once all dissatisfactions have been at least partially alleviated to reach some level which is tolerable.

The scales for levels of satisfaction and dissatisfaction both start at zero but have no upper limit. The scales are quite separate and are not extensions of each other. Practical upper limits are imposed indirectly only by an individual's capacity to feel. The only maximum limit to hunger is the indirect limit set by starvation and death but once hunger is satiated, the dissatisfaction is at zero and cannot be further reduced into negative territory. Levels of satisfaction similarly have a zero which signifies an absence of satisfaction but have no upper limit. But this zero of the satisfaction scale which represents its absence cannot be further reduced or assumed to continue onto the scale of dissatisfaction. Once dissatisfactions have reduced to be at a tolerable level for the individual, the drive (the force causing acceleration and giving velocity) to avoid them reduces. Similarly, once some threshold levels of satisfaction are achieved the drive to achieve further satisfaction reduces but depends upon the individual.

What constitutes satisfaction or dissatisfaction varies from one individual to the next. What levels of these are considered acute or tolerable or acceptable or unacceptable or mild satisfaction or ecstasy, also vary with the individual. To what extent and with what velocity a change of state will drive an individual towards reaching a different state of satisfaction or dissatisfaction also depends upon the individual. With this level of variation, and with this dependence upon the individual, motivating people is in the realm of art and is still a long way from being an exact science. The use of rewards and penalties to achieve the actions chosen to be elicited from specific individuals is the art of motivation.

There are a wealth of studies and literature regarding the psychology of motivation and proposing theories of motivation, but I confine myself to the practical aspects of exercising motivation. For a manager, the exercise of the art is crucial. Just as a painter needs to know something about the mathematics of perspective, but does not need to be an expert geometrician, the manager must know something about the theories of motivation but does not need to be a psychologist. He needs to be expert at practicing motivation but does not need to be a scholar of the science. To motivate himself and all those who may be involved in the chains of actions that he must mobilize, becomes crucial. To be effective, motivation must always apply at the level of the individual. Where he can, the manager must ensure that the art applied is appropriate to the individual. In many cases he will not be able to deal individually and then he may have to generalize and deal with groups of people, knowing full well that the individuals in the group will each be affected differently. His knowledge of the current state of satisfactions and dissatisfactions will vary from detailed knowledge of those close to him to virtually nothing about others. He may need to motivate people who are virtually strangers. Where he does not know the current state of an individual, the impact of rewards and penalties as motivators will be unknown. He may have to guess at these.

Of Psychology and Theories of Motivation

To practice the art of motivation, it is of some use for a manager to keep up to date with the state of the science. Motivation theory is an expanding branch of psychology and of social science though it is a long way from being an exact science. There is no single universally accepted theory of motivation but most theories generally fall into one of two groups; content or need theories and process theories.

Most of the need theories build on Abraham Maslow's classical work of 1943, *A Theory of Human Motivation*, developing the "hierarchy of needs". He identified five classes of human needs ranging from lower order to higher order needs and defined the terms physiological, safety, love, self-esteem and self-actualization needs. The hierarchy was such that a higher-order need would only come into play if the lower-order need was sufficiently satisfied. The physiological needs are the basic needs for survival such as for food, water, shelter and clothing. The needs for long-term safety come next and would include for example, housing, economic security, job security, health coverage, children's education and retirement plans. Under love Maslow grouped the social needs of humans to belong to the group and to have some status and liking within the group. These have been called "affiliation" needs by others and include the needs of the individual to being a valued participant in the family group or in friendship groups or in work-related groupings. The human needs for the approval of others and especially of superiors lies here.

Maslow's higher-order needs then comprised first the self-esteem needs (also called the "ego" needs) for freedom of action, appreciation, recognition and respect. At the highest hierarchical level, Maslow placed the needs for self-actualization consisting of intellectual and physical challenge, the need to excel or innovate or create and of achieving demanding goals.

He further grouped these into two and called the lower-order group as "deficiency needs" and the higher-order needs as "growth needs". He considered the deficiency needs as more potent and dominating but only until they were reasonably satisfied. Thus social motivators do not come into play until any acute deficiencies of physiological or safety needs are reduced and have reached some tolerable level. Effectively, higher-order needs are ignored and motivations are rendered ineffective until all lower-order deficiency needs are reasonably satisfied.

Many psychologists and management researchers have developed this basic concept to give more elaborate or more specialized need theories covering job satisfaction, motivation within the performing arts and in the workplace. These various need theories do not contradict each other and the fundamental theory developed by Maslow, with some variations, seems intuitively sound. I find the need theories particularly useful in application to the workplace when considering the content of what could be a motivator. All the deficiency needs are then to be measured on the dissatisfaction scale while the growth needs move the state of an individual along the satisfaction scale. I also find that the distinction made by the theories between the deficiency and growth needs is then well paralleled by the differentiation between the separate scales for satisfaction and dissatisfaction.

The second group contains the so-called process theories which focus on the cognitive process preceding and leading to behaviour. These include the equity theory, reinforcement theory, expectancy theory and goal-setting theory to name but a few. The common thread running through these theories is that they try to explain the thought process – the "how" – by which a need is converted into behaviour or actions. It has been proposed, for example, that goal setting is very effective but only when goals are concrete, reachable and not too far away in time. Performance improvements seem to be very amenable to such goal setting. Reinforcement theory considers motivation of human behaviour in terms of psychological conditioning and suggests that behaviour can be controlled by rewarding or reinforcing positive behaviour and penalizing negative behaviour. Expectancy theory is similar but focuses on the use of rewards in creating the internal expectancy of a desirable state of satisfaction within the individual himself. Other cognitive theories suggest that some behaviour is so rooted in unconscious desires and that these are the real motivators and may be quite different to what appears on the surface. The need for self-esteem or making excuses to avoid blame or denying negative emotions are examples of such unconscious motivators.

From a manager's perspective of putting the art of motivation into practice, I find these two groups of theories are not in opposition to one another. They are complementary and to be used appropriately in combination with one another. The need based theories provide insight into the content of what can be used as motivators. It is only since Maslow's work and subsequent developments that it has come to be accepted in management that looking at the diverse needs of employees is important. Much attention is now also given to finding the dominant need of an individual at any particular time since this will control the impact of other motivators that may be applied. These theories therefore help to define what shape and form and colour the carrots and sticks need to have.

The process theories, on the other hand, are very instructive in considering the thought process that is initiated within particular individuals or groups of individuals when a carrot or a stick is applied. The different theories each seem to have their most suitable areas of application. The thought process triggered, if and when it is triggered, will determine the actions actually taken by an individual. A manager will need to bear in mind though, that some people will have unconscious motivators and that it cannot just be assumed that what appears on the surface is the real driver. It is also relevant for a manager to consider the actions themselves and whether or not they can provide an intrinsic satisfaction and thereby reinforce the planned motivation.

Motivation is sometimes classified as being either intrinsic or extrinsic. Here intrinsic motivation is used to describe rewards from actions which are inherently satisfying (reading, playing a musical instrument, or solving a puzzle for example). Extrinsic motivation then is from outside the individual and could be a reward or a threat of a penalty. This is just a classification of different types of motivators and as such something to be taken into account by a manager when considering the actions he must mobilize. Where the choice is available, actions that are intrinsically satisfying are to be preferred.

A manager is primarily concerned with motivating others and therefore in applying extrinsic motivations. However, he needs also to motivate himself and here it becomes relevant to be able to achieve satisfaction in his own actions. Clearly if he can see to it that actions that he must necessarily take become inherently satisfying, he makes his own tasks easier. In my experience the key enabler to convert an action into an intrinsic motivator is most often knowledge and skill. The more one learns about food the easier it is to be a connoisseur; the more skilful one is at playing chess the greater the inherent satisfaction in playing chess. The more skilled a manager is at conversation the greater the inherent satisfaction in conversing for communication or for building a relationship. The act of learning itself can be a very strong intrinsic motivator and to promote the quest for learning is a powerful indirect motivator. It can be of some advantage if the actions he is trying to mobilize as extrinsic motivations are inherently satisfying to the people he needs to carry out such actions.

Other theories deal with the linkage between performance and satisfaction and there is some debate as to whether satisfaction leads to performance or whether the reverse holds. I believe that this question is itself connected to the hierarchies of needs and the satisfaction of those needs. Where the lower-order deficiency needs are involved, I believe satisfaction of these needs leads to performance since actions are paralysed till these needs are sufficiently satisfied. However, with the higher-order growth needs, performance itself leads to satisfactions provided the actions involved have an intrinsic satisfaction.

There are also theories which deal with the perception of equitable treatment where an individual compares himself to his peers and judges his motivators against those of his fellows. A lower level of reward than that received by somebody else can then be taken to be a punishment. Perceptions of justice and fair play can clearly have major motivating or de-motivating impacts.

From Theory to Practice

In my judgment, the many different theories are not contradictory. Most complement one another and some are based on studies of people in particular situations or particular environments. They are the various descriptions of the complex reality of human motivations, as perceived by different observers in different situations and from different viewpoints.

It seems to be not unlike the six different descriptions of an elephant – as a wall, a snake, a tree, a rope, a fan and a spear – when studied by six blind people! Nobody was wrong, but no one was wholly right.

The application of the current state of motivational theory into the art and practice of motivation needs to involve three distinct steps:

1. The use of an appropriate need theory to define the content of the motivators to be applied for getting individuals to move by means of purposeful actions towards states of greater satisfaction or reduced dissatisfaction
2. The use of appropriate process theories to design the content of the motivators to suit the cognitive process within the individual which is initiated by the motivator
3. The selection of actions such that the substance of the actions can – wherever possible – provide additional intrinsic motivations

The purpose of motivation in the workplace is to:

1. Instigate chosen actions by particular individuals
2. When instigated, to enhance the speed with which these actions are performed, while
3. Maintaining or improving the quality of the outcome of such actions

In the case of a manager, the actions desired are those he has chosen as being necessary to his purpose and which are his responsibility to mobilize. The individuals to carry out these actions are those that he has selected as being capable and available for implementing the necessary actions.

To be able to consciously engage in motivation, which is a necessary task for a manager, it is vital that some assessment be made of the current status of satisfaction or dissatisfaction of the subject. This in turn determines whether some other state of satisfaction or reduced dissatisfaction will be sufficiently separated from the current state for any motivation to be feasible. This applies irrespective of whether the subject is a subordinate, a superior or a complete stranger. Without such an assessment the drive actually generated by any motivator that is applied, will be nothing more than a guess. The objective is of course, to intentionally provide sufficient drive to the subject such that the desired action results and is carried out forcefully. In a few cases the manager will have sufficient information to be able to make a fairly accurate assessment. In most cases however, he will only have partial information. Nevertheless, the starting point must be an assessment of the current status. Most importantly, the manager must assess if the subject is currently in such an acute state of dissatisfaction that all drivers except that which reduces the prevailing dissatisfaction will be ignored and ineffective.

Robert Green Ingersoll
Happiness is not a reward – it is a consequence. Suffering is not a punishment – it is a result.

If the subject is in severe pain, or suffering some acute emotional distress, then it is obvious that it would be quite wrong, and pointless, to offer him inducements at that particular time as motivation for some unrelated actions. In the work environment, a manager is more likely to come across less acute, but still serious and debilitating cases of dissatisfaction. If, for example the subject is particularly dissatisfied and resentful about his salary or a missed promotion or his heavy workload, he will not be very receptive of any motivators till that dissatisfaction has been reduced to a level where it is tolerable. This is where the manager needs to have a level of empathy to be able to discern if his subject is in such a state. It also then becomes part of a manager's responsibility, and a duty in the case of subordinates, to alleviate such a condition purely for the sake of his own effectiveness. It is a necessity because until he does so, the subject is unavailable to him in the mobilisation of further actions.

(Of course the selection of people to carry out actions is part of a manager's judgment and it is incumbent upon him not to select people who are not capable of acting. However, resources are always limited, and a manager must often enable and empower and motivate the available people to become capable.)

Once an assessment of an individual's current state has been made, it becomes possible to consider the motivators that can promise a changed state and thus provide the required motivation to implement the desired action. It is my contention that a good manager has always made such an assessment before entering into any promises of rewards or threats of penalty. The assessment does not have to take much time at all and a few minutes may suffice, but the essential point is that the assessment be made. The accuracy of the assessment may always be in doubt but without it the manager is merely "hoping" for a response rather than practicing the art of motivation. It is a common fault that the focus is often just on the content of the motivator (the amount of the bonus, the weekend break, the promotion or the increased budget for example) without any prior assessment of the current state. This is an over-simplification which assumes that all the subjects are in some average or "normal" state of satisfaction or dissatisfaction. It ignores a key aspect of the complexity and individual variation of what constitutes job satisfaction and motivation in the workplace as a trade-off for simplicity. It is always permissible for a manager to make this simplification, especially when dealing with large groups. The important thing is that he be aware that he is making a simplification. This simplification is not ineffective, especially with "standard" rewards applied to large "standard" groups but, not surprisingly, gives average results with a wide spread. But the quality of motivation being exercised can be greatly enhanced by taking the extra step of first assessing the current state of the individual or the group.

To put the theory into practice the manager must eventually apply motivators. He needs to choose the motivators either for individuals or for groups of individuals. Using specific and well-directed motivators minimises the risk of collateral damage where the motivators for one person are perceived as unfair or unjust or, by comparison, as a penalty by someone else.

The Size of the Stick

Albert Einstein
If people are good only because they fear punishment, and hope for reward, then we are a sorry lot indeed.

There is a school of thought that rewards should never be offered without also having a balancing penalty; never a carrot alone but always a carrot with a stick. However, it does not seem rational to have a penalty based on the non-performance of a desired action merely to balance a reward for exceptional performance of the same action. But I believe the stick is needed, not as a balance for reward, but to set boundaries for acceptable behaviour. The danger with any rewards system is that the drive generated can be so strong that it leads to a distorted behaviour in which fulfilment of ego needs subordinate everything else. To have a reward system but where the behaviour is unbounded then panders to greed, selfishness, self-interest and a disregard for others in the workplace. A penalty or punishment system is thus necessary to establish a framework within which the rewards can function properly, not to limit the extent of the reward but to set the limits of acceptable behaviour. We must therefore distinguish between the punishments and penalties to constrain unacceptable behaviour and the absence of reward or other penalty associated with improving performance.

In recent times the unlimited nature of rewards in the financial sector and the absence of any penalties for unethical behaviour have demonstrated the ugliness of unfettered greed. There has been little motivation to exercise the traditional values of prudence or diligence or even to comply with fiduciary duties. The rewards offered as motivation of the higher-order needs have resulted in the fantastic creativity used in devising derivative financial instruments and the sub-prime mortgage bubble. In these newly invented areas of financial behaviour there was no tradition or background of constraints set by punishments or penalties for unethical behaviour, either internally within organisations or externally from a rather lax Securities and Exchange Commission (SEC). The financial systems across the world were in free-fall when, in 2008, Bear Stearns and Merrill Lynch collapsed, Lehman Brothers filed for bankruptcy and the American Insurance Group had to be bailed out. The banking sector all across Europe exhibited the same profligate behaviour and many went bankrupt or had to be bailed-out. The collapse of Iceland's three banks has virtually made the country bankrupt. In my view, it has been the combination of unlimited individual rewards on the one hand, together with the lack of constraints or significant penalties for unacceptable behaviour on the other, which bears much of the blame for the global financial meltdown of 2008. I would rephrase Einstein's quotation to be "When we are offered reward with no fear of punishment, then we show we are a sorry lot indeed".

I think penalties and punishments to restrain behaviour are absolutely necessary but must be restricted to the breach, by commission or by omission, of an expected behaviour. The expected behaviour must be comprehensively and clearly articulated and a mutually agreed thing. It cannot be that a penalty applies merely because the manager or an organisation had not made it clear as to what behaviour was expected. The expected norms of behaviour should be perfectly clear, and these should at least include:

1. A basic level of conscientiousness
2. A basic level of work performance
3. The level of cooperation with others
4. Standards of confidentiality
5. Standards of integrity
6. Standards of ethics

The penalties for breaching these norms need to be clearly spelled out and enforced. The ultimate sanction that can be applied in the workplace is termination of employment and the conditions for such termination need to be crystal clear. A breach of law invites immediate dismissal of course but any further sanctions are a matter of law and not for the organisation to impose. The penalties, apart from dismissal, to be applied in the workplace must not stray into the arena of cruel and unusual punishment.

The background of expected behaviour and the use of penalties to mark the boundaries of expected behaviour are crucial and necessary to be able to apply rewards as motivators without unleashing the destructive behaviour of accompanying greed. Without this background, every reward offered to an individual drives towards the most selfish and self-serving way of achieving that reward. It is this background which also contributes to establishing the relative value of the carrot. Provided that penalties exist at the behavioural boundaries, some types of penalties can also be considered for performance improvement. An absence of reward for example, can then also be perceived as a de-motivator in being the award for non-performance. A carrot for one mode of behaviour can also then act as a stick for avoiding the non-performance. In this sense a carrot always contains within it, the stick represented by the absence of reward. But, absence of a reward or other de-motivators for a non-performance, do not address or restrain unacceptable behaviour. These cannot replace or substitute for the penalty or punishment framework which establishes the bounds of expected behaviour.

The Sweetness of the Carrots

The most basic motivators in the workplace lie in the fundamental compensation package for employment and the working environment. These typically include the base salary or wages, working conditions, the content of the job, health care benefits, pension benefits, a career path and continuing education. These generally cover, directly or indirectly, the basic deficiency needs – the physiological and safety needs as described by Maslow – of survival and maintenance. Food, clothing, housing and the basic needs of life are the needs indirectly met by salary and wages and these are the basic motivators which keep the employee functioning in his role. Health care, pension plans and tenure of appointment are examples of the motivators which also cater to the security needs of an individual. However an individual's perception of deficiency with security issues generally increase with age and can undergo step changes as he takes on more responsibilities in the home. Getting married, having children, children entering school or college or having parents to take care of can all create changes in feelings of deficiency. The greater the deficiency, the greater will be the opportunity for a motivator to elicit a response.

For a manager dealing with the motivation of subordinates, these background motivators – terms of employment, general working environment and the prevailing work culture – form the basis of ensuring that the lower-order needs are all at least at a tolerable level. However, all that these accomplish is just that the individual satisfies the minimum conditions of his employment. They just balance the lower-order needs against the basic employment conditions. It needs a great deal more to bring the best out of people and move them not only towards performing to their limits but also to continuously challenge and expand their limits. Once the background motivators have ensured that the acute needs of a group have been reasonably satisfied, it becomes practical to then consider the individual variations and the motivators which can be designed to satisfy the higher-order needs and thereby mobilise the desired actions.

One such example of adjusting the background motivators was in India where there is no welfare state to fall back on. Health care is then one of the key items that can be offered by an organisation in the employee's compensation package. The family tradition – still largely followed – of individuals taking responsibility for the care of elderly parents can be a real burden, especially as health care needs and costs increase with their age. In 2001 when renegotiating the company health care plan with insurance companies we contracted to include not only the standard coverage for the employee and his immediate family (wife and dependent children) but also for the parents of the individual and his wife. There were some medical conditions that were excluded but even coverage for these was made available as a subsidised personal option. The lightening of mood in the workplace was palpable. The additional security perceived was attractive enough to become a feature differentiating the company and this was, I believe, a significant contribution to a reduced staff turnover and an increase in the number of job applicants. In 2005 we reviewed the costs to the company of providing such health care and found that the addition of parents to the coverage had not added greatly to the costs per person or to the premiums paid by the company. Here the motivator had been offered equally to all employees even though only a few of them would have had any immediate benefit. Over the 4 years of the review less than 5% of the employees had actually utilised the provision. But the perception of enhanced security, I believe, extended over all the employees and even into the job market and the benefit to the company in having a motivated workforce was far in excess of any increased cost of premiums.

Given that unacceptable behaviour is restrained by a punishment framework and that the lower-order needs are sufficiently satisfied so as not to disqualify other motivators, the manager can then consider higher-order motivators. In my experience the motivators are very similar across countries and cultures. There are differences due to the different individual perceptions of needs and satisfactions and some care is needed to ensure that the motivators will create the intended drive. Some examples of the motivators available to a manager, ranked in increasing order of hierarchical needs are:

- Security needs
  - Transparency in evaluation criteria and evaluations
  - Clarity of expectations of the individual and the group
  - Clear and realistic information regarding the opportunities and risks facing the group and the entire organisation
  - Unambiguous policies regarding the sanctions applying to, bullying, slander, discrimination or breaches of integrity
- Social needs
  - Regular feedback when expectations are being met
  - Negative feedback always connected to an improvement plan
  - Social events outside the workplace
  - Family events
  - Team building events or programmes
  - Building common values through group participations in charity or civic or community events ("adopt a village" or raising funds for a good cause)

- Opportunities to work jointly with others
- Inter-departmental sports competitions
* Ego needs
  - Awards as recognition for a job well done (for example, as employee of the month, salesman of the year or "best" performance of the week or month in any field)
  - Designation as a department or division or company "expert" in a particular field
  - On the job training for new skills
  - Participation in training courses especially in new fields of study
  - Subsidising part-time study
  - Appointment as the group representative towards the outside world
  - Additional responsibilities or expanded work content
  - Cash bonuses for extraordinary achievements
  - Bonuses in kind for extraordinary achievement (ranging say from a dinner for two to a paid vacation at a holiday resort but always based on achievement and not on effort)
  - Promotions
* Self-actualisation needs
  - Special assignments or challenges
  - Given goals and targets rather than tasks
  - Additional responsibility with freedom to choose the means to achieve an end
  - Granted a budget to maintain expertise (freedom to choose training courses, seminars or conferences)
  - Appointment as a mentor for someone else
  - Appointment to conduct training courses
  - Participation in brain-storming sessions regarding innovation or long-term goals or company strategy

When applying motivators it is essential to check that they are not being perceived as unfair by others. A feeling of a lack of equity or of being unfairly treated, whether true or not, can de-motivate even the most senior of managers. This becomes a dissatisfaction of an ego need and can occur even when all the lower-order needs are satisfied.

Setting targets and goals to enhance performance needs to be done individually and preferably where the individual participates in establishing the targets. Targets must be real and owned to be taken seriously; they must be challenging but doable within a reasonable length of time. Targets set from the top-down, or without the individual's involvement, will always lack ownership. Rewards must preferably be related to results and not on effort expended. The individual must be able to visualise himself attaining the target and whatever benefit is associated with it.

Management by Objective (MBO) is a powerful tool which shows excellent results when used consistently across an organisation. But such schemes can let themselves down when the cascade of objectives across the management hierarchy flows in the wrong direction or makes no arithmetic sense. Wherever I have seen "inverted pyramids" of objectives, where the objectives at the top of the hierarchy are greater than the objectives summed up from the bottom, it is apparent that the process has degenerated to become some form filling exercise and has no connection with genuine target setting for the motivation of performance. Balanced Score Cards can also be very effective when properly used but have a tendency to be degraded into a pro forma report rather than providing the intrinsic motivation that they can.

Short term target setting (typically periods of less than 12 months) seem to be helped by reinforcement in the form of constant monitoring of progress, showing proper appreciation when appropriate and reiteration of the goals. Reinforcement of this kind leads, I think, to a higher probability of achieving performance superior to the goals and often a steady increase in the goals set.

A manager needs to be wary of de-motivating influences and especially of situations where motivation intended for one person can cause de-motivation in another. The de-motivators which are particularly dangerous are those where a lower order deficiency is increased to the point where it nullifies all other motivators. Not all motivators are universally applicable across all individuals and this is why the initial assessment of the individual's current state and his desired states becomes so important.

When I first moved to Japan I had been familiar with and had successfully used "monthly achievement awards" to show appreciation of an individual's performance. This had been effective in Sweden and in the US. But I realised very quickly that singling out an individual for an award in Japan was causing embarrassment for the individual and in some cases was alienating the individual from the group he belonged to – and needed to belong to. The individual award was effectively threatening his affiliation needs. This motivator became much more effective when it was modified to be a quarterly award for a team performance instead of a monthly award for an individual.

There is a thin line separating motivation from manipulation. Having a healthy rivalry among subordinates can be enormously constructive. Where there is an element of humour involved in the rivalry this can lead very rapidly to a spiral of success. But, if the rivalry becomes threatening to ego needs it can very quickly become the source of conflict between individuals and turn destructive. It can become unhealthy and contagious when a performance rivalry becomes instead a rivalry for becoming a favourite of the manager. This is especially hazardous if the awards are large and there is some subjectivity involved in choosing the winner.

Wherever I have used such awards the monetary value of the award has generally been low and largely symbolic. Making the award with some ceremony and publicising the award with the winner's peers and superiors has much more impact than the value of the award. The criteria for selecting the winner must also have been pre-established and the selection must be transparent. I have spent much time in choosing unambiguous and easily measured criteria which could be seen to be objective. It has been more difficult, but not impossible, to choose award conditions such that the chances of having a perennial loser have also been minimised.

A manager must also take into account the visibility of rewards, the substance of the reward and the motivating effect it has on some and the potential de-motivation in others. Should he use a large bunch of carrots visible to all or should he use just one incredibly sweet and almost invisible carrot? Any awards system will mark the winners, but it equally marks the losers. In a country like India where nepotism and favouritism is rather common, it is vital that the winning criteria be tamper-proof and that the selection of the winner is done transparently and objectively. It seems obvious to me now, but it was not so obvious when I was starting my career, that the introduction of any awards system must also necessarily have a plan for taking care of the losers; either for developing them or for eliminating them as low performers.

Variable pay for performance related measures have been used as a motivator probably for as long as the employment of one person by another has existed. Variable payments in kind, as quantities of grain, to serfs and farm peasants have been known to have been used as rewards for good harvests from the earliest known times, and probably existed even before coinage had been invented. In today's world bonuses are usually associated in the public mind with excessive and obscene payments in the financial world, but having an element of variable pay is widespread in all fields and is commonly used at all hierarchical levels in organisations. Piecework in factories, additional payments to translators for the number of extra words translated, payments to doctors for number of patients treated above some minimum, extra pay to a shop salesman for the number of articles sold, all sales commissions and royalties or quarterly or annual performance bonuses for a manager are all examples of variable, incentive payments tied to some performance parameter. Remarkably there is much folklore and anecdotal evidence but not much measured evidence regarding the efficacy of such bonuses. It is extremely difficult to isolate just the effect of the bonus on performance since, in most cases the surrounding circumstances have changed significantly over the bonus period.

Nevertheless, I am convinced that a good bonus system, tailored for an individual or a small team and connected to challenging performance improvements does operate at the level of the higher-level needs and can contribute to lifting performance from the routine to the spectacular. However, the operative words are "good" and "individual". I have found that the general bonuses applied across large groups of people in large organisations are often tied to company-wide performance parameters which cannot easily be linked to the individual's performance. These rewards become little more than an automatic payment and the bonus is just a part of the normal and expected salary. If an organisation goes through bad times with a deterioration of performance and a consequent reduction of the bonus, it is perceived as a salary cut, and since individual performance has little impact, the intended motivator ends up becoming a de-motivator. The incentive for doing any more than the minimum gets lost.

To make a bonus system practical, manageable and objective leads to the choice of simple-to-measure parameters but the consequence is that the parameters measured may no longer be relevant to a particular individual's performance. If the parameters chosen are too highly focused and specific it can lead to some people getting large bonuses even though the company as a whole may have suffered disastrous losses.

This in turn can lead to huge resentments between people within an organisation. The over-simplification of parameters together with a large potential bonus can lead to managers performing only to that parameter or to a manipulation of results. There are far too many cases of CEO's with bonuses connected to share price, who end up merely manipulating the stock price and losing sight of the business.

I take the example of salesmen in the infrastructure field selling power generation equipment. The front-end team was about 40 strong and situated in seven countries and covering the world market. Each sale was then a project sale worth many millions of euros and each salesman would typically sell between one and three projects annually. A single power plant project could even approach a total sales value of many hundred million euros and even approaching 1 billion euros. An individual salesman would probably have had support from 5 up to perhaps 20 people in such a sale. To have a bonus based just on the volume of the sale resulted in a concentration on the large "sexy" projects and smaller projects were ignored, and, on the other hand, a performance based on just the number of sales led to a focus on the smaller projects and the "quick" sales, leaving the larger projects unattended. Having only a profit margin as a parameter was also unsatisfactory since this led to the lower price countries being neglected, and this was unfair to salesmen responsible for those countries. Eventually we used all these parameters combined together with a predicted "profit margin to win" to evaluate the bonus for our salesmen, with great success. But while the same four parameters – volume, number, profit margin and expected profit margin – were used for all, the bonuses were tailored to suit each individual salesman and his area of responsibility for the business. A completely different team bonus system based on response times was used for the support teams to match the challenges that they faced in the "back office".

Handling team bonuses needs special care to avoid perceptions of unfairness since some measure of over-appreciation of some and under-appreciation of others is inevitable. A fundamental rule for me has been not to substitute effort as the parameter to be measured instead of result. Effort is visible and is less likely to cause feelings of inequity but is not very meaningful in evaluating a performance.

A bonus system, by itself, operates at the level of needs of the ego and therefore cannot compensate for deficiencies in the lower-order needs such as those due to a limited health care system or a poor working environment. It cannot either provide for the higher-level needs of self-actualisation. A bonus should only be used when it is part of a larger and more balanced rewards system. I believe a properly constructed rewards system containing both measurable, numerical targets with bonuses as well as soft, qualitative goals, can not only enhance people and performance but can be invaluable in the retention of the best talent. The challenge, the expectation and the opportunity to excel that can be on offer with a properly balanced reward system is particularly attractive especially for the top performers. Reward systems, I think, are less effective in recruitment because it is difficult for a newcomer to fully visualise the satisfactions involved.

Triggering self-actualisation or other higher order needs is remarkably effective provided the lower-order needs are reasonably satisfied.

Personally, I have found the challenge of something which had been judged by a peer or a superior as being "impossible to do", to be an irresistible challenge. I suspect that some of my superiors realised this very well when they put the bait in front of me and warned me that down-sizing in Japan or India would be extremely difficult. Or when a faceless but senior civil servant pontificated to me that challenging the State Bank of India in a court of law in India was futile.

I take another example from my sales team that I have mentioned earlier. We noticed a wide variation in the quality of contracts (terms and conditions) that were negotiated and finalised by our salesmen. I was well aware that "goodness of contracts" is a very nebulous thing. This was especially so in the infrastructure sector where contracts could run for long periods and the final judgment of the goodness of a contract could be made only 5 years or more after the point of sale. We introduced two actions simultaneously. First, we made it extremely bureaucratic and almost painful for a salesman to get approval for changes to terms and conditions after he had first declared and received approval for the conditions he thought necessary to win a contract. Second, we invented a "Goodness of Contract Index" which had no statistical significance whatever, but was very easily measured as deviations from our "standard" set of conditions. We challenged all the salesmen merely to improve on their own track record with no specific targets and no other rewards than those intrinsically available. We published the performance every month among the sales fraternity to create some peer pressure. The challenge became to show sound initial judgment and resulted in a quest for excellence in negotiation. Within 2 years our salesmen had honed their negotiation skills, had learned a great deal about contract risks and contract language and our contracts – as sold – had improved beyond recognition and not one penny of a bonus was involved.

Retaining the best talent and the top performers is one of the key challenges facing a manager. The most effective motivators are now those addressing the higher-level growth needs and the manager has to factor in the inevitable loss of such perfomers as they develop and move on to greater responsibilities. Paradoxically, the best motivators are the addition of responsibilities, new and intellectually challenging assignments and the training and mentoring of newcomers; all of which only hasten the time when he must move on. But that in itself is a natural progression that a manager can be justly proud of and his own motivator.

When performance penalties are applied they should preferably be in the form of a motivator which induces actions to eliminate whatever invited the penalty. The manager must always have a purpose with such penalties. It must be a corrective action and not a vindictive one. For example if the penalty is to be for getting into conflicts with others, then it could be in the form of compulsory counselling or even attending a course on people skills. If the penalty is to be for a lack of some particular competence then it should obviously be in the form of training or education to increase that competence. And there is nothing wrong in generating a little bit of embarrassment when the non-performer has to attend a class for beginners. If the failure lies in a lack of cooperation with others or a failure to share information within a team, the best penalty may be to send him on an awareness development or a leadership course. Provided that a positive motivator is also being used, then some monetary penalty can also be attached, usually as the denial of an expected award. But the monetary penalty must not be such that he cannot feed or clothe himself.

When Carrots Rot

I have seen some managers revel in the "divide and rule" concept. They seem to enjoy promoting conflict situations where they can be judge, jury and executioner. This is especially true when their own insecurities about their capabilities and competence are pronounced and they have a fear of a subordinate taking away their jobs or have a kind of paranoia which is also based on insecurity. A clear sign of insecurity and incompetence is also when a manager quotes rules and regulations or company policy as his only reason for requiring some particular action or for denying a request. I take the view that when someone, at any level in an organisation, quotes a rule but cannot explain why the rule is beneficial to the organisation then he does not add value and has no reason to be where he is. Any insecurity in a manager – which is a deficiency of a lower-order need – spreads quickly among subordinates and is debilitating. Some managers seem to believe that threats and fear are the only real motivators. In fact, some try to manage entirely on the basis of de-motivators rather than motivators. They may deliberately set out to increase a lower-order need as a way of penalising an individual. This could take the form of placing him in an isolated corner, taking away any meaningful work, not inviting him to staff functions or meetings, affording him no protection from abuse or criticism and generally ignoring him. But these people do not qualify for me even as managers, let alone as "good" managers. Penalties for performance related matters are not unacceptable but these differ in character to the punishments and penalties for unacceptable behaviour. But, even when these are justified, they must never stray into the area where a physiological or a safety need is increased. To my way of thinking that kind of behaviour leaves the area of management practice and enters into the realm of what is inhumane behaviour. For the perennial low performer the remedy – when improvement is not possible – is a direct and reasoned and open dismissal or relocation, but without ever sinking to the level of application of cruel and unusual punishments.

A bonus system alone based on narrow performance results can often be very damaging. When targets are too narrow the focus on that specific target dominates to the detriment of other soft goals. If the time period used is too short then long-term goals suffer. As we have seen earlier, if the rewards are or can be very high, then cheating and manipulation can be irresistible temptations. Unethical behaviour is promoted and company goals become the excuse. Normally unacceptable behaviour is rationalised on the grounds of some greater duty. Enron is a case in point. The narrow focus on increased revenues which were rewarded by huge bonuses, led to imaginative book-keeping and the inflation – by fair means and foul – of the revenue numbers. A bonus system inevitably distracts and detracts from the higher-order needs which are satisfied by intellectual challenge, the pursuit of excellence, altruism and learning.

A bonus system provided it is contained within a well balanced rewards system and constrained by penalties and punishments which define the underlying ethical framework of behaviour can be highly effective.

But beware the rotten carrots in a bad bonus system or a bonus system gone bad.

Chapter 9
No Confidence Without Integrity

*A manager's **integrity** is bound up with his identity and his values. It is what underpins all the actions he mobilises. Integrity comes in two parts; there is the inner sense of integrity which is personal to an individual, and there is his integrity as observed by an external party or by the surrounding society. Being consistent with his own set of values is what preserves his inner personal integrity, his sense of wholeness, his ethical code and even his identity. It is independent of what is observed. Being lawful in his actions and following the direction of the integrated ethical code determines the external judgment of his integrity. His inner integrity allows him to prioritise and discriminate between conflicting needs or commitments or different courses of action. His ethical code – when engaged – provides direction to his actions by defining what is correct and desirable to do.*

My Integrity or Yours

A lie is a construct of language.

If I dislike someone but knowingly state the opposite, is my integrity impugned by the false statement even if the purpose was to spare someone some pain? And would my integrity be compromised any less if I told the truth and caused unnecessary pain?

Whether integrity is entirely inherent within an individual and exists even if the individual is a solitary being, or whether it can have meaning as an inherent attribute of an individual only when existing within a society of fellow beings, is a distinction that can only ever be a matter of opinion and unlikely ever to be proven. If integrity is "always doing the right thing", then the judgment of the person defining right and wrong is brought into the definition. If integrity is honesty, sincerity, consistency with one's own moral and value judgments, consistency with some surrounding society's value judgments, compliance with an observer's moral values or some combination of all of these then, the individual and the perceptions of these virtues by an observer become integral to the definition.

> Samuel Johnson
> There can be no friendship without confidence and no confidence without integrity.

Attempts to define integrity very quickly enter into a metaphysical plane and are very difficult to articulate. It seems easier and more practical for me to first consider the consequences of a lack of integrity rather than trying to define what integrity is in some absolute way. If an observer felt I was lacking in some particular virtue then he would not trust or have confidence in my actions connected to that virtue. If he felt I was lacking in courage he would not trust my actions in a position of stress but he probably would not question my integrity. But I find it undeniable that if I am judged by anyone not to have integrity, then all of my actions and all of my behaviour become suspect. Clearly my integrity, in an observer's perception, is something holistic which includes within it all the virtues he wishes to ascribe to it. But my actions and behaviour are controlled by the virtues I have and the values that I ascribe to my own integrity. This suggests to me that one way of describing integrity is that it is always, and can only be, manifested in an individual's actions. It is independent of whether it is being observed or not, but it can only be perceived by an observer. If an individual acts to be perceived as having integrity, but his actions are not consistent with his own values, then it cannot be integrity. But if a person acts consistently with his own values but his acts are considered to be without integrity by society at large (say the actions of a criminal), then it is still not a case of integrity. It would seem therefore that for a person to have integrity, his actions must first be consistent with his own values but must also pass the test – in respect of some critical values – of being consistent with those of some larger surrounding society that he belongs to. These important critical values are those fundamental values which define what is "right" or "good" or "just". At the individual level these would be termed his moral or his ethical values. For a religion they would usually be termed moral values based on a concept of morality whereas other non-religious societies would use the term "ethics" rather than "morality".

It also seems self-evident to me that every individual does have some measure of integrity. At worst someone may be said to have no integrity, but there is no such thing as a negative integrity. So while the cup of integrity can never be less than empty, I am unsure as to whether it can ever be full; and then whether there is a cup at all. This is no closer to a definition but it allows me to distinguish between what an individual with integrity does and how an individual with integrity is perceived.

Honesty and truthfulness are usually considered as being essential to integrity. But this requires some further examination. Honesty and truth as statements are entirely dependent upon the existence of language. I distinguish here between truth as a physical fact which could be observed or verified by any observer, and truth as a statement using language. A lie is a construct of language. It is claimed that some animals also display types of behaviours which could be considered lying, but I find that this form of lying is always as deception connected to survival (either to escape a predator or to get food or to mate). Deception is behaviour designed to divert some other entity from its actual or perceived purpose by suggesting that some state, other than the actual state, exists. I therefore take deception to be something other than lying but which may include lies if language exists. Cases of chimpanzees and gorillas using rudimentary sign language to effectively "lie" are reported, but the lie is entirely contained within their rudimentary language, and only reinforces my belief that without language, deception may be present but a lie is undefined. As soon as language comes into play, variability is introduced at the point where language is used and at the point where that use of language is perceived. There can be no absoluteness about statements about honesty or truth if they are dependent upon how they are stated and how the statements are then perceived. The focus immediately shifts from the content of the statement to the purpose of the statement. This automatically raises the question whether it is the honesty – or perceived honesty – of a statement which is a matter of integrity, or whether it is the purpose of the statement, or whether it is both. I return to the case where I dislike someone but knowingly state the opposite. Is my integrity impugned by the false statement when my purpose was to spare someone some pain? And would my integrity have been compromised any less if I had told the truth and caused unnecessary pain? And should my action then look for the approval of an outside observer? In this case the outside world may not be much interested in or concerned about my statement and the problem is entirely created by my own values being in conflict. The dilemma is then only because I attach value to both telling the truth and to not causing pain, but the two cannot be satisfied at the same time.

The practical view of this situation is actually quite uncomplicated. I take it as self-evident that my integrity remains uncompromised as long as I remain consistent to my values even if the values may sometimes be in conflict with each other. That is a conflict that only I can resolve and only within myself. However I may choose to resolve it the resolution also represents my values. How my actions may be perceived by an observer however, is outside my control. The outside perception is irrelevant to my actions provided that my internal value system tells me that it is. On the other hand, if the particular situation was such that my own internal values acknowledged the relevance of the outside perception, then my actions would need to be consistent also with that outside view. To complete the loop, it is then also necessary that my internal values be consistent on critical ethical or moral matters – such as rightness or wrongness or fairness or goodness – with those of the society within which I function or wish to function. If on a critical moral issue my values are in conflict with those of the society in which I function, then the only choices open to me are:

1. To compromise my values and live with that, or
2. To maintain my values and accept any strictures placed on me by the surrounding society

In either case I could try to change society to resolve the conflict. If I maintain my values and do not wish to accept the penalties or strictures of society then my only option is to opt out or to instigate a revolution.

For a person to have integrity therefore, his actions must be consistent with his own values, where for the critical moral values his values are consistent with those of the larger society he functions in or wishes to function in. To be able to take this further in trying to describe integrity we need to be able to describe how an internal set of values would be connected to the moral or ethical values which must be shared with the larger society.

Values, Morals, Law and Ethics

Every person has some set of internal values or standards. These are the standards he applies to make comparisons which then form the basis of his behaviour and actions. All comparative adjectives such as beautiful or tasty or hot or clever or strong are judged against these standards. He may have as many or as few standards as he feels necessary to function. People with very few standards of their own are often labelled as being "shallow" while those with a broad range of standards can be perceived as being "deep" or having a rich character. But even if my values may say that one is better than the other, I cannot say whether "shallow" or "deep" is better for him. I observe merely that someone with few values of his own is unlikely to experience many value conflicts with surrounding society. The set of individual standards may include aesthetic standards of appreciation for food or art or literature or music. The standards could be based on his religious or political or intellectual beliefs. The individual values usually include a sub-set of critical standards of morality or ethics, which distinguish good from bad and separate right from wrong or justice from injustice. These standards then enable his application of comparatives to draw conclusions as to what may be for example, useful or sound or beautiful or just or right or good. Together these make up the set of values that is inherent to him and which he considers important. A person's individuality and his identity are closely intertwined with his set of values. To some extent the value set is his identity. Behaviour which deviates from his values can lead to self-doubt, guilt, shame, self-reproach and a certain loss of integrity and identity.

A set of values should not be confused with laws or rules and regulations. Laws and rules specify the limits of acceptable behaviour. They usually do this by defining behaviour which is unacceptable and specify penalties and punishments for non-compliance. What is acceptable or compliant behaviour then, by exclusion, becomes all behaviour that is not unacceptable. Values, on the other hand, can be better described as standard methodologies or standard principles for making comparisons and leading to behaviour. Values cause behaviour whereas laws define the limits where behaviour becomes unacceptable such that society may levy a penalty. There are areas of human behaviour which are not covered by laws and therefore where all behaviour is – in consequence of not being unlawful – lawful.

Values can cover every aspect of human behaviour and this gives a very wide range of potential values. Certain values are then common to groupings of people whether in a family or different kinds of communities or societies or countries. A commonality in a set of values can then be said to be the culture of the relevant group. The values considered most important in a shared set of values – the moral or ethical values of that society – do not allow of deviation by group members and can even define membership of the society, especially in political and religious societies. This applies even if the behaviour in question is not unlawful. Critical deviations can lead to penalties such as public ridicule, expulsions, excommunications, inquisitions, witch-hunts, fatwas, honour-killings and even executions. In other societies, membership is conferred by birth (including the groupings of race, family, parents, ancestors or nationality) and cannot be disallowed but deviations of an individual's value set from the most important values of the group can lead to penalties and sanctions and the status of an "outcast". The most important values in all societies are usually those connected with morality and judgments of "right" and "wrong". Generally however, members of a society are permitted to have individual values which deviate from the shared set if the particular value is not considered a critical moral value. Equally if a value is not included within a particular shared set, the society is indifferent to an individual having such a value. The moral values — fundamental questions of "right" and "wrong" — are quite similar in most countries. There is no country or society which does not have the fundamental moral or ethical value that doing harm to other members of the same society is "wrong". Variations enter by way of the differences in the exceptions by which harm to others may be permitted (self-defence or during war or in support of a righteous cause, or to those who are not members of the same society for example). However there is considerable variation in the other less critical values and it is this variation in the value sets which contributes most to the variation of cultures.

Moral values are a subset of the total set of values possible and concepts of morality govern what are considered moral values. All definitions of morality consider it to be a code of conduct but whether it is a code specified by the individual or put forward by a society (such as a religion) or an absolute code applicable to humans universally is a matter of great debate. Some believe that a moral code can only be derived from a religion and others assert that it is independent of any religious concepts. Nevertheless, all moral codes are made up of moral values and these are those values considered, by the individual or by a society or universally, as being the most important in distinguishing between "right" and "wrong". We can also observe that concepts of "right" and "wrong" are all fundamentally based on harm to others being classified as "wrong" and, in consequence, not causing harm will always be "right". It should be noted though, that "not causing harm" is not equivalent to doing "good". The distinction between "good" and "bad" is a separate moral value which along with "just" and "unjust" are most commonly the important moral values. The content of these values, that is what constitutes "right" or "good" or "just", varies from one society to the next and one individual to another.

While his internal values govern an individual's behaviour, his morality only judges whether the behaviour is right or wrong. Laws may have moral concepts involved but they only define the limits of acceptable behaviour. Though illegal behaviour can be penalised, laws do not govern behaviour directly, except inasmuch as the penalties are a coercive force against illegal behaviour. Neither his internal set of values which tell him what to do, or his moral values which tell him what he ought or ought not to do, or law which tells him what he may not do address the question of what is correct to do. What is correct for him to do is the realm of his ethics. For a society, ethics represent both correct and desirable behaviour.

An ethical system can exist at the level of the individual or can apply to any group or community or society. For a society of individuals it represents not only what is correct behaviour but also the desirable behaviour of its members.

The Hippocratic Oath was one such ethical system. Many professions and societies (lawyers, doctors, engineers and nurses for example) have formulated ethical codes as applying to their members. Religious organisations tend to see morality and ethics as being synonymous and usually refer to their moral code as being their code of ethics. For most religions, moral behaviour is the same as ethical behaviour and represents correct behaviour which is always desirable behaviour. The whole field of all possible human behaviour is neatly divided into only two – moral and immoral. Professional organisations, on the other hand, may have ethical codes for their members to follow, but then rarely infringe into the area of morality. For example the medical profession would not trespass into moral judgments of their members but may have much to say about the ethical standards of a member. An enterprise may develop a code of ethics for its employees, but would not presume to infringe into the moral space. Many organisations have so-called ethical codes which are no more than rules and regulations and do not really address the correctness of behaviour. Others take compliance with laws or compliance with rules to be a code of ethics. Most ethical codes will generally be compliant with law.

This view provides me with a way of looking at behaviour which allows me to avoid getting entangled in the complex philosophical aspects while still affording a practical way to apply these complex concepts.

1. An individual's internal value system leads to all his actual behaviour.
2. Lawful behaviour represents the limits of behaviour which is acceptable to society at large by defining what is not lawful. Individual behaviour may or may not be lawful but behaviour deemed unlawful is subject to the penalties of law. A code of law is often based on moral precepts but lawful behaviour is not always moral behaviour. Much individual behaviour is not addressed by law and is therefore lawful.
3. Moral values are those related to differentiating between "right" and "wrong", "good" and "bad", and "just" and "unjust". The most important moral values of the individual are usually consistent with those of the society he functions in. Moral behaviour is usually lawful but is not always so. Behaviour which does not raise or impact the fundamental moral questions is, by default, usually taken to be moral.
4. Ethical behaviour is that which the individual considers as correct in the prevailing circumstances and which his moral values do not disqualify as being "wrong" or "bad" or "unjust". For a society, the ethical behaviour of its members is both correct and desirable behaviour. For the individual, ethical behaviour will always be related to the same or a larger set of values than those he considers moral values. By this definition then, an individual's behaviour, if ethical, will also be moral but may or may not be lawful behaviour. But ethical behaviour always requires a positive choice to be made. Behaviour which is not unethical does not, by default, become ethical behaviour.

While the range of all possible human behaviour is generated by the individual's values, it is subject to:

- Law, which defines what a person may not do
- Morals, which define what a person ought not to do whether or not it is lawful
- Ethics, which describe what, is correct and desirable for a person to do; which will always be moral and will usually be lawful

With this framework we can consider an individual's ethics and integrity of behaviour in the workplace. However we should first establish if a business or other organisation within which an individual functions, can or should have a code of ethics and how such a code may relate to the larger surrounding environment and the rule of law.

Business Ethics on the Grand Scale

We have become almost immune to seeing new headlines every other day about political and corporate scandals regarding corruption, fraud, pollution, child labour, discrimination and the like.

- "Arthur Andersen guilty in Enron case"
- "Record US fine ends Siemens bribery scandal"
- "Investigators search Defense Ministry in Japanese bribery scandal"
- "Bosses jailed in South Korean bribery scandal"
- "Daiwa Bank Bosses Pay $775m Fraud Charge"
- "Corruption scandal looms over ABB"
- "Alstom Raided in Swiss Probe Into Contract Bribery"
- "Boeing, the Pentagon and the tanker scandal that won't go away"
- "Campaigners' fury at £286m deal to end corruption probe after BAE Systems admits using cash to win contracts"
- "Pfizer Drugs-Hit with Billion Dollar Fines"
- "India's Madoff? Satyam Scandal Rocks Outsourcing Industry"
- "Shell in U.S. Gov. Sex, Drugs and Corruption Scandal"

Many people are no doubt involved, but the overwhelming majority of business activities and the overwhelming majority of people are not involved in these scandals. However, even though they represent a relatively small percentage of all the business that humans transact, the scale and volume of all that is done on the grand scale, albeit by a relatively few people, does trickle down the chain and does impact everyday life and behaviour.

The headlines in the newspapers refer only to the few cases which are in the public eye and where a prosecution is taking place or being attempted. Small corporations rarely make the headlines and all the instances where illegality or non-compliance cannot be proven are taken to be perfectly acceptable and continue unchecked. The true volume of cases exhibiting a lack of ethical standards, like some mammoth unseen iceberg, is probably some orders of magnitude larger than what is visible. But the headlines do not give a full picture of the little that does get disclosed.

Two aspects are usually missing. One is that people can exhibit a total lack of ethics and integrity with respect to some particular behaviour or when dealing with certain people while upholding the highest standards in other behaviour or with different people. One kind of behaviour may prevail within the family or within a closed society and a quite different standard may apply to those outside.

The other aspect that is usually missing is that behind every such "scandal" is usually an attempt by a political party or politicians to raise party funds. It is often the competition between political parties to win elections that creates a pressure to collect funds which, in turn, may provide a decisive competitive edge in getting the most votes. The fund collectors are usually the politicians themselves, lobbyists, bureaucrats, political agents, consultants and middlemen. Since corporations and "high net-worth individuals" are seen as the primary source of such funds, then the provision of such funds leads to corporations demanding a quid pro quo in the form of contracts or some other form of benefit which is in the grant of the political establishment. Bridges to nowhere get built, taxes are waived, zoning regulations suddenly change, infrastructure projects for power or transport or roads cost more than originally planned, trading scams are developed and there is always an upcoming election and a political party initiating the process.

There are probably many politicians who do have admirable intentions and who do not get involved with the murkier side of political funding. There are many more that feel trapped in and cannot avoid perpetuating the existing system. But politicians whether in the US or Europe or in Asia do sell "access" into the world of lawmaking, regulations and approvals. At one time laws – as with the Ten Commandments – were primarily concerned with establishing limits of behaviour. Lawmaking today is concerned a great deal with channelling the flow of tax or other revenues.

Ministers in India have their performance ranked according to how much they raise for the party coffers. When I was first appointed to lead the Alstom Group in India in early 2000, I made a courtesy call on the then Minister of Power in the BJP (Bharatiya Janata Party) Government, Rangarajan Kumaramangalam. We found we had a number of common friends and even that my father had once served in the Indian Army under his uncle General K. Kumaramangalam. We met socially on a number of occasions until his untimely death of blood cancer in August 2000 (and some people still suspect something untoward in his sudden illness and death). Ranga's roots were in the student wing of the Indian Congress Party and he had even served as a Minister in the Congress Government of the early 1990s. However he had become disillusioned with the pace of reform and had resigned to join the BJP in 1997. Though he had demonstrated great energy and skill in implementing reforms and in getting difficult bills passed through Parliament, there were many factions within the BJP which considered him merely an opportunist, resented his presence in the party and were highly suspicious of his very high profile and his popularity. Through many conversations Ranga tried to explain to me the realities of political life in India which required him continuously to "prove" his value to the party to remain in the position he had. "Within the party," he would explain "it is not what I may achieve for the country or in parliament that matters; it is only what funds I can bring to the party that count. The skill in politics lies in achieving other things while meeting the funding expectations of the party". Ranga was highly intelligent, cultivated, energetic and immensely likable. He would surely have contributed a great deal more to the process of reforms in India if not for his untimely death. He represented a new dynamism in Indian politics but it is not for nothing that he was known within the power generation industry as "Mr. Five Percent".

After Ranga's death the Ministry was handed over by the BJP to one of its coalition partners, the Shiv Sena party. Though the new Minister, Suresh Prabhu was also popular and had a reputation for getting things done, the period with the Shiv Sena in charge was not very productive. Stagnation occurred probably because of internecine disputes not only between the two political parties but also between the Minister and his party leader as to the choice of contractors to be favoured and the sharing of the "contributions" from the contracts awarded. Some contracts for large power plants were awarded during this period but were accompanied by scandals concerning bribery. I suspect that this got into the open only because one of the parties felt hard done by!!

It is almost a required tradition for Japanese politicians to approve bridges and highways in their constituencies that nobody needs, except the party, the civil contractors, their employees and their shareholders. Contractors of course show their appreciation in the usual way. In the last 20 years Japan has built up the largest public debt in the developed world which is now in excess of $10 trillion.

Parliamentarians across the world offer their services to raise questions in parliament or in parliamentary committees. Heads of Government can be heavily involved and Jacques Chirac and Helmut Kohl are only examples. UK Parliamentarians pad their expenses regularly and Ministers sell their services and their parliamentary questions. There is a venal attitude exhibited unashamedly by many Members of the European Parliament. Brussels may once have been a centre of commerce and for the production of lace but today is probably the centre for all EU subsidy scams. The skimming off of funds, misuse of subsidies and dubious regulatory schemes such as for farming subsidies and Carbon Trading are legendary in the European Union. All over the world many politicians propose the "pork belly" projects in their own constituencies, sometimes with little competition, to add to appropriations legislation. Just in the US alone there has been between US$13 and 27 billion of appropriations for "pork" projects for each year between 2005 and 2009. Assuming that these projects just followed the OECD 3% guidelines on corruption, but made use of all the loopholes available, the contract awards could have legitimised between US$400 million and US$800 million every year which could have – and probably has – ended up in the funds of political parties and their lobbyists. A large number of the people involved in these channels have rather "sticky fingers" which allows the amassing of individual wealth as it flows.

Large private infrastructure projects are not immune either. When project financing is involved for the construction of power plants or bridges or highways, the developer's equity can often flow as part of the main contract. Effectively the politically approved tariff for power or the toll to be charged is set higher than it needs to be for the developer to "create something from nothing" both for himself and the friendly politician.

I observe that it is nearly always elections and the seeking of positions of power which follow elections, which create the financial demands, which in turn then result in corporations seeing and taking available opportunities to gain a competitive advantage. In my experience, which is limited to contracting in the power generation industry, the reverse sequence, where corporations initiate the whole process while seeking competitive advantage and offer payoffs to politicians or contributions to their party funds, is not unknown but probably not as prevalent. The combination of an unscrupulous businessman together with an avaricious politician is difficult to detect and almost impossible to avoid. This phenomenon is not limited by geography or country or culture. Culture only seems to affect the methods and channels used. There are probably many politicians who are genuinely trying to serve society but there are very few who have not abdicated their personal codes of ethics in regard to political funding.

Nevertheless, large corporations are usually willing parties to the bribery or corruption or fraud and are far from being blameless. Where actions are illegal, and they get found out and sufficient evidence which will stand up in court is available, then a few managers get prosecuted as officers of the corporation and the corporations get fined. Corporations are very quick to term such managers as "rogue" managers and wash their hands off them, but only when they get found out. It is merely a convenient pretence that the rogue managers had operated in some isolated bubble. On very rare occasions a politician or two may get slapped on the wrist. Shareholders, though they are owners of the corporation, may suffer some minor inconvenience when the stock price drops somewhat, but they escape all moral or ethical or legal strictures for the actions of their corporations. In a few cases some shareholders and pension funds may lose a great deal and complain bitterly about the frauds perpetrated but they rarely shoulder any responsibility as part-owners of the offending corporation.

Over the years I have also been party to paying commissions to agents and paying consultants for various "services". The two dozen or so such cases I have been involved in have all been of the relatively simple kind where we have been bidding against competitors for the supply of some equipment to a customer in the public sector. When contract volumes have been sufficiently large they have attracted the attention of politicians and the consultants and lobbyists who are their symbiotic parasites. Usually a politician or some senior bureaucrat has then indicated the level of contribution needed – everything else being equal against the competitors – to win the award. The favoured consultant or lobbyist or building sub-contractor has generally also been identified to us and he becomes the contracting party for a consulting agreement or an agency agreement or a subcontract. The cases I have been involved with have all been, at least superficially, "fully compliant" with prevailing laws and regulations but have not always conformed to what I would consider my own ethical standards. I have generally been aware in such cases that the services contracted for in consultancy agreements have been largely fabricated. The documentation to "prove" the delivery of non-existent services is not hard to create. Over-invoicing by a sub-contractor of the amount of concrete and steel actually used for the foundations of a building is not easily discernible once the building is complete. Invoices from IT sub-contractors for "software development" are not easy to penetrate. When the construction site is remote in Africa or Asia a building contractor may invoice for the construction of temporary (but imaginary) roads and bridges which are inevitably "washed away without trace" when the next rains arrive. It is not something I am terribly proud of and I have compromised my own standards, which is something I will just have to live with. I draw whatever comfort I can from the fact that I have never initiated such discussions, have never gone looking for where I could use undue influence and have always kept within the OECD guidelines for commissions or consultants' fees not exceeding 3% of a contract value (as if being lower than this magic number of 3% absolves one of any lack of ethics).

Sometimes the undue influence is obtained not by making payments but by waiving debt or some other valid contractual dues from other corporations. The writing off of loans as bad debts by banks to certain favoured clients happens all over the world. Apparent losses due to bad business decisions are sometimes used to camouflage such flow of funds. It is strange that improper and even fraudulent payments – or waiving of debt – to a corporation rather than to an individual, which are well documented in all details except as to the true purpose, can escape their proper label of bribery and are accounted for as business losses.

In one case while at Siemens, I declined to waive cancellation charges – of many millions – due from a major US utility for a very clear contractual breach but I was overruled by our US management and this debt was waived anyway for the sake of winning some other order. It was not strictly illegal but it was an attempt to exert undue influence and was not wholly ethical either.

The rationalisation – which I know is rationalisation – is that if I had not participated in these cases, I would probably have lost some orders, would not have stopped the project from being awarded to a competitor, would have made no impression on the system whatsoever, would have jeopardised my own targets and would have made life more difficult for our own employees. It has never been my ambition or intent to be a crusader or a martyr and I have no regrets for not trying to change the world on this grand scale. If I was in the same position today I would probably do the same all over again. My biggest regrets are that such systems are still so pervasive and that I was not clever enough to figure out a way of defeating the system and not compromising my values.

I have declined to participate in many more cases than the cases where I have made commitments and where commissions or fees were actually paid, but the truth is that my non-participation has usually been on economic or practical grounds and only sometimes on ethical principles.

I have stepped aside in Taiwan and Indonesia and declined to bid. This allowed the potential orders to go to Japanese competitors, but I declined only because the politicians were demanding too much – over 5% of contracts worth several hundred million dollars. I have declined the offer of a senior Indonesian bureaucrat to "help in getting a project included in the National Plan", not because of any ethical consideration but because I didn't think he had the competence to do it. I have declined to offer personal kick-backs to the executives of Chinese and Israeli corporations and have lost the orders – in both cases, but at very different times – to US competitors. I have declined to offer for some projects in India in the States of Uttar Pradesh and Chhattisgarh where the Chief Ministers and their fund collectors – who happened to be the Chairmen of the State Electricity Boards – demanded respectively, 10% and 7% of the contract value as their cut. I was well aware that the Chairmen had made commitments to party funds for getting their jobs and that they were required – and expected – to fulfil their obligations by means of the contracts awarded during their tenures. Most of the CMDs (Chairman and Managing Directors) of Indian nationalised concerns are political appointees. They only get their appointments confirmed when they have made their political commitments to the ruling party in the State concerned or to the ruling party in the Central Government and sometimes to both. Some part of their political dues has to be paid up-front, and the rest has to be fulfilled through the contracts they award during their tenures. It becomes effectively a "contract award tax" which no supplier can avoid and which is to the benefit of the ruling party.

While the anti-corruption legislation and guidelines introduced around the world have certainly reduced the political demands from the 7 to 10% of contract value that used to be demanded in the 1970s to the more typical 2–4% today, the legislation and guidelines have actually served to legitimise the demands at this level. The legislation seems to be intentionally designed to include sufficient loopholes such that political funding is not impaired. The political will to really introduce an ethical code for politicians to live by does not exist – it does not exist in the US or in Europe and certainly not in Asia or Africa or the Middle-East.

I have even been given a lecture by the Private Secretary of an Energy Minister in Europe explaining the flexibility available in the OECD anti-corruption guidelines and how they could be utilised in favour of the political party concerned, such that all the paperwork would be fully compliant and no money-laundering regulations would be broken.

Corruption is equated only with non-compliance and by default, compliance – even while exploiting the loopholes available – is deemed sufficient to prove that there is no corruption. Ethics has degenerated to meaning compliance. As if you could not be fully compliant and totally corrupt.

The absence of ethics in the political world sets the tone for all institutions and corporations. There is a pervasive atmosphere within the business world today taking the view that ethics is not a matter for corporations. Milton Friedman, Peter Drucker and others must bear their share of the responsibility for having propagated the view that corporations should only be concerned with the profit they deliver to shareholders. They have – maybe inadvertently – supported the view that humans in a corporate setting can and should abdicate their own ethical codes. The *Wall Street Journal* has declared from on high that ethics cannot be learned and ethics courses are irrelevant to business. Utter rubbish of course, but even the "newspapers of record" such as the *New York Times* or *The Times* or *Der Spiegel* or the *Wall Street Journal* have lost their famed objectivity and have become political advocacy channels. It is such high-profile and basically amoral views which have been greatly responsible for providing a cloak of respectability for the attitude that:

1. Corporations have no business to concern themselves with ethics.
2. Even if ethics is important then compliance with law is a sufficient substitute for having a code of ethics.
3. If an action is seen to be compliant with laws then this is sufficient.

It appears to me that this attitude has been a retrograde step over the last 40 years and especially since the 1970s, which is only now – after the global financial meltdown of 2008 – beginning to be redressed. Large corporations, ably assisted by the Big Four auditing firms, have fine-tuned the processes and documentation needed to show compliance.

After Siemens experienced their scandals in 2007, anti-corruption training courses were held compulsorily throughout the company – mainly, I think, to assist in the negotiations with the SEC and to minimise the extent of the inevitable fine. The training courses were conducted by staff from KPMG and I was disappointed, but not surprised, that the trainers either did not have the intellectual capacity to see – or perhaps did not want to see – the distinction between corruption and non-compliance. The ethics content of the so-called training was non-existent and as anti-corruption training the courses were meaningless. They probably did have some value in defining the paperwork needed to show compliance in the event of an audit, and the fact that the courses were held probably helped in the negotiations with the SEC. But the entire exercise and even the accusations against retired Siemens executives by the company itself was entirely for damage control and image management purposes and had little to do with ethics. When scandal erupted in the media and Alstom turned on its former Chairman, Pierre Bilger and when Siemens turned on Heinrich von Pirer, it was damage control and investors and stock price that was at stake – not ethics.

There is still reluctance among businesses to address the fundamental cause – which is their own codes of ethics that they live by. While the absence of ethics at the political level may be responsible for putting temptation in their path, there is no excuse for corporations to abdicate and satisfy themselves with the appearance of compliance. By taking the position that unacceptable behaviour is only that which is non-compliant they have, of course, also defined everything else that can be done as being acceptable. But it does not stop with just the officers of the corporation. It extends to ownership. Normally an owner is expected to take some responsibility for his property. An owner cannot abdicate his responsibility for the consequences of, say, his vicious pit bull terrier which is out of control or even for an unsafe sidewalk on his property's frontage. But yet, no shareholder is really willing or able or required to take his share of the responsibility for the ethical conduct of a corporation he partially owns. And this is so even though the shareholder, as an individual, may well have an admirable code of ethics of his own. It is a lazy attitude to claim that the multiplicity of shareholders or the transient nature of their holding makes it impossible for this responsibility to be taken.

Perhaps someday politicians and corporations will give value to being clean and not only in seeming to be clean. Ethics develops in children initially by being told by parents what is right and what is wrong. As it matures the child accepts the views of some larger society to define right from wrong. In time, the child grows up, and with education and thought and maturity an individual develops his own concepts of right and wrong and integrates these with those of the surrounding society. Politicians and corporations are still content, it seems, to be told – by law – what is wrong. They take the simplistic, child-like and easy view that everything else is legal and therefore right. When forced to, usually only by disclosure, they accept the ethical codes, albeit temporarily, of the surrounding society. But most have yet to develop their own codes and to develop their own positions differentiating between what is merely compliant and what is right. As an association of people, corporations already lag far behind the majority of their own employees in the development of their ethical concepts. It seems that they provide a melting pot where the codes of ethics of members are taken down to their lowest common level. They need to and will eventually grow up, but this will probably need a step change in the evolution of corporations and will not happen anytime soon. Till then corporations will continue to seize whatever opportunities are presented by the needs of the politicians and they will not take the risk of allowing any codes of ethics of their own to deny such needs or to pass up such opportunities.

Ethics in the Workplace

But most managers will not need to concern themselves about the grand questions of the ethics of high politics and big business and corporate funding of political parties.

> Albert Einstein
> Relativity applies to physics, not ethics

They will be concerned with the more mundane questions of ethics which continuously crop up in their everyday behaviour. Even though a vacuum of ethical values may characterise the corporate position, managers will need to apply their own code of ethics together with that of the larger society outside the corporation to a multitude of actions and behaviour. A manager, to be true to his own values, cannot merely fall back on some action being lawful to justify it. He needs to take a position on the correctness and rightness and fairness of his actions and behaviour. He cannot victimise some of his subordinates or make favourites of others even if his actions are all perfectly lawful. He cannot mobilise those actions, that may well be lawful and which his organisation may have no ethical opinion about, if they lead to a result he himself judges to be unjust or wrong. That he has a code of ethics which allows him and enables him to take a position is vital. Even if his own code is rudimentary and not very well developed then, by default, it is the code of ethics of the larger society surrounding the corporation which must come into play.

Ethical considerations can arise often in everyday matters of human relations and in interpersonal interaction. To play on people's fears as a form of motivation would be unethical for most people, but a manager must have his own values on the basis of which he can set his own limits of what is correct and what is not. A universal base-line for ethical codes is the concept of not causing harm to someone. His values will determine what he considers to be harmful and whether he makes exceptions to his own rules. Varying definitions of causing harm can lead to uncertainty and even conflicts with both subordinates and with superiors. Is causing discomfort the same as causing harm? Is causing embarrassment the same as causing harm? The critical point is that the manager should take a position on this and any other ethical issues arising. If necessary he will need to persuade others to his point of view or he must compromise his own. To deceive or betray someone's trust as a means of mobilising actions would always cross a line and becomes manipulation, but he needs to decide where to draw his own line. Providing negative feedback about someone's performance is a basic requirement for a manager but the manner in which he does it is his choice. Whether it should always be in private or whether sarcasm is allowed and what level of penalty can be proposed, are all matters that every individual manager must take a position on. Ethical considerations can, and should, be involved to define his own "right and correct" way to do this. Privacy and confidentiality issues often crop up and have ethical implications. How far can a manager go in spying on employees and their e-mails and their conversations? Can it be acceptable to buy information about a competitor from a consultant? And is it any different if information is bought from an employee of the competitor? Is it ethical to accept information or documents which have been stolen? Maintaining confidentiality about corporate plans about downsizing for example, can come into conflict with norms of fairness or justice. Labour relations and dealings with trades union can be complicated by the injection of political ideology. It can become difficult to maintain personal ethical standards when they come into conflict with a political objective, for example in a confrontation with a union during a strike or when using non-union labour to defeat a strike. In a heated labour dispute it is easy to put ethical codes to one side and it can provide a real test for a manager in maintaining his own values. In an atmosphere of external pressure, to pressurise subordinates to the point of their breaking stress could be in conflict with ethical values of not causing harm. It is not at all uncommon that a superior's view of correct behaviour may not coincide with the manager's views. Such divergence must be addressed and it is not necessary to treat every such divergence as a resigning issue. In most matters it is perfectly permissible to agree to disagree but the critical point is that the disagreement be visible and acknowledged. I have generally found that to suggest an alternative way of reaching the same objective, and one which satisfies any ethical concern I may have, is more likely to be listened to and then adopted than merely to reject some action required by a superior. I have also taken the approach with one particular superior that I could not follow his instruction because I felt it was wrong, and that if he wanted it performed in that manner I would prefer he ask someone else. Fortunately he was open enough that we could still maintain a working relationship and I did not have to resign. But the subjects and limits of compromise, and at what level confrontation is required and should be resorted to, are intensely personal to the manager. But the simple rule I would advise for any manager to apply is the age old "do unto others as you would have them do unto you".

Ethical issues arise across all functions in an enterprise. From purchasing procedures to customer service to methods of accounting to marketing and advertising practices the drive for the good of the organisation can lead to conflicts with personal standards. Purchasing managers will always have pressure from vendors which may require an ethical position to be taken. For example, it may not always be fair to one vendor that his price or other terms and conditions are disclosed to his competitor. If competing vendors make the same promises (for example in guarantees being offered), how can you ethically take into account the fact that you believe one of them but not another? Similarly, a Service manager will face ethical issues with customers and the corporate behaviour in dealing with them. He may need to take his own position when making excuses which are not wholly truthful or when charging for repairs which should properly be the responsibility of the seller. An Advertising manager must be able to distinguish when promotional statements have crossed the line to become deceit. He may need to decide when negative or misleading advertising exaggerating a competitor's faults is no longer ethical.

Marketing potentially dangerous products (such as drugs or weapons or addictive materials) to vulnerable sections of society raise obvious ethical issues in areas where the law may not extend. Dumping dangerous waste products in an African country which has no environmental protection laws or Union Carbide manufacturing dangerous chemicals in Bhopal may never have happened if there had been space for the ethical standards of individuals to have been engaged. Questions of fairness arise with medical tourism to countries where costs are low but where the resources used are then not available to the less affluent people in that country. Indian hospitals established for medical tourists perform the most advanced surgery and organ transplants but have increased the growth of an illegal organ trade exploiting the poor or those enmeshed in debt. Japanese health insurance companies run excellent hospitals in the Philippines, but the local employees at such hospitals may have to get their health care elsewhere. Should a franchise owner or a licensor be held responsible for the working practices used by a franchisee or a licensee? Certain kinds of international cartels are allowed by law but could well be unethical. OPEC and the International Diamond Cartel are examples. Others are disallowed by laws but raise no ethical issues. Others are unofficial and a natural consequence of strategies within a free competition. I find it quite unremarkable, for example, that pizzerias all across Sweden have the same price for their products but doubt that any formal price-fixing has taken place or that any profound ethical issues are involved.

The wasteful use of non-renewable resources or environmentally unsound practices in manufacturing may not be regulated by law but deserve the exercise of mind and application of values to determine the correct thing to do. Intellectual property concepts and definitions of what constitutes intellectual piracy can be extremely contentious, and here too the manager should be ready and willing to apply his values and ethical code to determine the right and correct behaviour. Manufacturing generic drugs without paying licence fees may be unethical but it can be equally unethical for environmental activists and other "do-gooders" to resort to alarmism and pseudo-science and subsidy misuse. Recourse to alarmism and scare-tactics whether about global warming to develop the carbon trading market or about coming influenza pandemics to sell unnecessary vaccinations and drugs have a clear ethical dimension.

While the grand scale of corruption appears everywhere, it is the less developed countries which exhibit the more mundane, unspectacular and everyday occurrences of petty bribes and payments of so-called facilitation fees. The amounts involved can range from small change to a government official to jump a queue and up to large amounts extorted by tax officials to look the other way. Generally all such actions are illegal but many are ingrained in the "system" and may form an integral part of the remuneration of relatively poorly paid jobs. However, they still pose ethical questions for a manager which he must take his own position on.

I have never had any time for tax officials making fabricated demands of excise duty through extortion, but I have sometimes paid a "facilitation-fee" to sea-port customs officials to expedite the clearance of a consignment. I have had no qualms in paying a small fee to the clerk in the visa office to speed up my visa renewal but have refused to succumb to a bureaucrat who wanted to sell access to his Minister.

A manager must draw his own lines to govern his own behaviour.

The financial world has been particularly aggressive in promoting the notion that ethics has no place in business, and only the limits set by law have been acknowledged and accepted as constraints on behaviour. Since law is often reactive this has allowed the creation of strange and wonderful financial and trading products in areas where the law has been silent and lawmakers have not yet written any laws. In such areas, where there is also an absence of any guidance from any ethical code, financial bubbles and dubious practices have grown unfettered by any constraints. Stock exchange bubbles, real estate bubbles, currency speculation, speculation in metals and grains, the mortgage bubbles and the sub-prime mortgage bubble have all been concerned with redistributing an inflated value of the existing pool of wealth but not often in creating any new wealth. It was concepts of the creation of wealth together with the industrial revolution which helped establish modern economics in the nineteenth century. But, in recent times the governing theme has been the accumulation by redistribution of existing riches without necessarily any corresponding increase of total wealth (whether by increased trade or increased production or increased services). The bubbles have all burst and while some fortunes have been made, others have been lost and much pain and suffering and collateral damage has been evident. The backlash to the financial excesses seems to be now leading to the acceptance of the necessity of having some codes of conduct. Together with increased self-regulation and some legal regulation, unofficial codes of conduct resemble the beginnings of an ethical code. There seems to be a drift back to the idea that financial and economic activity are fundamentally social activities and cannot be divorced from or immune to the values and ethics of the surrounding society.

In the absence of any ethical code of his employer a manager must fall back on to his own code, and where necessary, integrate it with that of the society surrounding his organisation. If a company's primary purpose is considered to be solely to deliver profit and shareholder value to its shareholders, then a manager needs to not only follow all legal constraints but also to use his own code of ethics to establish his own view of the correct and desired behaviour to achieve such a purpose.

The narrow definition of a company's purpose as being restricted to just making profit is evolving and it is now becoming more acceptable to talk about stakeholders rather than just shareholders. Stakeholders include not only shareholders and employees but also customers, suppliers and the society surrounding a company's establishments.

> WE Henley, 1849–1903, from *Invictus*
> It matters not how strait the gait, how charged with punishments the scroll, I am the master of my fate: I am the captain of my soul.

The concept of a corporate social responsibility is gaining acceptance – even if primarily as a public relations exercise – and seems to be a sign of corporate growing-up. There is much discussion and development of arguments which try to show the benefits to a corporation of having a code of ethics. But I find this a little unnecessary. The fundamental reason for behaviour to be ethical is not I think, because of some collateral benefit it may bring but simply because it is the right and proper thing to do. The ethically right and correct thing to do is sufficient in itself and does not need excuses or justification. In spite of the Wall Street Journal's opinion, ethics can indeed be taught, should be taught and can be developed. Teaching by example, with a superior as a role-model for a subordinate, is perhaps the most powerful way of developing ethics. But an individual still needs to make the shift from following what his parents told him, or what his superior told him, to making the code of ethics his own. What is yet to be brought into the picture is how an individual's code of ethics may be integrated with that of his employer and how that is influenced by the values of the owners.

Managing with Integrity

We can now return to a manager's integrity of behaviour in the workplace. To maintain his integrity he must then ensure that his behaviour and actions:

1. Whether voluntary or imposed, are consistent with his own set of values
2. Are never unlawful
3. Are consistent with the right and correct behaviour indicated by the code of ethics resulting from integrating his own with that of the surrounding society he operates in

I take the following as being axiomatic:

1. Ethical values are a sub-set of an individual's or a society's values and represent the most important values about rightness, goodness and justice.
2. All ethical codes include the fundamental requirement of not causing harm.

Where the organisation or corporation he operates in, does not have an ethical code, it becomes the manager's responsibility to bring in his own ethical code or that of the society surrounding the corporation.

Integrity comes in two parts; there is the inner sense of integrity which is personal to an individual, and there is his integrity as observed by an external party or by the surrounding society. Being consistent with his own set of values is what preserves his inner personal integrity, his sense of wholeness and even his identity. It is independent of what is observed. Being lawful in his actions and following the direction of the integrated ethical code determines the external judgment of his integrity. Honesty and truth and sincerity then fall into place. They are not to be measured on some absolute scales, but are to be measured and compared in the light of the desired and correct behaviour (given by ethics) or forbidden behaviour (defined by law). There is no longer any ethical dilemma then posed by the telling of "white lies", but the limits of what is a "white lie" is defined by the prevailing ethical code.

A lack of inner integrity undermines a person's strength of character, his self-confidence, his self-image and then can damage even his own sense of identity. His inner integrity allows him to prioritise and discriminate between conflicting needs or commitments or different courses of action. His ethical code – when engaged – provides direction to his actions by defining what is correct and desirable to do.

The observation of integrity is based upon a code of ethics external to the individual and then becomes crucially dependent upon whether his own code is sufficiently integrated with the surrounding code. This becomes a measure of the extent to which he has, and is perceived to have, consideration for the surrounding society. A lack of perceived integrity in an individual or, by extension, in an organisation, destroys trust and reputation. It is taken to be a deficiency of wholeness and evidence of internal corruption or corrosion of the persona and, as such, a fundamental flaw.

Perceptions of integrity sometimes distinguish between different types of integrity though it seems unlikely that an individual makes these same distinctions internally. Thus integrity may be termed intellectual or professional or artistic or moral. This is not perhaps surprising because observations are usually limited to certain kinds of behaviour and perceptions are inevitably limited to those areas observed. I am of the opinion that these are mainly labels and that they are not different types of integrity but merely the different facets of integrity which can be observed. A lack of intellectual integrity could just as well be a lack or professional or artistic or ethical integrity (for example with a scientist who fabricates his results or with an author who plagiarizes another). Integrity is not, I think, divisible into separate parts but can be observed from the different viewpoints of morality or ethics or scientific or artistic rigour or a professional code of conduct.

Alan K Simpson
> If you have integrity, nothing else matters. If you don't have integrity, nothing else matters.

Ethics and integrity have generally not been recognised as everyday management topics and have often been avoided in the workplace. In my view, an organisation cannot isolate itself from the social environment it is surrounded by. It must have an explicit view of its own integrity and therefore of its own ethical code. Merely being compliant with law is insufficient. The owners must be party to this. When an investor buys shares in a company then, as with any other purchase, he must take responsibility for what he owns. The individual must also be given the space to engage his own code and to integrate his code with that of the organisation, and if this cannot be achieved then the only rational consequence is that the two must part. It is time to bring these into the main-stream of management and into the fundamental vocabulary of a manager. Not for the sake of public relations or for avoiding criticism but because it is the right thing to do. This shift will be characterised by no longer having Compliance managers who act as policemen but instead having Ethics managers who act as a coach. If ethics are sound, compliance will become a natural and automatic consequence and a non-issue. With ethics and integrity, corporate governance and corporate social responsibility follow naturally.

But no matter what exists or is lacking in his surroundings, the manager remains the master of his fate and the captain of his soul.

Chapter 10
A Touch of Class

Class is not appearance and it is not personality or charisma; it is a style and an elegance of behaviour and a consistency of actions. It is the final attribute of the nine which I consider the fundamental characteristics of a good manager. It is separate to the other eight but represents the harmonious combination of the others. It requires that the other eight attributes be present all at some reasonable values. It is the completeness and balance of the package of attributes which represents the wholeness and totality of a persona.

"A Man for All Seasons"

Robert Whittington was a schoolmaster and grammarian who lived in the time of Henry VIII in England. He was a contemporary of Sir Thomas More who he described in his *Vulgaria* of 1520.

> Robert Whittington
> And, as time requireth, a man of marvelous mirth and pastimes, and sometime of as sad gravity. A man for all seasons.

Thomas More reeked of class.

It is this completeness of a person, a roundness of attributes, and a uniformity of surface which I try to articulate by using the word "class" to portray the package which makes up a good manager. It is not just an arithmetic summation of the other eight fundamental attributes that I have identified, but is a separate attribute which describes the harmonious composition and combination of these eight. Class does not require that the other attributes all be at very high levels. But they do all need to be above some threshold level, and class requires that they present a well-balanced whole. Someone who is exceedingly brave for example, but whose other attributes are less developed, lacks this balance and inevitably skews towards recklessness. Equally, somebody with very sound judgment, but whose communication skills are not as strong, will lack this balance, and his judgments will not be matched by a corresponding mobilisation of actions. A good communicator without a corresponding strength of character will soon be revealed to "be all sound without substance". Great strength of character which is not matched by soundness of judgment is likely to show up as very stubborn behaviour. Having great social power but with poor judgment could mean a dangerous person to be associated with. Great power without integrity would lead to demagoguery. Over-abundance or a relative deficiency of one or more of the attributes will produce a lop-sided combination and this will detract from class.

Just as a brave person is not usually conscious of being brave, or a person of great strength does not consciously choose to apply strength of character, so a classy person is not aware of having or exhibiting class. To him his behaviour is just his normal behaviour reflecting what he considers the right and proper thing to do. But it is his attributes which lead to his behaviour and by which his class can then be observed. Class is not appearance and it is not personality or charisma; it is a style and an elegance of behaviour and a consistency of actions. It is a generosity of spirit and of time and of wisdom rather than just charity. It is not sophistry or eloquence but it is innocence and sophistication simultaneously. It is not the arrogance of superior intelligence but it is the retaining of the sense of wonder and being always ready to learn or to teach. It is being true to oneself such that the external perception of the persona and the reality of the persona converge.

It is sometimes easier to put into words what it is not. It is the opposite of being uncouth or arrogant or mean-spirited or cruel but it is never weakness or cowardice. It is questioning and scepticism rather than suspicion and mistrust. It is trusting and being trusted. It is having strength in a velvet glove and compassion encased in steel. It is a balanced exposition of intelligence and knowledge and spontaneity and rationality. It is being unafraid of showing emotion but rarely discomposed by it. It is being unhurried and confident and sure. It is without noise.

Such perfect paragons of virtues are few and far between.

Kipling's words from his poem "If" seem appropriate for Sir Thomas More who "neither foes nor loving friends could hurt", and who could "meet with Triumph and Disaster and treat those two impostors just the same". Thomas More lived a long time ago and he could "talk with crowds and keep his virtue, or walk with Kings – nor lose the common touch". Perhaps he would not recognise the picture we have of him today, but what we know of his life truly describes "A man for all seasons".

But classy behaviour is not as uncommon as it might seem. Almost everybody has their moments of class; situations in which their behaviour or actions are observed and experienced as being classy. Some people have more of these moments of classiness than others and for the good manager a large number of his actions or his behaviour will exhibit class. We observe others only through their behaviour in particular situations and these observations can only represent a small part of all their behaviours. We may not always be able to extrapolate from a few observations, but if someone exhibits a consistent pattern of classy behaviour, it is not unreasonable to draw the conclusion that a person is classy.

Class in a person is reminiscent to me of the cut of a diamond. A master diamond cutter chooses the facets he cuts to give the most pleasing whole in accordance with his own aesthetics and to suit a particular stone. He tries to create his composition of cuts to get the most impressive combination of the brilliance (due to light reflected out from the interior) and fire (due to refracted light within the stone) that he can. He polishes the facets to get the lustre (light reflected from the surface) he wants. Raw stones have their internal characteristics and colour and flaws, which both enable and restrict what cuts are possible. The master cutter's level of skill may further define the type and fineness and symmetry of the cuts that are feasible. He optimises between waste reductions on the one hand against size and cut of the gems resulting from a single raw stone on the other. Sometimes, and especially if some flaw exists in the stone, the cutter will sacrifice size to get an improved brilliance or fire or scintillation. He may even deliberately use a flaw to enhance the fire or he may cut away a flaw to enhance the brilliance. He may vary the cut and polish depending upon the colour and clarity of the stone. He may design his cuts to enhance the colour which is near the surface of the stone. He combines and compounds his skills with the characteristics of the stone and compensates for its flaws to create the finished gem-stone. The value of a finished diamond rests in its size and clarity and colour and above all, in its cut.

A good manager is his own master diamond cutter. His fundamental attributes are his various facets and his weaknesses are his flaws. It is his own aesthetics and his awareness of his strengths and weaknesses which lead to the manner in which he combines, compounds or compensates for his attributes. The manner of their combination leads to his behaviour which when it is then observed in the light of the society he operates in shows up as his class. His behaviour defines his class. Therefore class is not something which is or can be developed explicitly, but it develops as a consequence of an individual's awareness of his own strengths and weaknesses. An imperfect balance of his attributes improves as he develops his weak points or compensates for them. Inevitably his behaviour develops and matures. But classy behaviour, when observed, can be emulated. Feedback from the surrounding society about the behaviour observed can be built upon. Emulation requires more than superficial replication of a behaviour pattern. It needs the development of the fundamental attributes as well. Merely copying behaviour which is not backed up by the soundness of the underlying attributes is not sustainable. Classy behaviour when it is just faked is undertaken for the sake of appearance and not because of any conviction of what is considered the right and correct thing to do. It is then like having fake diamonds of cubic zirconia or of silicon carbide, which glitter and can deceive but which shatter if subjected to impact stress. There is no upper limit I think to the scale of class and the development of attributes and the consequent increase of classiness is wholly open-ended.

Classy Is as Classy Does

We have all experienced examples of classy behaviour. They can be isolated examples or they may be the regular behaviour of an individual but only in some particular circumstances, or they could be the consistent behaviour in all circumstances. We often refer to sportsmen as being classy in the particular circumstances of their sport.

I saw Rod Laver play towards the end of his playing career. There have been many great tennis players since. John Newcombe was strenuous, Bjorn Borg was icy, Jimmy Connors was energetic, John McEnroe was fiery, Pete Sampras was workmanlike and Roger Federer is effortless. But for all their tennis skill and all their great records I would hesitate to call them classy as I would with Rod Laver. I never met him and know very little about the rest of his life, but on the tennis court he just oozed class. This accolade covers not only his skill at tennis but his demeanour, his interactions with competitors and the entire pattern of his behaviour on court. While I have insufficient information to extrapolate the accolade to him as a person, it is a distinct possibility that he was not just a classy tennis player but also a person of class. Among the other great sportsmen I have been privileged to watch, Sir Garfield Sobers was another such "man of all seasons" – both on the cricket pitch and off it.

In the 1980s when I had just moved to Sweden to ASEA Stal in Finspång and was making the transition from having been a research engineer to becoming a salesman, I was greatly encouraged and influenced and coached by Carsten Olesen who was the Managing Director at the time. Initially I thought that the time Carsten spent with me and the patience with which he explained the rationale behind his decisions was just kindness to help a newcomer to settle in. But when I saw him spend the same effort with many others, at various hierarchical levels and both within and outside the organisation, I realised that it was just his way and pretty classy.

Class can be exhibited by anyone, of any station, in any job and at any age. It is not something reserved for the powerful or the famous or the rich. It does not demand extraordinary levels of courage or judgment or any other attribute. It does demand a harmonious combination of the fundamental attributes. It does require a resulting behaviour which is consistent and not capricious. The behaviour is characterised by an internal conviction of doing the right and correct things but with no compulsion to show bravado or to appear heroic. When it comes about as a pursuit of internal goals which are more demanding than the expectations of surrounding society then it is manifested and observed as classy behaviour.

I was once travelling from Madras to Neyveli in Southern India to visit the site of a power plant we were constructing – about 10 h away by car. On Indian roads and with Indian traffic this was a bumpy and gruelling journey. A few hours into the journey, Sundar, the chauffeur, suddenly stopped and asked for a break which I readily agreed to. While I was stretching my legs I watched as Sundar spent the entire 20 min or so, with his tool-box helping a farmer fix the loose wheel of his bullock-cart. I never knew Sundar outside of that journey and cannot comment on his character outside that incident, but for a city chauffeur in the midst of rural India, to voluntarily stop during a tiring journey and help a farmer by the wayside, on a fairly busy highway, was highly unusual. I asked him later why he had stopped for a complete stranger when he had no obligation to do so and nobody else had stopped, and he said simply "Because nobody else would – and I could".

A class act.

George Bernard Shaw in *Pygmalion*
The great secret, Eliza, is not having bad manners or good manners or any other particular sort of manners, but having the same manner for all human souls

No doubt we would all define what constitutes classy behaviour differently, and a general definition which is universally applicable is difficult. But it is not so difficult to specify the behaviour that would cast a veto and disqualify an individual from being considered classy. Rudeness or selfishness or being uncouth or unjustifiable arrogance or being abusive, even in isolated behaviour cannot be reconciled with having class. Ingratiating or servile actions are incompatible with class. This does not however mean that a classy person may not at times be very emotional or show great anger or deep sorrow. But it will very seldom be irrational. An innate fairness is a key characteristic and this will show up as behaviour which does not change just because a different person is being addressed.

To assess whether a prospective manager has this mysterious quality of class based on a very limited observation of his behaviour is almost impossible. This must therefore be addressed indirectly by assessing the other fundamental attributes. The challenge then is to judge whether these attributes are in sufficiently good balance with each other or that they can come to be developed to become well-balanced. Since such assessments are inevitably subjective and there may be many assessors involved it becomes important to be able to communicate and compare the different assessments. Insisting therefore on quantifying these attributes by way of a bar chart or a radial plot allows not only the comparison of assessments by different people but also the visualisation of a complete profile of the subject. The smoothness of the surface represented by the tops of the columns of the bar chart or the roundedness of the shape of a radial plot gives a measure, albeit crude, of the subject's wholeness and his potential to be "a man of all seasons".

In the late 1980s and early 1990s I was involved with an ABB – Babcock & Wilcox joint venture company established in Ohio to develop a clean coal technology for power generation. A demonstration power plant was being built at Tidd, Ohio for American Electric Power. Robert Donovan was one of the B & W board members serving on the board of the joint venture. As with most 50/50 joint ventures any non-alignment of the promoters' strategies and goals can be magnified within the venture. We had many heated discussions and arguments between the ABB personnel and the B & W personnel about strategic directions, technology, engineering designs and about marketing. At one time the arguments had reached a very acrimonious and contentious stage and over a period of about 12 months, positions had become entrenched and the disputes were growing. The differences were sufficiently serious that the future of the venture itself was threatened. We convened a 2 day meeting in Akron to either settle our differences or to decide to terminate the venture. The 20 or so people involved who gathered were fully charged and well prepared with drawings and arguments and presentations supporting their respective positions and to shoot down the opposition. Bob Donovan opened the meeting and asked all gathered to do him a favour. Since he had come on board only recently he proposed a small change to the agenda and requested that we take 1 h just to prepare and give him a summary of all the potential benefits of the venture and all that we were agreed upon. He then left and returned an hour later to a room where the brittle and charged atmosphere had completely changed once the goals of the venture had been reaffirmed and we could see that we actually agreed on a majority of the issues. Bob insisted we document all our areas of agreement before starting the discussions on our areas of disagreement. He kept entering the room every few hours for the next 2 days but said very little – he just listened. We did not resolve all our differences at that meeting, but we resolved some and the reaffirmation of goals led to an approach which had suddenly turned constructive and was no longer destructive. Bob Donovan's reading of the situation, his change of the game being played and his approach and behaviour were pure class. I met him a few more times in the following year and learnt a great deal from his quiet and assured way. In 1994, Bob joined the board of ABB and was actually appointed the head of operations in the Americas. Sadly, in 1996, he was on the military plane, carrying the US Commerce Secretary and a business delegation to the Balkans, which crashed in Croatia without any survivors. But my memory of Bob Donovan is of those 2 days in Akron where he converted a poisoned and infected atmosphere into a creative one within the space of 60 min.

Perhaps what I call "class" is what others may call "flair" or "style" or "dignity" or "graciousness". These are surely all facets of class. But beyond semantics, my main contention is that it is an inherent human quality, which describes that behaviour which is a consequence of the manner in which the fundamental attributes combine and mesh with each other. It is the whole which is greater than the sum of the parts. But it does not carry any overtones of privilege or caste or "noblesse oblige".

After the Great Hanshin earthquake struck Kobe in 1995, it was an act of pure class when Bo Dankis got on his motor-bike and negotiated his way through the rubble and collapsing buildings to check up on affected employees.

But classy behaviour does not need extraordinary events to be manifested. It can be observed in ordinary people and in the most unremarkable of situations and in the most commonplace of interactions. It could be the waitress rushed off her feet in a busy New York restaurant but who did not just rattle through the nine specials of the day but actually guided us through the entire menu. It could be one of the Lufthansa ground staff at Frankfurt Airport when a flight had been cancelled, not losing her temper but patiently explaining and keeping her composure when faced by a mob of irate passengers. Or it could be Queen Sylvia of Sweden when opening an environmental conference in Zaragosa in 1986, not just "kissing hands" with all of us in the reception line, but actually taking the time to ask authors of the papers to be presented about the significance of their research efforts.

Classy behaviour is being serious without needing to be sad. It does not recognise and is oblivious to class distinctions. It treats with crowds and Kings alike.

Index

A
ABB, v, vi, 36, 68, 87, 101, 102, 151, 169, 170
Action requests, 26–32, 35, 64, 119
A "good" manager, 1, 14–21, 27, 29, 32, 36, 38, 39, 45, 47–51, 68, 75, 91, 104, 107, 113, 114, 116, 122, 123, 132, 142, 165–167
American Insurance Group, 134
Alstom, v, vi, 12, 68, 117, 151, 152, 157
Amakudari, 85
American Electric Power, 169
Analysis paralysis, 46–48
Angelo, E., 91
Apathetic bystanders, 120
Aptitude tests, 16, 20, 30
Aristotle, 24, 112
Arthur Andersen, 151
ASEA Stal, 168
Assessment
 by hypothetical scenarios, 30, 33–34

B
Babcock & Wilcox, 169
BAE systems, 151
Balanced score cards, 138
Barnevik, P., 36
BCA. *See* Business Consultancy Agreement
Becket, T., 27, 32
Beethoven
 Waldstein Sonata, 36
Belfort Bax, E., 109
Bell, A.G., 39
Bharatiya Janata Party (BJP), 152, 153
Bhopal, 160
Bilger, P., 157
BJP. *See* Bharatiya Janata Party
Boeing, 151
Bombay High Court, 117
Bonaparte, N., 38

Bonus system, 139, 140, 142–143
Bravery and risk, 112
Brendel, A., 36
Bribery and corruption, x, 9–10, 154, 155
Bucho, 13
Burke, E., 24, 27
Busby, M., 36
Bushido, 115, 124
Business Consultancy Agreement (BCA), 10
Business ethics, 151–158

C
Carbon trading, 153, 161
Carrot and a stick, 125–128, 130, 133, 135
Cartels
 International Diamond Cartel, 160
 OPEC, 160
Casual Fridays, 12
Character
 attributes, 14, 17, 93, 96, 97, 165
 materials analogy, 93–96
 strength of, 18–20, 93, 95, 97–101, 103–108, 120, 163, 165–166
 traits, 93, 95–100, 105, 106
Chirac, J., 153
Class, 19–20, 27, 64, 141, 165–170
 analogy with diamond, 166–167
 as attribute, 19–20, 165–168
Classy behaviour, 166–170
Collateral damage, 32, 36, 115, 161
Communication, 19, 25, 29, 31, 34, 35, 57–73, 82, 89, 91, 106, 130–131, 165
 across cultures, 67, 68
 conversations for, 70–72
 elements of, 57–60
 feedback, 57, 59–61, 64–66, 68–70, 73
 feedback loop, 59–61, 64, 69–70
 intended, 18, 57–63, 65–66

Communication (*cont.*)
    for the manager, 60–65
    message, 57–62, 65–67, 69
    recipients, 18, 32, 57–62, 64–67, 69, 82
    skills, 29, 32, 34, 72–73, 106, 165
Compliance, 10, 122, 145, 150, 156, 157, 164
Conditions of satisfaction, 40–42, 52, 54
Consensus creation, 9, 17
Corporate rules, 6, 7
Corporate social responsibility, 162, 164
Corporate values, 7
Cosby, B., 40
Courage, 19, 20, 25, 27, 48, 51, 109–124, 146, 168
    across cultures, 114–116
    and bravery, 19, 109–115, 117, 119
    culture and language, 19, 109, 114–116, 119–122
    definition, 19, 109
    and duty, 114, 122, 124
    and endurance, 113
    every-day kind, 113
    false, 110–111
    and fear, 109–122, 124
    and heroes, 111
    metaphors for, 114, 115
    with peers and superiors, 120, 122–124
    samurai, 115, 124
    scales, 112
    space, 120, 121, 123
    and thrill-seeking, 113
    in the work place, 115–119
Crane, S., 111
Culture
    of courage, 109, 115, 119–122
    of shame, 90
    and values, x, 59, 148, 149
Cut of a diamond, 166

D

Daiwa Bank, 151
Dankis, B., 102, 170
Darwin, C., 1
Deficiency needs, 129, 131, 135
Degrees of separation, 78
De-motivation, 131, 135, 137–139, 142
De-motivators, 135, 138, 139, 142
Dharma, 85, 115
Dilbert, 7
Diotisalvi, 39
Diwali, 8
Donovan, R., 169
Downsizing, 11–12, 37, 38, 72, 141, 159

Drucker, P., 156
Dunbar number, 81
Durgapur, 37
Duties and rights, 83, 84

E

Einstein, A., 54, 133, 134, 158
Elliott, D., 44
Empowerment, 27, 28, 86, 121
Enron, 116, 142, 151
EPDC, 37
Escalation of engagement, 75, 86–89, 91
Ethical behaviour, 150
Ethics
    absence of, 156, 157, 161, 162
    and business, 151–158, 161
    and compliance, 10, 150, 156, 157
    corporate vacuum, 158
    for a manager, 10, 158, 160–164
    in society, 146, 149, 158, 161–162
    in the work place, 105, 158–162, 164
Exercise of power, 17, 18, 23–26, 30–32, 34–38
    as a vector, 31
Extinction by instinct, 46, 47
Exxon, 33

F

Facilitation-fee, 161
Finspång, 168
Firing process, 10
First Brno, 68
Form and substance, 7–8
Foucault, M., 24
Friedman, M., 156

G

Geneva bible, 75
Giri, 85, 90, 124
GKN, 62
Goodness of contract index, 141
Grapevine, 67, 71–72, 121
Great Hanshin earthquake, 102, 170
Group-think, 47, 52

H

Habit, 4–14, 42–45, 47, 49–51, 54, 69, 107
Harley-Davidson, 33
Henry II, 27, 32
Henry VIII, 165
Higher-order needs, 129, 134, 135
Hindi, 71
Hippocratic oath, 150

Hitachi, 37
Honne, 67
Hood, R., 99
Hoy, R., 123
Human breakdowns, 101
Human satisfaction, 127
Hurricane Katrina, 119

I
Iceland, 134
Ishikawajima-Harima Heavy Industries, 101
Indian Congress Party, 152
Informal conversations, 70–73
Integrity, 7, 8, 10, 17, 19, 20, 25, 29, 34, 51, 54, 65, 66, 82, 89, 95, 96, 99, 105, 106, 123, 124, 134, 136, 145–164, 166
   definitions, 54, 145
   and human behaviour, 148, 150–151
   and value conflicts, 148
   and values, 148–151
Internal values, 147–150
Inwha, 9
Izzat, 7

J
Jicho, 13
Judgment, 14, 18–20, 25, 27, 29, 30, 32, 34–36, 39–55, 60, 69, 72–73, 86, 94–96, 98–101, 110, 112–114, 117–118, 121, 122, 131, 132, 141, 145, 149, 150, 163, 165–166, 168
   assessment of, 45, 50, 54
   "bad", 39, 40, 51–54
   characteristics of, 32, 42
   in a court of law, 41
   and habit, 42, 43, 45, 47, 49–51
   in a manager, 44–46
   managerial, 34, 41
   in managers, 44–46
   nature of, 40–44
   paralysis, 35, 43, 44, 47
   process, 40, 41, 43, 45, 47–51, 53, 54
   quality gates, 51
   soundness, 18, 45, 49–51, 54, 166
   timing of, 49
   unconscious, 41–45, 47, 49, 50, 72–73

K
Kacho, 13
Karita, 101
Key account managers (KAMs), 81
Kawasaki Heavy Industries, 6
King Priam, 39

Kipling, R., 166
Kobe, 11, 33, 101–104, 170
Kohl, H., 153
Key Performance Indicators, 6
KPMG, 157
Kumaramangalam, R., 152

L
Lapland, 71
Laver, R., 168
Laws
   vs. values, 148
Lehman brothers, 138
Lord Kelvin, 40
Lufthansa, 103, 170
Lundberg, G., 37
Lying and deception, 146
Lynch, M., 134

M
Machiavelli, N., 24
Management by Objective (MBO), 137–138
Manager
   behaviour, 4, 8, 14, 15, 18, 24, 107, 117, 120, 158–162, 169
   brave actions by, 114
   claims, 6, 15, 33, 41
   and comfort zone, 119, 121
   compliance, 2, 10, 164
   and courage, 17, 19, 20, 45, 48, 50, 51, 113, 114, 120–123
   courage characteristics, 48, 112
   definition, 3–4
   dissent, 46, 47, 108, 122–124
   dress code, 12
   duties and rights, 83, 84
   ethics, 10, 159, 161–164
   functional titles, 2
   general, 2, 3, 13
   grades, 12
   habitat, 4–14
   integrity of behaviour, 162
   judgment, 18–20, 27, 32, 34, 35, 44–49, 51, 69, 132
   by location, 2, 33
   nine key characteristics, 20
   by process, 2, 8, 47, 51, 61, 62
   as process keeper, 9
   profile, 17–20
   qualities, 2, 5, 16–18, 20, 35, 61, 82, 113, 169
   sales, 2, 6, 33, 69, 89
   as a species, 1–21

Manager (*cont.*)
  title as rank, 2, 3
Managerial behaviour, 4, 14, 24
Managerial communications, 60, 62, 66
Maslow, A., 97, 129, 130, 135
Materials science, 93–95, 103
MBO. *See* Management by Objective
McCloskey, R., 61
McLuhan, M., 59
Meaning to message, 65–66
Medical tourists, 160
Ministry of Trade and Industry (MITI), 37
Morality, 68, 99, 110, 146, 148–150, 163
More, T., 165, 166
Motivation, 19, 27, 35, 106, 107, 114, 125–143, 159
  definition, 125–126
  as a force, 125, 126
  for a manager, 126, 128, 130, 132, 133, 135, 138, 159
  and manipulation, 138
  need theories, 128, 129
  practice of, 128, 130, 131
  process theories, 128
Motivators, 126, 128–139, 141–142
Motivators available to a manager, 136
Mr. Five Percent, 153

N
Nemawashi, 9
Networks, 18, 20, 28–30, 35, 36, 63–65, 72, 75–91
  flow in, 79, 80, 87
  human, 78–82, 91
  nature of, 75–78, 81
  purpose, 75, 77–80
  size of, 79
  social, 72, 76, 78–80, 82, 86
  strength, 79, 81, 82
Newton's First Law of Motion, 15

O
OECD. *See* Organisation for Economic Co-operation and Development
Olesen, C., 37, 168
Organisation for Economic Co-operation and Development (OECD), 153, 155, 156

P
Penalties, 26, 126, 128, 130, 132–135, 141–143, 147–150, 159
  for unacceptable behaviour, 133, 134, 142
Peter principle, 16

Pfizer drugs, 151
Political funding, 152, 154, 156
Port Island, 102, 103
Positive psychology, 97
Power, 6, 17–20, 23–38, 41, 47, 78, 86, 114, 152–154, 166, 168
  analogy with physics, 23–24, 26, 27, 29
  assessment of, 28–30, 33–34
  definition, 23–24, 26
  empowerment, 27, 28
  exercise of, 17, 18, 23–26, 30–32, 34–38, 41, 47
  managerial, 26, 29–30
  music of, 36, 38
  proper exercise of, 17, 24–26, 34–38
  social, 23–26, 28, 30–31
Prabhu, S., 153
Practice of motivation, 128, 131
Pressure tactics, 107
Proper exercise of power, 17, 24–26, 34–38
První Brněnská, 68
Psychological universals, 89
Purpose of motivation, 125, 131

Q
Queen Sylvia of Sweden, 170
Quotations
  Aurelius, M., 105
  Bonaparte, N., 38
  Brown, R.M., 51
  Burke, E., 24, 27
  Carrol, L., 110
  Catherine the great, 126
  de Saint-Exupéry, A., 82
  Drucker, P.F., 60, 156
  Einstein, A., 54, 133, 134, 158
  Gini, Al., 34
  Henley, W.E., 162
  Hill, N., 93
  Ingersoll, R.G., 132
  Johnson, S., 145
  Kelly, K., 76
  Khayyam, O., 16
  King, M.L. Jr., 78
  McCloskey, R., 61
  Milne, A.A., 84
  Neuman, A.E., 40
  Nietzsche, F., 24, 104
  Rockefeller, J.D., 17
  Scudder, S.F., 58
  Shakespeare, W., 42, 70, 114
  Shaw, G.B., 124, 169
  Signoff, D., 59

Simon, H., 44
Simpson, A.K., 164
Smith, F.W., 1
Tennyson, A.L., 98
Truman, M., 112
Twain, M., 109
Whittington, R., 165
The Wizard of Oz, 124

R

Relationships, x, 5, 8, 10, 18, 20, 23, 25, 28, 29, 35, 52, 75–91, 96, 105, 115, 130–131
  across cultures, 89–91
  across departments, 91
  development of, 85, 86
  pairings, 82, 83, 85, 87
  types of, 82, 83, 85, 89
Request for action, 26–28, 30–32, 119
Rewards, 3, 4, 6, 26, 28, 36, 107–108, 116, 121, 125, 126, 128, 130–135, 137, 139–143
  and penalty, 26, 125, 126, 128, 130, 132, 133, 143
Rights, x, 1–4, 7, 10, 13, 15, 18, 33, 34, 36, 39, 43, 48–50, 71, 83–85, 91, 98, 99, 109, 110, 117, 118, 123, 124, 131, 145–150, 158–164, 166–168
Rosetta stone, 90
Rowe, D., 40
Royal Society, 40, 80

S

Sakura, 115
Sales manager, 2, 6, 33, 89
Salmon, N., v, 118
Sami language, 71
Sapience, ix
Sapir–Whorf hypothesis, 71
Satisfaction and dissatisfaction, 126–129, 131–133, 137
Satyam, 151
  computers, 116
SBI. *See* State Bank of India
Scudder, F.S., 58
Securities and Exchange Commission (SEC), 134, 157
Seken-tei, 90
Shell, 151
Shinkansen, 101

Shiv Sena, 153
Siemens, 68, 107, 151, 155, 157
Small world hypothesis, 78
Sobers, G., 168
State Bank of India (SBI), 117–118, 141
Stieler, F., 68
Strength of character, 18, 19, 97–101, 103–108, 120, 163, 165–166
  definition, 93, 99
  development, 105–108
  functions of, 98–99
  managerial, 20, 95, 99–100, 108
  sufficiency of, 98–99
Stress and strength, 100–105
Stressors, 101
Stress perception, 101, 104, 110
Success and goodness, 1, 15, 16
Sumo, 88
Supreme Court of India, 117

T

Tatemae, 67
Theories of motivation, 125, 128–131
The Red Badge of Courage, 109–124
Tidd, 169
Tower of Pisa, 39
Track record, 15–16, 20, 30, 35, 49, 54, 55, 141
True voice, 67, 70, 71, 89
Types of English, 90

U

Uchida, S., 6
Undue influence, 8, 10, 155
Union carbide, 160

V

Virgil, 39
Von Pirer, H., 157

W

Wakamatsu, 36
Wall Street Journal, 156–157, 162
West Bengal, 37
Western Union, 39
Whistleblower, 115, 117
Whittington, R., 165
Wittgenstein, L., ix, xi